Catherine Carswell

LYING AWAKE

*An unfinished autobiography and
other posthumous papers*

Edited with an Introduction by
JOHN CARSWELL

D1493913

CANONGATE
CLASSICS
76

First published in 1950 by Secker & Warburg. This edition first published as a Canongate Classic in 1997 by Canongate Books, 14 High Street, Edinburgh EHI ITE. Copyright © Catherine Carswell 1950. Introduction copyright © John Carswell 1997.

The publishers gratefully acknowledge general subsidy from the Scottish Arts Council towards the Canongate Classics series and a specific grant towards the publication of this volume.

Set in 10pt Plantin by Hewer Text Composition Services. Printed and bound by Caledonian Book Manufacturing, Bishopbriggs, Glasgow.

Canongate Classics
Series Editor: Roderick Watson
Editorial board: J. B. Pick and Cairns Craig

British Library Cataloguing in Publication Data
A catalogue record for this book is available on request from the British Library.

ISBN 0 86241 683 3

Catherine Carswell (1879–1946) was born in Glasgow, one of the four children of George and Mary Anne Macfarlane. On leaving school she attended classes in English literature at Glasgow University, but could not in those days be admitted for a degree. In 1904, after a brief engagement, she married Herbert Jackson. When, in 1905, she told him of her pregnancy, he tried to kill her. Declared insane, he spent the rest of his life in a mental hospital. Catherine returned to Glasgow where her daughter was born and worked, first in Glasgow and then in London, as dramatic and literary critic, for the *Glasgow Herald*. In 1907 she began legal proceedings for the anulment of her marriage. She won the case, making legal history.

Her friendship with D. H. Lawrence was kindled by her favourable review of *The White Peacock* (1911). They met in 1914 and their relationship lasted until Lawrence's death. In 1915 she married Donald Carswell, with whom she had one son, and in the same year she lost her job at the *Glasgow Herald* for praising *The Rainbow*. Soon after this the Carswells moved briefly from London to Bournemouth. She became an assistant dramatic critic at the *Observer* and continued working on the novel which would become *Open the Door!* In 1916 she and Lawrence exchanged manuscripts of *Open the Door!* and *Women in Love*. Her novel was completed in 1918 and won the Melrose Prize on publication in 1920. Her only other novel, *The Camomile*, was published two years later and she then devoted herself to *The Life of Robert Burns* which made her name in 1930. This was quickly followed by a biography of Lawrence, *The Savage Pilgrimage* (1932), a number of anthologies and a life of Boccaccio, *The Tranquil Heart* (1937).

After her husband's death during the black-out in 1940, Catherine Carswell lived alone in London. She worked with John Buchan's widow on his memorial anthology, *The Clearing House* (1946) and on her own autobiography which was published, incomplete, as *Lying Awake* in 1950. Her friends included Vita Sackville-West, Edwin Muir, Rose Macaulay, Storm Jameson, Hugh Macdiarmid, John Buchan and Aldous Huxley. Catherine Carswell died in Oxford at the age of sixty-six.

Si l'usage l'eût permis, j'aurais dû écrire plus
d'une fois à la marge: *'cum grano salis'*.
RENAN: *Souvenirs d'Enfance et de Jeunesse*

To be bound for ever by the arbitrary accident
of one's memories: what an idea of immortality!

Author's Note

Contents

Introduction

MY mother left this book unfinished. She did not wish the work of her last years to be published until after her death, and although she worked persistently at it until her last illness, she refused to think of this book 'about herself' as pressing, but rather as a reflective and prolonged spinning of the various threads of her life.[1] However long she had lived, I think she would still have left the book behind still incomplete. In one of the many notes found among the material for this book – notes meant for her own guidance but also serving as finger-posts for a future editor – she says as much: '*End*. Make it abrupt; no reason why it should ever end. Not in any form though informed by a theme. Merely an attempt to give the texture.'

She died in 1946, a few weeks before her sixty-seventh birthday and very nearly three years after writing to me that she was 'working on something longer for which I've been making notes for years.' Every now and then she sent me a passage or referred to the tussle with 'the book I'm trying to write', and the value she put upon it was a strange one. She mentioned once with mild disdain an excited author she had met purring over his first proofs; but after an air-raid she wrote that, 'What I think of most at the moment is how disgusting it would be for my papers and bits of things to be destroyed.' She set no store by her book (though she had lived by letters for many years past) but she valued it, perhaps, more than any of her previous work. During three difficult years, this book, 'so eagerly begun', and pressed on – 'today I *made* myself write for some hours at my book'

1. A single chapter, however, the first, was published in *Windmill* No. 4, and is here reproduced by courtesy of Messrs. W. Heinemann.

– was the recurring ground-bass of her life. The war, her friends, her movements about England, even her illnesses – and she had one serious illness during this time – never succeeded in diverting her from this work. They were built into it, as suited her purpose.

During most of this time I was serving in the East, and heard, though constantly, only by letter. I knew, or had been told, that some day I should be the editor of this book, but I had every reason for hoping that day would not be soon. Although, when I returned to England in 1945, my mother was sixty-six, it never struck me that she was old; and her last illness was sudden and catastrophic. Not long before its onset she had been through and destroyed a great number of her many papers; but I am certain that everything she meant for this book survived. She had not yet given it a title, nor had she ever drawn up (so far as I have been able to discover) any complete scheme of the way in which she saw the book as a whole. She left me, too early, to understand and make good her intentions.

Before I went abroad I would neither have hoped nor have dared to attempt to do this; but four years of absence and constant correspondence brought me to know my mother and to understand her better, perhaps, than all the years that I had till then spent close to her. I began to understand how she had made a calling, not a profession of letters – the distinction, of which my mother would have approved, is Virginia Woolf's; and in some ways I had always accepted this fact, as children and adolescents do. But then I came to see how it had been achieved, and at what expense and labour. The reading and editing of the material for this book have enlarged that awareness still more. As she says in the course of the book itself, and in many of her letters, she could not but be a writer, and though she once exclaimed to me, 'It is awful feeling that one would rather do anything than write!' She immediately added, 'But one has to set against this the undoubted sense of conquest in *having written*'.

She was a frank critic, both of her own and other people's work, particularly when it smacked of the kind of 'intellectualising' (as she called it) which marred a hopeful essay I once sent her from abroad: 'too many thoughts in it and not enough thought' was her comment. She believed that successful writing demanded the history of 'thought, effort, secret failure' which had been her own experience. 'How ill-read some of these lads are,' she wrote to me once of that one among my contemporaries whom I had always thought the best read man I knew. He had, I think, owned up to having read only one novel by George Eliot. Her own reading, while she was writing this book, was wide, various and largely unfashionable – Herzen, Alfred de Vigny, the Prince de Ligne, Dickens, Rabelais and T. S. Eliot, and 'for several weeks *nothing* but a small French dictionary – every word from A to Z' – are random samples from a single year's correspondence. 'As it is I rarely get started to the book till after supper, and my reading is done mostly in bed between 1 and 2.30 a.m. Then, though I don't usually get up at all early, I get sleepy during the day. Yesterday I lay on the floor and slept for two solid hours.'

The book she was writing at this time – this book – was not intended to be a simple narrative of her own life. Even if she had lived to finish it I do not think she would have tried to give anything like a description of her most active years. The plan was rather to stake out her position in childhood and in old age, and to weave across the years which lay between, from one charted position to the other. 'I was *meant*,' she wrote, 'if I may use a questionable expression which sadly dates – I was meant perhaps to be a child and an old woman. I did my best in between, but in age the ecstasy returns without the agony, though it is not forgotten.' This was the theme she hoped would inform the book, and even in this unfinished state one can see that she was successful. The two positions are clearly stated in detail; the process of casting threads between them has been begun; the texture can be discerned. Its author would have expanded and improved this book if she had lived, but she would not have wanted to alter its nature.

Some of the letters collected at the end of this book – particularly those to Florence McNeill, will help to supply those middle and active years which my mother deliberately passes over almost in silence. The account which she gives stops short at the moment her career was beginning, when,

beautiful and talented, she had just come back to Glasgow after
studying music for two years at Frankfort. But instead of teaching music she turned to the Glasgow School of Art and then to
Glasgow University then for the first time admitting women.
She was studying English Literature and at the end of her first
year was promoted to read honours under one of the university's stars, Professor Walter Raleigh. She was twenty-four.

In 1904 she made her first, and an unhappy, marriage,
which, after an early separation, was in the end annulled.[1]
She returned to Glasgow with her daughter Diana, and
began a serious career as dramatic and literary critic, becoming a regular member of the staff of the *Glasgow Herald*. In
1912 the death of her mother dissolved the household in
which she had been brought up (her father was already
dead), and with her daughter she moved to London.

As a literary reviewer and dramatic critic on *The Observer*
under St John Irvine she began to make a name. With
Ivy Low, later the wife of Maxim Litvinov, she came to
know D. H. Lawrence – she describes the beginning of
this friendship in the early pages of *The Savage Pilgrimage*,
the narrative of Lawrence which she wrote shortly after his
death. The friendship between them was one of the closest
of both their lives. It was Lawrence who encouraged her to
press on with the novel she had already begun about her
youth in Glasgow, and in 1920 *Open The Door!* appeared
as a prize-winning first novel.

In 1915, five years before the publication of *Open The
Door!*, she married Donald Carswell, whom she had known
in Glasgow before he too left Scottish for London journalism.
But though they had the profession of letters in common, his
approach to it was very different from hers. His training and
interests were more academic, and his ambition in writing
was to express his knowledge – which was great – rather

1. *Jackson v Jackson* (1908) A sensational case and also a
leading one. She had to prove the man had been insane
at the time of the marriage. A little after the marriage
he tried to kill her. He had been at the early stages of
dementia praecox which gives the patient delusions. Her
pregnancy challenged his delusion of impotence and he
became homicidal; he was never released from hospital.

than his experience or his imagination. He was a literary craftsman with a high standard of style, perfected over years and maintained with patient care. Like many craftsmen, too, he was by modern standards unproductive, working when he felt inclined and refusing to part with his work until it had undergone all the processes which his skill could supply. This technical skill he put at the disposal of the native literary ability which he found in his wife, and considered greater than his own.

It was a happy marriage, both of talent and temperament, even though the talent and temperament brought by each partner were so different. They were complementary to each other, and each entered into the other's work not only as critic (friendly, often severe), but, in my mother's case, as typist, and in my father's as legal adviser (he was a barrister who had early given up practice). The work of each passed under the other's eye, yet they remained distinct authors. It was on one occasion only that they ostensibly joined forces to produce an anthology on their common Scottish background.

The success of *Open The Door!* and the encouragement of Lawrence set my mother to work on her second novel, *The Camomile*, also based on her life in Glasgow: it appeared in 1923. Other novels were intended, including one in which Lawrence was to collaborate; but Lawrence was now a wanderer in search of health, and never returned to England for long enough to take part seriously in the plan: there were difficulties with publishers, and above all a family divided her attention.

For a year or two she wrote little, contributing only the essay on Proust's women to the memorial volume on Proust which was collected by C. K. Scott-Moncrieff – she had been among the first admirers of Proust in this country. But after a few years of housekeeping and journalism, she decided to write another book; and this time to turn her back on fiction and produce instead a full-length biography of Scotland's greatest literary figure, Robert Burns. Much later, when she was writing her life of Boccaccio, she commended her latest subject's admirable foolhardiness in undertaking a translation of Homer (though he knew no Greek), with no better a collaborator than a mendicant

Orthodox monk who knew next to no Italian. She had some of the equipment and much of the instinct of a biographer, but she turned to biography in much the same spirit as she praises in Boccaccio: by academic or traditional standards she was not the person to reassess Burns.

The spirit in which she set herself to this book – it took almost five years to write – is summed up in what she wrote in 1929, when it was almost finished: 'For some reason – perhaps for many – this Burns book has turned out more than a mere book for me and has definitely been life-giving in the stangest ways. I shall have had *this* out of it whatever else may happen.' The growth of the *Life of Robert Burns* can be followed step by step in the letters to Florence McNeill written between 1926 and 1930, and with it the author's awareness that the popular legend of Burns, encouraged by former biographers, gave an idealised and emasculated hero. Again encouraged by Lawrence, who was consulted about the book, she was determined to get at Burns the man. Her view of him has since been sustained by later academic work, but in 1930 its publication caused an explosion of anger, and sometimes venom among the more orthodox Burnsites. By one correspondent (who enclosed a bullet and signed himself 'Holy Willy') she was urged to use the enclosure 'in a quiet corner and leave the world a better and cleaner place'.

To escape her house, family and friends, and find time to write, my mother had the habit of hiring a room at some distance from her home and keeping its address a secret. Much of her Burns had been punched out on an old Corona portable in a room in Keats Grove, almost opposite the house where Keats had lived, in Hampstead; and about the time the Burns was published she decided to take the whole house and establish her family there. It was a tall, narrow building, about a hundred and fifty years old, which had been let out in single rooms to poor lodgers by a retired music hall comedienne. An earlier landlord had been an amateur gasfitter, and gas-pipes appeared and disappeared in strange festoons sprouting from ceiling or floor; sixteen layers of wallpaper were removed from the walls, an operation which the builders thought would endanger the structure. Here, doing much of the work with her own hands, she created the household in which many of her friends best remember her; and when, long afterwards, she wrote to me that she 'still maintained' (there had been no opportunity of demonstrating it for some time) 'that the best parties are dinner parties of not more than six or eight well chosen guests' it was of Keats Grove that I thought.

All her life she made fresh friends, many of them surprising ones, and many of them outside her own literary circle. There were, for instance, two statesmen, both of whom she had known at the beginning of their careers, Maxim Litvinov and Salvador de Madariaga. Through Maxim Litvinov she came to know the successive Soviet Ambassadors in London, Krassin, Sokolnikov and Maisky, the last of whom she carried once to Hampstead Heath on a Bank Holiday and sent spinning on a merry-go-round. In her own profession there were few women writers, very few writing Scots, who were not among her friends. But she made as many friends in Camden Town and in her country village; and one of her last friends – and by this I do not mean protégés – was a stiff old country gardener, once a soldier, whom she liked better than most literary society.

About the time the Burns was published, the friendship which she valued above all the rest had been ended by D. H. Lawrence's death at Vence. Controversy divided his surviving friends, and it was to this controversy that my mother contributed her next book, *The Savage Pilgrimage*, in which she gave her narrative of D. H. Lawrence. By this book she divided herself deliberately, and without truce, from some of those who claimed to have an exclusive right to the understanding of Lawrence. Her book was withdrawn, but later reappeared from another publisher, in 1932. The controversy was still going on, and the attacks of the Burnsites on the earlier work were still being launched when she left both for a month and travelled to Berlin to look after the mother of Dimitrov. The Reichstag fire trial was then going on.[1]

1. G. Dimitrov, a Bulgarian Communist, was one of the principals accused of arson. The evidence against him was flimsy and he was acquitted. It was and is generally thought to have been a rather crude and ill-managed Nazi plot.

About this time, too, she found and furnished (she rode down in the van herself with the furniture, guiding the vanman through country by-roads) a cottage near Toppesfield, in the north of Essex, paying four shillings a week for it to a neighbouring farmer. From then on, though she never had a car, nor could drive one, she divided her life between town and country. Each was equally her home. Three anthologies belong to this period of her life. In two, *A National Gallery* and *The English in Love*, she collaborated with Daniel George, and in a third, *The Scots Weekend*, with her husband.

Like many other authors my parents found it difficult to earn a living in the years which followed the depression. Sales were poor and journalism was ill paid. In particular, high hopes which had been built on my father's play were not fulfilled. She decided to live on a more modest scale, and for reasons which will appear in this book, emotionally she almost welcomed this decision. Keeping always the country cottage, and moving most of our possessions to it, we gave up the Keats Grove house and moved to two rooms in a grimy, little-used crescent behind Camden High Street.[1] To reach them one climbed three flights of dark stairs, but when one entered, it was clear that here, with far less promising material, she had succeeded almost as she had succeeded in Keats Grove. 'If it hadn't been for my pleasure in dilapidated houses,' she wrote much later, when I protested against one of her war-time removals, 'we should not have had so many that were amusing. It has partly been imposed on me by circumstances, only partly by temperament.' At the time of this first move she was working at her biography of Boccaccio which in 1937 appeared as *The Tranquil Heart*.

The expenses of living were now less, and my father, after many years of literary hopes and disappointments had a regular post in the Home Office, so it seemed that the retreat to Gloucester Crescent might be only a temporary one. The war broke out, and a few months later my father was killed in a motor-car accident in the darkness, as he left his work. Not very long afterwards I was sent to the East on military

---

1. So at the time, but not now. It is called Gloucester Crescent.

service. This book was then taking shape in my mother's mind, and her ruling mood at that time can be seen in this, which she wrote not long after my father's death:

> I no longer need what I have always lacked, faith in myself. I have mostly lost what I once had, faith in other people. I have found and I possess faith in life to sustain and vindicate me and in death, into which before very long I shall most surely sink. I believe that there is behind and ordering both life and death a beneficent purpose beyond my comprehension.

The author was now living (apart from occasional journalistic earnings) on the civil list pension granted in recognition of her own and her husband's work, and she was sixty-two. She still entertained her friends, and still moved between town and country; but her life had contracted, and she now set out to sum up what she was and what she had been with that detachment on which Lawrence had commented during the previous great war:

> . . . you are the only woman I have ever met who is so intrinsically detached, so essentially separate and isolated as to be a real artist and recorder. Your relations with other people are only extensions from yourself.

'An old woman,' she now wrote, 'with a full life behind her, should make the best of spectators.'

Most of this book was written during the worst years of the war in what the author called 'a mixture of Franciscan austerity and the current bohemianism', between Camden Town (where she stoked the boilers as part of her tenancy in the basement), and her cottage in Essex. One Christmas she took a mail-sorter's job at the local post office – 'Anything,' she once said, 'rather than a desk and a chair in the Ministry of Information.' Towards the end of the war she helped Lady Tweedsmuir in the preparation of the two books commemorating John Buchan – *The Clearing House* and *John Buchan, by his Wife and Friends*. She decided at last to live settled in an old house at Wallingford, in Berkshire, which others (but, I think, not she herself) thought would allow her to write more easily than her old irregular and comet-like existence. She began to lay plans for other books, considering this one as a kind of continuum, to be worked on occasionally, and never to the exclusion of other work. She chose Calvin for her fourth biography, and had already begun to gather material.

> One's past [runs one of the notes for her autobi-ography] is like a lot of old songs of which one has forgotten the words, even the titles. Emotions, conditions, follies, joys of former years are brought to life again by those tunes with something ineffable added from the present and by the passage of time, but the words themselves are gone. Not Proust himself can recall them. Instead he has to concentrate on the accretions instead of the thing itself, the experience as it happened. Knowing this he has to excuse himself for his falsification. Anything said in words of the past can be only half true, and there is something of hell in the half that is true. It is not for nothing that heaven is imagined by us as a place of music without words other than hosannahs and amens, a place of blissful being rather than of rapturous speech. True, in the beginning was the Word, and the Word was God, but, whatever that Word may be it is in the singular. Wit and wordiness both are excluded. I imagine, on the other hand, that hell is a babel of voices where sinners spend eternity striving to write apologetic accounts of their lives on earth, which they are not permitted to forget. No doubt there is wit of a sort in hell, still more, wordiness. Perhaps dwellers therein are compelled to peruse each other's autobiographies. I hope to attain heaven and the forfeit of verbal language where music, motion and the glance will say all there is to be said.

She died at Oxford in February 1946, shortly before her sixty-seventh birthday. All her literary life she had been a great collector of papers, but at her death she left little except the collection on which this book is based.

Knowing the way my mother worked and her ruthlessness

in discarding those efforts at expression that did not please her, I can only hope that proper editorial piety has not been affected by my awareness that the author would have had little respect for the manuscript as I found it. I have, I confess, allowed this awareness to assist me in marshalling and selecting from five or six hundred separate pieces of prose and verse ranging from complete chapters to a few words on the back of an envelope. Some of the best and most pregnant things are on the backs of envelopes.

The manuscript, or rather the collection of papers on which this book is based, was, as I have said, being worked upon when the author died. I inherited a desk rather than a book. The work of editing has been rather like the wandering of an apprentice through a half-built house when the master builders have gone leaving their tools and materials ready for the morning. From a finished chapter one can, if one chooses, follow the provenance of a paragraph apparently embedded neatly between its two fellows, through successive typed and written drafts, perhaps in different juxtapositions, back to component sentences and even phrases scribbled on a railway journey (as is clear from the writing). More often the series is incomplete – there are notes, and perhaps drafts incorporating the notes, but no finished chapter – bricks but no walls; sometimes there are only notes, longer or shorter, connected or disconnected; and there are what can only be described as technical flourishes, literary doodles, ornaments laid by for a later stage. Where can the apprentice assign (it stands on a piece of paper by itself) 'Astute but gullible, gifted but uninspired, worthy but silly, noble but without wisdom'? Or this, again by itself? 'The irritability of diffidence'.

Each chapter, and many lesser fragments have their substructure of drafts and notes; but not every fragment has a superstructure, or even an indication of what that superstructure was to be. Every part of the manuscript bears signs of careful revision, even the roughest notes sometimes showing alterations in a later hand. The sureness of touch with which these alterations are made, and their consistency in strengthening where they displace, is one of the most striking and most instructive things about the

manuscript and the author's habits of mind. While she loved
composition, she felt as Dr Johnson did about its intolerable
labour: 'I have begun to hate this book,' says one of her notes,
'to hate writing it, to hate my clock, which is silent in its glass
case – ever since Mr Jankosky from upstairs examined it,
offered me five times what I gave for it, turned it upside
down and replaced it. No amount of coaxing has made it
go since that evening.'

Her sureness of touch in revision has strengthened me in
holding to one principle of editorship – never to reinstate
a passage or phrase through which the author's dissatisfied
pen has been drawn. I have, however, been rather more
lax if the rejection has been by implication only – *i.e.*
I have sometimes admitted a paragraph which exists in
draft but has found no place in the chapter to which it
had been assigned. Nevertheless I have not allowed earlier
drafts to appear which actually duplicate passages appearing
(though in a different form) in what can be established as a
later text.

Given these rules, the establishment of the completed[1]
and all but completed[2] chapters has been a fairly simple
matter. There remained the mass of drafts, sketches and
notes, some federated with others and looking forward to
a place in an already intended chapter, others picked up, as
it were, in passing, and laid by with no very clear indication
of their future use. In dealing with all these I have had to use
rather different principles, and have allowed myself rather
more discretion. I have not tried to place this residue in
order of composition, nor necessarily to reject an earlier in
favour of what appears to be a later draft. It has been a
freer, and so perhaps faultier choice, between five hundred
or so competing pieces; and it is principles of rejection rather.
than principles of selection that have been employed.

Some fragments, without expansion or support, would
have been obscure; others, without mutilation, would
have been libellous; many could not stand alone; others
were purely factual. After severe sorting, a field was

1. I, II, VIII, XIV, XV.
2. IV, V, VII, IX, X.

left, every member of which, I felt, deserved a place in the book.

The field chosen, there remained the question of arrangement. Here I had some help from the author, who, both in rough schemes of the shape that parts of the book were to take, and at the heads of many (but not all) of the notes themselves, had given possible chapter headings. Where a large body of cognate fragments existed, I have been able to federate them into a single section. Such, for instance, has been the case with the chapters on 'Men and Women' and 'Letters and Women'; but within these composite chapters[1] the arrangement of the fragments has necessarily been my own.

It can be seen from Lawrence's correspondence with her that my mother wrote poetry, though she rarely published, and never in book form. The few poems I have found – presumably all she thought worth keeping – have never, I think, been published before. Most of them are contemporary with the rest of the book, but one or two are very much earlier in date, and for want of a better principle they (except the sonnet on March, which seemed to be intended for the section in which I have placed it) are all arranged in a single section in approximate chronological order of composition.

So far as they would carry me, therefore, I have relied on my mother's own rough schemes; and beyond that point on my recollection of her intentions and in the last resort on my own discretion. The title of the book (since she left the matter open) is of my choosing, and in a few instances I have silently corrected obvious slips; otherwise every word, including the title page, is the author's own. It may be felt that in including so much on which my mother had not passed final judgement I have done her a disservice. But to me the fragments and her letters reflect her gifts and her character with especial sharpness. For this reason in particular I owe a considerable debt of gratitude to Miss F. Marian McNeil and Mrs. Ferrucio Bonavia for allowing me to print a number of my mother's letters to them.

1. III, VI, XI, XII, XIII.

The task of editing has been hard, and the writing of this introduction harder, for I have not my mother's secret for combining objectivity with emotion, and it would be wrong for me to try to describe here what the author so well describes for herself. One thing, however, which many will answer for, she omits altogether when she speaks of her youth and her old age. I have said earlier that she was beautiful when she began her career – an important thing to report of any woman – and beautiful she remained until her death, with the beauty of a younger woman.

NOTE TO THE SECOND EDITION

THIS, Catherine Carswell's last work, reappears after half a century with the original text I inherited and my introduction corrected only in minor respects. I add this note to remove a number of errors in Catherine's account of the Haskard family which she gives in Chapter IX ('Florence: the Bank') and offer a new generation of readers some thoughts about her development which have struck me forcibly in recent years as more about her youth and upbringing have been established.

Soon after this book was first published I had a sorrowful letter from General Haskard, who was then living in retirement in Ireland after a distinguished military career, and had been Catherine's cousin and inseparable play-fellow Dugal, as described elsewhere in this book. Being in the direct line of descent from Timothy Haskard, the one-legged man who crossed the Alps and founded the family fortunes in Italy, General Haskard's information is undoubtedly correct.

Timothy was originally of Leicestershire yeoman stock who ran away to sea at an early age (as many boys then did) but when quite a young man lost a leg in an accident, returned to his native county and gained some knowledge of the wool trade. But the spirit of adventure had not left him so he set out for Italy and settled in Florence about 1823. This, of course, was long before the unification of Italy, and Florence was the capital of Tuscany under an Austrian Grand Duke, under whom the one-legged Timothy obtained employment. He prospered, and when, some twenty-five years later, the Grand Dukes were ejected by the forces of liberation, Timothy retired with considerable savings with which he built up a business importing and re-exporting wool.

Timothy married an Englishwoman in Florence, and had a son, William, who founded a bank to finance the trade his father had started: Haskard's Bank developed into one of the strongest in Northern Italy, but even so could not withstand the financial hurricane of 1929.

The relevance of this remarkable story is that William, founder of the bank, married Catherine's mother's sister, and so was her uncle by marriage. Nor was this connection the only window on Italy through which Catherine was to look as a child. More and bigger ones had been opened by the departure of her maternal grandfather and his brother – both of them Disruption Ministers – to Italy, there to found congregations of the new Free Church of Scotland. The Rev. George settled in Florence, where his daughter married William Haskard; and the Rev. John chose Rome. From them issued a growing cousinhood, some of whom Catherine met when still a child; and visited in Italy when emerging from her teens for the prolonged visit to Tuscany which provided the vivid Italian experience for *Open The Door!*

Then, at eighteen, she was sent to Frankfort to study music at its famous Conservatorium. She was there for two years, an experience which provides the major episode of *The Camomile*. Then the University of Glasgow.

Clearly her father was an exceptionally broad-minded man for his time, religion, and station in life. He was entirely self-made, and had himself travelled widely, mainly to America, building up his export business.

She found in the Italians and Germans an unaffected warmth and love of culture which inspired the rest of her life. I think it helps to account for the rapidity and endurance of her friendship with Lawrence, who liked Italy, perhaps, better than most of the many countries he lived in; and I am sure explains her otherwise inexplicable decision to embark on her biography of Boccaccio.

When the thirties came, and she became famous in her

native country for her Life of Burns, she sorrowed over the fanatical nationalism of Mussolini and Hitler, and the harm they were doing to their peoples, the ordinary Germans and Italians she knew and loved. She detested the stridency of nationalism. She had, too, lived through the First World War. So, although she loved Scotland, and remained noticeably Scottish in her speech to the end of her life, she had reservations about the nationalist content of the Scottish Renascence. She admired the work of Lewis Grassic Gibbon and William Soutar, and indeed MacDiarmid, from whom she had many friendly letters and presentation copies of most of his works. She valued his courage, I think, but had doubts about him as a man. She remained very much on the fringe of the movement. She was certainly a convinced Socialist, but not in any way a political animal. She knew and valued the distinctiveness of Scotland and its culture, but I never heard a word breathed by her in support of a political separation.

While a good deal has come to light about the author since my edition of 1950, I have strictly maintained the two principles of altering nothing Catherine herself wrote, or departing from what I knew of her intentions and the editorial method I followed in framing this book, as stated in this Introduction of forty-seven years ago. I have however included some new information about her first marriage which would have been hurtful to some then alive, and have elsewhere corrected a number of errors and obscurities in my original text of this Introduction. Most of these have been detected by the unflagging and highly professional work of Dr Jan Pilditch, who is at present in Scotland researching a biography of Catherine Carswell. To her my warmest thanks are due, with my very best wishes for the future of her work.

John Carswell
Hampstead, November 1996

PART I
AUTOBIOGRAPHY

CHAPTER ONE

The Clock

Nor dare she look upon her winter face.

AS I walked through the wilderness of mean streets which bound on three sides that part of London where I now live, I looked about me thinking and speaking within myself.

I looked at the people passing, intent on their various business: young people gazing only at each other and quick under the impact; middle-aged people striving, absorbed under their burdens of success or failure; old people with the past in their preoccupied eyes. Now and again one of these infirm waifs bestowed on me a ghostly regard, a distant or searching query, a piercing glance of recognition, by all of which I knew myself hailed as a new inhabitant of their hidden realm – the realm of the husk that has known seed and blossom even if no fruitage. But the others looked past or through me, so that I felt myself to be invisible to their fantasy of seeing, as once the old – unless known personally – were invisible to mine. 'Even of present things we have no other holde but by our fantazie', I thought with Montaigne: and even in the little life of the weakest individual like myself there are many worlds of fantasy before we finish, given only enough years.

In this year and on that day, something in the air, in me, in all these faces, told me that I had left my latest fantasy so full of joy and anguish, and that I was entering upon another unannounced. What was more, I was entering upon that phase for which least guidance exists. Youth, after all, is proffered advice, middle-age compulsion. But reports concerning old age are so vague and various that each entrant is at liberty to seek a personal procedure. It might be well, I thought, to set about my own before the limits imposed by decay become too pressing. Best make a premature submission, if only to prolong the capacity – indubitable perquisite of the elderly – to cock a snook at life. If there be indeed any wisdom to be had from the condition of old age, let me survey it at leisure. If not, let me grow used, without repining, to a childish existence of sensation enriched, it may be hoped, by memory, yet undisturbed by thought.

I found comfort as I walked along – feeling the air and the sun as extraordinary pleasures – in the knowledge that my legs, my eyes and my ears were still serviceable. I could, without mishap, have walked along the wall of the canal bridge on my right or sprung upon the moving trolley-bus on my left. Only the other day, in a hawthorn-littered glade in East Anglia, I had set myself to vault a fence, and had found my limbs obedient. True, the fence was not a high one, and the fact that I had to dare myself to it without witnesses for a fall, has significance. But I cleared it, if I then stood trembling on the other side. And not long ago – this time with deprecating onlookers – I dropped from the footboard of a train which would have carried me, squeezed into its wrong portion, through and far beyond my station. Not bravado but inconvenience inspired that jump. Laden with baggage and faced with the choice between the jump and a fifteen-mile walk, or a night in a haystack, I chose the jump. 'She'll be electrocuted,' I heard somebody say with relish as I dropped towards a tangle of brake wires on the track. Then the voice of a travelling soldier – 'the old girl has done it, by God,' as I landed without a fall. Never yet in my life have I broken a bone, nor so much as sprained a muscle. My body deserves better of me than that I should do so now. There must be an end of this, I said, as I gathered my shaken self and my scattered belongings. The old girl will jump no more. It is some consolation that, even as a child, I disliked jumping or dropping almost as much as I liked climbing or balancing.

I thought, as I walked along: it is not entirely bad to see again while being oneself virtually unseen. 'Everybody used to turn and look at you when we went about together,' my sister, Fanny, complained some time ago (Fanny says things like this), 'but now nobody gives you a glance.' I apologised. I am apt to apologise when my toes are trodden on; besides, I was less concerned by the remark than by the unresolved sisterly grudge by which it was dictated. 'After all,' I said, 'it's their loss. I don't see what I can do about it.' 'You might at least powder your nose, smoke less and wear a proper hat,' she scolded. 'Ah, if only I could find one that didn't make me feel a guy! Do you remember that wonderful creation with the shot bronze-and-green ribbon bows you once chose for me at Miss Sinclair's in Glasgow? That *was* a hat!' We recalled with laughter how, meeting for the first time in twenty years, my mother and one of her sisters from Italy had spent their meeting deploring each other's deteriorated looks and unbecoming apparel. And so we parted in amity.

But, I repeat, it isn't sheer loss to become invisible to the casual eye. The young woman may hardly walk without attracting attention: the woman wearing age's disguise goes about unnoted and underanged. Here she is like the child again, but with experience behind her eyes. What first appeared as a deprivation, I thought, I may now bring myself to welcome as a benefit. At least I begin to detect in it certain advantages. Observation is purged and sharpened. A refuge is bestowed, a novel entertainment, a release, sometimes a revelation. I can, I thought, count this ghostliness, this new species of truancy, as on the credit side. The world remembering I am by the world forgot. There is comfort, too, in being well past improvement.

I thought; it is no doubt shocking, when for years on years one has functioned as the mainspring of a household, the punctual nerve on which the well-being of a home has reposed, to become inessential. No creature at this moment knows or is concerned with my whereabouts, my time of day, my doings. These no longer matter to anybody, scarcely to myself. From such a dismay men are known to have languished, even to have died. But still suffering from this loss and because I have suffered it, I begin to perceive that from it in season a small gain may grow.

So here, I said, is another handful to be garnered from my stubble field.

As I thus thought and spoke with myself – much more having now escaped my memory – I looked at the traffic, at the houses, at the evocative names over the poor little war-denuded shops. *Miller, Lewis, Sandler, Donald, Daniel, Gray, Maurice.* And there, above the shops, and below them behind pavement gratings, were homes. Token homes perhaps, but triumphant; homes of people – a shell or pot-plant on the sill, a cat or a canary enjoying the window, a reassuring flicker of flame in the fireplace or reflected from a treasured piano-front. Such homes, I know, must be swept away as unworthy of civilisation. They are on many accounts to be deplored. Yet they have been dearly loved. Men and women innumerable dream of returning to them as to a paradise. They are still lovable and most profoundly touching. They have crystallised character, created eccentricity. I shall miss them when they go.

How many homes, I thought; how many faces, streets, names, shells, plants (including several aspidistras I was allowed to wash once a week as a child); how many hearths and cats and cage-birds have gone into the texture of my life! This it is, I said, to be old. At least it purports to age. This is the nostalgia not known to youth, but something different, diffused, detached; not a true nostalgia, because free from desire. Vigny, when he was only twenty-three, foretasted it when he wrote in his journal, '*Ah! Combien j'ai vécu! N'y a-t-il pas deux cents ans que cela est ainsi?*' But Vigny was that rare thing, a poet born with an old heart, and his sophisticated eye received impressions which had at once the weariness and the clarity of age.

My own vision, with what seemed like centuries behind it, was at this moment not joined with fatigue. Indeed it had become infantine to a degree that nothing came to it tarnished, nothing staled. But, being not an infant, I saw the present and the past partaking together in a third figment. As in a symphony the opening notes come dawn-fresh; then make way for other new-born themes, only to recur and build themselves again unpredictably with these; then stride through transpositions of key, find transforming counter-points and, at last, gather up everything for the hidden yet predestined finale; so now my sight played for me. Mine was the summary movement – the fastest, too – with the conclusion anticipated though not yet in the ear, and with the earlier movements revealed in their relation to the whole. While this mood lasts, I thought, age is consummated, even acquitted.

It does not last. How should it? Nor do I – ecstasy being a grave danger in my family – ask that it should, though I have often imagined this to be the appropriate music for those insatiable listeners of the old-fashioned interminable heaven. I ask only that it should, upon occasion, sound for me in sudden concert.

I noticed a hairpin lying on the pavement – precisely the kind of hairpin I wanted; bronze, with wavy ends. Stooping to pick it up, my symphony forgotten, I saw into a basement room beneath the grating of a shop.

In such a darkly shining little room as this, I thought, but high in the shocking tenement of a Glasgow slum, where it was set like a gem, I had first conceived my love of the poorest sort of home which good women inhabit and cherish. It was in the religious humour of my parents that we children should often go with them from our own large house to visit needy but exemplary Friends in the Lord, whose lot had been cast in a single room in the Gorbals or the Saltmarket. An unforeseen result was that I was ravished by admiration and imbued with affectionate envy. Could anything be more desirable than some day to possess just such a tiny home oneself? Its ardent perfection within, heightened by the noise and filth of every approach, filled me less with reformatory or compassionate, than with emulative zeal. I still find it difficult to traverse any slum without prospecting there for a room which I could 'make nice' and occupy. Here my practical experiments have varied from wasteful expense of energy to moderate success, enjoyable in either outcome.

But perhaps the obsession might be traced to a deeper, an ancestral source. Because, as I stooped for that hairpin and saw into that basement room between Camden and

Kentish Towns, I found myself also thinking that into some such living apartment off the old Glasgow High Street, long before I was born and before the industrial slums of Glasgow existed, my maternal great-grandfather must have entered to make the single remark recorded of him. My mother liked to tell us of it and it made upon me, as so many of her words did, a deep impression. If I prove to be something disposed to ancestor worship, this derives from her. She would, I think, have endorsed Anthony Trollope's observation, 'It is certainly of service to a man to know who were his grandfathers if he entertain an ambition to move in the upper circles of society, and also of service to be able to speak of them as persons who were themselves somebodies in their time . . . It is certainly convenient to be able to allude, if it be but once in a year, to some blood relation.' But her principles would have led her to excise the phrase regarding social ambitions.

Certainly the grandfather of whom she most loved to speak was unlike her mother's father in that he lacked distinction of blood. His name was Lewis. He was a Welsh soldier, most likely a mercenary of the Continental wars. When his regiment came to be stationed at Stirling Castle he loved and married Janet Inglis, the farmer's daughter who brought the milk each morning to the barracks. Upon leaving the army he set up shop as a grocer in Glasgow, prospered, and became a burgess of the City. Coming suddenly into the room behind, below or over the shop one day, he found his two sons poring over their forbidden books. 'Books or business!' he exclaimed in exasperation. 'Business or books! But it cannot be the both of them. You must take your choice.'

Each boy, George Lewis, my grandfather, and James, his younger brother, chose books and went to Glasgow College. George took degrees at Edinburgh and at St. Andrews as well. Both became eminent ministers of the Scottish Church, married above them (as Scots ministers, forming a sort of aristocracy of the intellect, commonly did), 'came out' at the Disruption in 1843, died in elegant Continental beds, lie buried near to Keats and Shelley in Rome. George wrote a number of books in virile English, books which display an open and enterprising mind. He made the first complete translation from Latin of the Breviary and the Missal with copious notes which lack neither appreciation nor humour. He edited a newspaper. He visited America and wrote about his visit. He brought up his daughters on Shakespeare, the Bible and the news of each day, deeply impressing upon them his firm, expository character. Would the great-grandfather condone, the grandfather condemn my picking up a hairpin from the pavement of Camden Town? No matter; I am of both, if less decisive than either. It may be because my paternal grandfather was yet another pulpiteer that I find a homily even harder than a hairpin to resist.

A tiny boy, almost a baby, stared up at me without criticism from the edge of the kerb where he sat. He had been singing to himself, that song of the happy small boy – mindless, tuneless, timeless, without beginning or ending. My stooping and smiling struck him into silence. From a window above came a burst of radio music followed by full-throated adult laughter. Throughout the world human beings were killing and being killed, torturing and being tortured, undergoing nameless agonies, tasting hatred or despair, welcoming death in the widest of all wars. In this street there was strain, sorrow, heartbreak. I know most of the dealers. Two, within a week, had lost only sons. There were gaps between houses where the bombs had fallen wiping out many families. Within the past twenty-four hours some of our hospital ships had been destroyed.

Yet the air of this street, and all the air round the world vibrated with laughter and with music. That same morning, after leaving home, I had called at my fried fish-and-chips shop and at my grocer's. In the first, the handsome, clean, efficient Jewess, who is in full charge since her husband's enlistment in the R.A.F., was sweetly singing as she tested her fry with the drainer. 'Pedro, the Fisherman', she warbled, and the queue joined in. 'You're happy!' remarked one of them who wore the grimed uniform of a fire-fighter. 'Yes, I'm happy this morning,' she admitted with her radiant smile. 'For *once* not a thing in the papers this morning to make me sad.' She paused.

Her face clouded. 'Oh, I forgot. There was one thing – those hospital ships!' After a moment of silent attention to her vats, she was again humming the catchy tune where she had left off. Soon she was in full song. The fire-fighter whistled the chorus.

And in the grocer's. 'Cold this morning,' remarked a customer. 'Coldish, yes,' replied the tradesman, 'but d'you know, when I set out from home there was a white rime over the grass. It crunched under my feet at each step. That "crunch,"' his eyes beamed. 'Makes you feel good for the day, that crunch of the grass under your boots.' He smiled with happiness. We all smiled with happiness. And here were this baby and I smiling in perfect momentary contentment, eyeing each other over nothing more than a hairpin; and in our ears the voices of soldiers and munition makers shouting with laughter over some new song or old joke.

Is this illogical human capacity horrible or to be praised? I have wondered, if all could be truly reckoned up (not Mass Observation, but God alone could do it because, while pain is mostly conscious, pleasure is as often not) would grief or gaiety predominate in the worst moment throughout the existence of our planet? I have thought that perhaps, if the smallest and the commonest satisfaction might be included in the sum of happy rays, these would at any time outnumber the others, if only by a little.

I thought, Tomorrow will be different with me. Melancholy, resentment, anxiety or some other frenzy will preside. When I get home, I thought, I must make some rough notes by way of reminder. But why? They would only add to the disorderly heap that has for so long grown bigger and dustier, while afflicting me because I dare not examine it. Better break a futile habit, burn the lot unread, cease to be haunted by a project of which it is the flaccid symbol, lapse into what there is to be experienced from an unchronicled decline.

Then I saw a face look out at me from a shop window so that I stood still to return its gaze. The shop belonged to one of the two dealers, brothers known to me, who had lately lost their sons. I was already too familiar with most of the dejected and dismembered relics, scarcely to be named antiques, which formed this one's war-time display. But the face was the face of a clock not seen by me before.

The war had reached that stage when many chronometers, accustomed to be renewed from the Continent, were refusing to register our island hours. Mine had stopped beyond home repair, and I could not afford the price of a new one. This might serve my turn. It was a timepiece obviously French: the body and base ornate with gilded brass; decorations in Sèvres china – turquoise and white, with flower wreaths; on either side a lion's head menacing the pilgrim in relativity. I wanted it. But if it did not keep time, I was resolved to turn from it. I have often wished that I might have been a mender or maker of time pieces, thus joining the only body of craftsmen for whom time has no existence. But I am informed that it is too late for me to enter the fraternity. As things are, I cannot be bothered looking after the more perfect possessions I have too readily acquired, so that I usually end by giving them away; and already I have defective possessions enough to occupy an eternity of expertise. Perhaps this is a reason why I easily conceive of an eternity.

I entered the shop. My friend's wife was in charge, he being asleep after fire-watching. 'How's things, lovey?' she asked. 'Any news of your boy? Have one of my fags: yours is down to the root.'

We sat to talk before approaching the formula of a deal. The clock remained silent. But she said it was in going order, and it was priced – 'to you, ducks' – at three guineas. With this dealer I never 'bate'. Compliments were exchanged and the clock became my affair. I thought, as I paid for it, that there went a shilling for each year of my life.

Having borne it back to the war-crazed *conciergerie* where I was furnishing my second rent-free London home, I proceeded to improve the new acquaintance. It came alive, I found, only on a particular stance near my bed, ticked almost inaudibly, chimed the hours and half hours with unaggressive sweetness, needed winding only once in sixteen days of mild acceleration. Upon so merciful a companion in the voyage through time I

could surely rely without being startled or depressed by
its reminders.

But more was to follow. One night, soon afterwards, I lay
in bed reading after midnight had sounded. Presently I put
away my book and turned out the light. Through my first
drowse came the intimation that another hour was behind
us. 'One', I murmured settling farther down. 'Two', I heard.
Could I have heard aright? But the vagaries of time have
long been so familiar as scarcely to perturb me. 'Three',
sang the still small voice from under the glass shade which
guarded its larynx from the all-prevailing coke dust. With
sleep banished I listened for more. And I counted, while
the bell struck sixty-three and then ceased.

All next day the clock behaved normally. I searched the
innocent face, noting with new appreciation its elegant
frivolity; the figuring in gold and black, the bands and
circlets of small roses, violets, green leaves, tendrils, all
in their natural colours. But the dial remained enigmatic.
That night I stayed awake till 1 a.m. – no unusual delay –
to make sure. Perhaps I had been deluded or asleep. But
again the insistent chime was repeated, and I reckoned
sixty-three.

At the same hour, on seven successive days, I heard the
same tale of strokes. On the eighth day a single stroke
resumed for the advent of morning. Since then, there has
been no irregularity but for an occasional striking of a
hundred and three, which I have taken with unconcern.

The other did concern me. Omens are not in my line of
life. Wax to first impressions and subject to illusions, I yet
belong to the tribe of the tough, not the tender-minded. I
knew that any clockmaker could explain to my satisfaction
the behaviour of my clock. But I had to examine the
coincidence of my own response. The chime of my clock
is deliberate. Sixty-three notes occupy a full two minutes.
Hence, seven times in that distributed quarter-hour I had
heard a voice asseverate my years. *Seven multiplied by nine,*
it sang, *equals sixty-three; sixty-three, the grand climacteric of
a human life; sixty-three, presided over by Saturn: sixty-three,
your age.*

The voice did not recall the lugubrious croak of Poe's

raven. It conveyed neither melancholy, menace, nor despair. It came to the ear rather as the piping of some small species of water-fowl, reiterative but remote. It did not deny; it did not threaten; it merely affirmed.

And I argued with it. I argued across my pile of dusty notes not yet destroyed. Who cares, I said, that I have tried and failed to find an outline which would give those notes meaning? And without some such outline they are wearisome even to me. While I enjoy without fail the memoirs of other lives – pictures of childhood for its own sake, records of the most trivial, or the most important encounters – I disclaim them for myself. My venture, all too vaguely envisaged, was to be in a different mode, a mode I now see to be beyond my powers. I would have set out (if I could) on my petty peregrination because, like a greater pilgrim, 'I only thought to make I know not what', and I should have persevered (if I did) like that same greater pilgrim, only 'mine own self to gratifie'. If it gratify me no longer, why compel myself to pursue it, most likely without avail? Who will benefit? Not I. Composition has become for me a heavy toil, and the time for such discipline is surely past. Not a world in the re-making, which, less than a world at war, will be disposed to examine such a testament of age or old woman's trivia. My days, besides, are full. I had not foreseen how short and how full the days of a solitary can be as energy flags. I cannot even allege any new art in growing old, unless it be the elaboration of truancy from toil. But while, like Prescott the historian, I have always had 'a healthy aversion to persistent work', I doubt if I could conjure from that the history of my Peru.

Leaving these drawbacks aside, I have some friends and of relatives a host. I do not gladly shock, induce tedium or inflict disappointment. With Montaigne I had rather be difficult than tedious, but one may be both.

I have indeed a son – far away and battle-bound. Against his grand climacteric (God send it) the clumsiest attempt might provide occasional reading at once light and pious. But here, too, there is risk. I would not deface for him the sacred image of a mother, yet truthfulness alone is worth my effort.

Seven times I argued with the French clock. Seven times the distant, deaf, inhuman voice measured my living numerals. The voice prevailed.

I may hope to have come at least by a mounting stone. The enterprise looks hard: the course is obscure, the destination unknown. The beast that must carry me is spavined and given to pause. My seat is precarious. But my unrepining lot has mostly been to venture under poor conditions and to work with poor tools. Lacking these handicaps I might not feel impelled to set out.

The wise and fortunate, becoming soon aware of their limitations, refrain from tasks that are beyond their capacity. Others, like myself, can accomplish in any degree only by addressing themselves to the unattainable. Wasteful, exhausting, often fruitless, it is none the less our only way to do, the more because even the attainable got by less grandiose means tastes to us insipid.

This has been my tiresome fate: to admire magnitude and to desire perfection, yet to be baffled by almost every disadvantage of nature and circumstance; to covet method and order (yes, and to strive for them!), but to have a wandering mind and an erratic memory; to be full of occupations, profuse of interests, immoderate in foolish energy, while subject to confusions and lacking the capacity for proper habits. Whether it be from a sense of my inadequacy, which would provide an excuse beforehand against failure, or from some subtler scepticism, I am discouraged by the consideration of economical means and fine implements. Yet another defect is that in everything and at every point I am waylaid, bewildered, arrested or diverted by the mysteries of textures.

It sometimes happens, however, that disabilities are one with the nature of an essay. May it be so in this, my last. I propose to survey what is gone for the better regarding of what is immediately here, and what is present for the better knowledge of what is past. With eyes on the setting suns I shall try to examine former dawns. Looking back at the faces of youth I shall endeavour to see the more steadily my own winter face. In this dual undertaking I may well fail. But, while I have the sense to hear the French clock chime, I mean to do my best. At least there can be no harm in it. 'Who is entitled to write his reminiscences,' asks Alexander Herzen. And he replies, 'Everyone: because no one is obliged to read them.'

CHAPTER TWO

Glasgow

I WAS born towards the end of March, 1879, on top of a steep, grey, stony hill in and overlooking that 'seat of discipline' – as Henry James has called it – the city of Glasgow.

There have been times when I resented the place of my birth. Such resentment might have been more lasting and more just had I been one of those ragged, bare-legged, blue-footed, verminous and valgus children, whose condition, not far from our square-pillared portico, often aroused my envy while occupying much of my father's leisure and my mother's compassion.

George Eliot chose well when she lodged Felix Holt in a Glasgow slum to discover there that 'this world is not a very fine place for a good many people in it', and that countless people lived in streets where there was 'little more than a chink of daylight to show the hatred in women's faces'.

When I was born the shame of the slums, gaining tidal force from the industrial revolution, already lapped murkily round three sides of the eminence where our home stood. It was a tide all the more foul in that it was fed from the cleanly Scottish Highlands and the Irish East Coasts, polluting these innocent, if also idle feeders, within a generation of their entry. Yet they floated us and our like in arks of safety, industry, prosperity and hope.

In our particular ark we were taught to love, honour and entertain the poor. The poor, one might say, were our pets. Decidedly they were always with us. We were not taught that our own privileged nurture was largely sustained at the price of their poverty. How should we be taught by our parents what they themselves did not know? Both country born, upright, sensitive, lovers of their kind, they were oppressed as I now fully realise, by 'the stench of trade', besides which John Stuart Mill found 'little else . . . at Glasgow'. They were horrified by the conditions. They deplored the squalor and the hideous inequality. They lived without luxury, feeling, I think, that self-indulgence would be ill-mannered. In the thirty years I knew her, my mother had only one evening dress, and that her wedding dress of thick white Irish poplin which, as she aged, she veiled with black lace. They strove hard and constantly to ameliorate and to reform. True, they had the vaguest comprehension of the economic implications of the position in which they found themselves. Their souls were noble, their hearts Christian, their actions consistent. But they had been reared in a conventional social and religious code which on the whole commended itself to their reason. Poorly read outside the Bible and a few major classics, their intellectual equipment was meagre in spite of educations on which some thought had been expended. And my father had his living, and ours to get. Like most sons of Scottish country ministers he had gone out into the world when still in his teens (to be circumstantial, he had been shipped to Trinidad upon leaving Merchiston School) with scarcely more in his purse than any Highland or Irish immigrant to Glasgow.

No doubt it was a fault to be so little capable of economic thought; to see so clearly the wrongness of the situation, yet so obscurely the proper remedy. Myself becoming at fourteen a lifelong socialist (through reading Robert Blatchford) I have blamed them.

But I cannot claim an effort towards a fairer society comparable with their effort towards the coming of God's kingdom on earth. Those of a similar inheritance with mine who were able to carry on the example and transfer the impulse were the salt of the next generation. But I notice that, upon a further remove, where the religious and humanist elements are not merely repudiated but became inoperative (two very different states), many who think with economic correctness excuse in themselves much personal selfishness and ill behaviour on the ground of a wrong social system. I cannot judge them or my parents for these different failures. None the less I hold it a calumny to say that the Christian philanthropists of the nineteenth century prolonged the shames of the industrial revolution by a sop of charity. Those like my parents (there were many) were inspired to most practical and most handsome energies by their leaders – men such as Shaftesbury, Wilberforce, Livingstone, Chalmers, Candlish. They stood for social justice. They fought against evil, ignorance and greed. They served their generation and every cause of progress. And they did all with graciousness, with modesty, with lives that were personally scrupulous at home and in the market-place. They were good. And I have come to think more highly of goodness than of anything else. Nothing can take the place of goodness.

Besides, of course, Mill was wrong. There was much in Glasgow besides the stench of trade. Even omitting the estimable aspects, which I did not appreciate until my childhood was past, there was life, fierce, reckless and abundant, more especially when this life was low.

I have said that I was sometimes envious. I envied most of all the tattered, bare-headed, bare-footed trace-boys (fortunate in having neither hats, shoes, nor any new clothes) who waited with their powerful horses at the St. Vincent Street crossing for the two-horse cars which it was their work to help uphill to Sauchiehall Street. While the car was moving, a boy, running alongside, hitched his trailing trace to an outside hook, hurled himself with a wild cry upon his steed, and cantered up abreast of the car horses, sitting sideways almost on the tail of his own beast, till they reached the top. There he unhitched again without stopping the car, and returned at leisure to his former station. I greatly admired this feat of horsemanship, and gladly would I have spent my days in its acquisition and practice.

Again, I envied those children, poorest of the poor, who were not on the platform and wearing detestable Sunday clothes, but down in the body of the City Hall upon occasions of Mr. McKeith's Children's Dinner Table. Their enjoyment seemed as great as my discomfort. The appetising smell of thick hot pea soup and chunks of new bread, which ran among them in trolleys, rose in my nostrils. We had already attended St. John's Church that morning and, after nibbling an unsatisfactory sandwich in the vestry there, had walked to the City Hall. After a long hour and more of hymns and hunger, we should walk all the way home again, to sit down to the tureen of rice-and-milk soup – a favourite with my father and decreed for our Sunday dinner 'to save the servants'. I liked pea soup very much. I hated rice-and-milk soup – hence proving that I was no worthy member of my father's family, because he said that 'all Macfarlanes love rice'. I could well have done with even a chunk of the new bread (unwholesome, my mother would have said) of which the aroma almost unendurably stimulated my hunger, while I saw it being snatched by a thousand small hands from the passing trolleys.

Already I have said how attractive I found the homes of our poorest friends among the godly. I found a different, perhaps even more powerful attraction where no godliness was in evidence. Sometimes of a Saturday night my father took us down with him to walk about one of the worst, most crowded neighbourhoods so that we might see 'the heathen at our doors' and, no doubt, that we might conceive a horror of strong drink which never entered our house except for jam-making, when it was my mother's country habit to dip the pot covers in brandy for the better preservation of the fruit. Our parents had not been brought up as teetotallers. My father had keenly enjoyed good wines, and my mother had a liking for ales and cider. Both worked and spoke always for the open tavern service of food with liquor for everybody. But, seeing the drunkenness of the Glasgow poor under only the lowest conditions, the absurd licensing laws, the clandestine drinking of the obscure, and the privileged sideboards of the richer citizens, they felt that circumstances forbade any self-indulgence no matter how innocent and temperate. Every Sunday afternoon, for some years, my father went a round of the cells in the police station, baling out the week-end drunks with half-crowns so that they might not lose their jobs on the Monday morning. He asked each one to sign the pledge and to return his half-crown out of the next week's wages. The pledges were often broken, though once only was a half-crown not repaid. But how, he asked, could he even suggest to one of these men the giving up of drink if he himself were going home to refresh himself with a glass of port?

So far as I was concerned, however, a horror of drunkenness would better have been attained had my father gone on the Greek model and shown us some of the servants at home in a state of intoxication. When such a misfortune arose, as it did, though not often, it was concealed from us if possible by charitable mis-statements. But in the teeming Saturday night crowd, where all the men and women, and even children at the breast, were openly drunk, drunkenness assumed an epic quality. It was an orgy, an abandon, a bacchannal, a celebration, a wild defiance. Shawled women fought, screaming and tearing out each other's hair, while the men stood round roaring them on with laughter. Other men and women reeled along in song or reclined oblivious in gutters. At that date – round about 1890 – whisky, gin, even brandy, could be bought by the lowest wage-earner, and cheaper, more potent liquids were to be had for a few pence. No alternative pleasures were offered except for a hard thrift. The spectacle was shocking. But it had a sordid splendour, a whole-hearted, ruinous contempt which, for the moment, excluded other considerations in at least one beholder. Hence, my father's morality play miscarried. I was of course frightened. I clung to my father's hand. My heart bled for the children of my own age who dodged or trembled unshielded in the gas-lit, milling, vociferous throng. But, though I did not then, and do not now analyse my emotion, I know that I partook in some sort in a triumph. Being a child I was unaffected by the frightful hygienic and sociological implications of the scene, and in spirit I inclined rather to applaud than to censure the actors in it. I remained almost untouched by the simple missionary passion by which my parents were informed. I breathed more easily in the Trongate on a Saturday night than when joining in the hymns at a meeting of the Grove Street Institute (my father presiding) or at a 'Happy Sunday Afternoon' for the Canal Boatmen, or helping arrange the flowers for a soirée at the Y.M.C.A. of which my father was the president and one of the initiators.

If we had been in Central Africa and I had been given the choice between a native dance and a service in the mission hall, I cannot doubt which would have had my preference. In spite of our mother's prayers and our father's heartfelt dedication, none of us were born to be missionaries.

The long humped thoroughfare, on which we lived, afforded endless interest to me throughout my childhood. Running from poor and shabby regions in the east to genteel ones – becoming shabby too – each way by considerable inclines, it looked down abruptly from our summit upon districts even more sharply contrasted. Our big blackened stone house, bearing the number 127, was at the westernmost corner of half a dozen similar houses cut off by cross-roads and dominating the height. The house at the easternmost corner was inhabited by priests of the Jesuit College behind it, on the backside of the lane which ran all along the wall and ashpits of a row of back-greens.

The priests' house (which we always ran past on tiptoe), and ours were the two biggest houses of the six, but we felt ours to be superior because it had a small railed square of green separating the end from the cross-roads pavement. This green, together with the world of wall, lane and ashpits (large as some of the slum rooms housing whole families) made part of a happy hunting ground for us children. In addition we had in our back-green, which was divided into two parts on different levels, what we called 'the woodhouse'. This was made over to us to do with as we liked. We painted it all pale blue enamel inside, furnished it from the boxroom, lighted the vile-smelling stove, made feasts there with cousins who came to us on holiday from their boarding schools, and found in it innumerable sources of enjoyment. So strong were my home-making instincts that I seriously considered converting our ashpit into an annexe for myself and my dolls.

Below and behind, to the north, lay the furtive steeps of Garnethill leading precipitously to the denser purlieus of the Cowcaddens. For a solitary child these were not without dangers to explore, and I still sometimes find myself there in bewildered, though not painful, dreams. In front, to the south, the life of Sauchiehall Street clanged and sauntered past, well within sight of our windows across an exciting waste piece of land, where later we watched the building of a panorama. This duly opened to display the Battle of Bannockburn, which we enormously admired, especially the 'real' grass and twigs in the foreground. We were near enough to Sauchiehall Street to have a detailed view of Queen Victoria when the little, bonneted, old lady drove past on her Diamond Jubilee visit. Indeed we were sure that she responded with a special smile and wave of her hand to our frantic greetings from the top of our porch, upon which we had assembled with flags by getting out of one of the drawing-room windows. From farther off we could hear the sounds of the river: sirens and steam-whistles on foggy days, the clangor of the shipyards when the wind was set from there. From a nursery window we watched the first illumination of the town by electricity, and we saw the fireworks of the Exhibition. In every direction we had wide and eventful prospects.

Though this was the earliest home in Glasgow that I can remember, my sister and I had been born round the corner on that same hill in a house, or rather half house, where our parents had begun their married life with the modesty demanded by their circumstances. Those houses now are mostly theatrical lodgings. But in the last quarter of the nineteenth century, Hill Street still displayed well-polished brass plates on many glossy doors, and housed some of our near acquaintance. Hector Cameron, the celebrated surgeon, was one of these; and our only Glasgow relatives, the Roxburghs, had lived next door to us.

Of these Roxburghs I have no very early memories. They were of a generation older than my parents, and their numerous children and grandchildren, whom we came later to know, were then already winning distinction in England and in more distant parts of the world. With old Dr. Roxburgh I became acquainted only from his portraits (we had a remarkably vivid oil painting of him and several photographs), and from talk. He looks stuffy, choleric, and almost too full of irritable character, with a crumpled red Ibsenish face round which white tufts of hair stuck out irascibly, and I have heard it said with smiling tolerance that, in his later years, he liked surreptitious draughts of whisky 'behind the cupboard door'. He had been the minister of our church, Free St. John's, which was engulfed in slumdom and trade traffic to the East before ever I sat sleeping against my mother's shoulder in one of its dark pews.

St. John's had an interesting history and bulked large in our lives. It was one of the twenty new churches built in Glasgow by the great Thomas Chalmers, and the one which he chose as the first centre for his great social experiments when he left the Old Tron Church to occupy its pulpit in 1819, by which date he was already famous as a preacher in London and as a mathematician in Scotland.

In a population largely composed of weavers, labourers and operatives, Chalmers found that of 3000 families more than 800 had no contact with any church, much less with any culture. Children attended no school. Poverty and drunkenness ruled. He divided the parish of St. John's into districts, setting over each a deacon and an elder to be responsible for the temporal and spiritual care of its inhabitants, and in the course of each year he visited every family himself at least once. He founded two day schools, at fees of two shillings to three shillings a quarter, and several Sunday and mission schools. Seven hundred children attended the day schools. The others had free instruction. He issued quarterly publications on *The Christian and Civic Economy of Large Towns*, and in four years had substantially reduced the pauper expenditure of Glasgow. After he left to become Professor of Moral Philosophy at St. Andrews University the work at St. John's was carried on successively by three men of strongly contrasted characters: Dr. Roxburgh, Dr. Alexander Whyte, and Dr. John Carroll. Dr. Roxburgh, my great-uncle, baptised me; Dr. Whyte married my parents and later supplied me with godly books by himself; Dr. Carroll was our minister at St. John's, where my father was a leading elder. At the Disruption of 1843, in which Chalmers acted as the spearhead, both my grandfathers and both my great-uncles were among the 450 ministers who withdrew with him from the Church of Scotland, forsaking their comfortable manses and stipends at what they felt to be the call of duty. If, when success rewarded their hardihood, they tended to become a trifle smug, perhaps they may be forgiven by lesser men who claim lack of smugness but never risked their all for a principle.

When I was born Dr. Roxburgh was on the eve of retirement, and my baptism must have been one of the last offices he performed. He being infirm and I frail, the ceremony took place in one of the Hill Street drawing-rooms. I was named Catherine Roxburgh, after old Dr. Roxburgh's wife – Aunt Roxburgh as we came to call her. Soon afterwards they left Glasgow with their one remaining and only unmarried daughter, Cousin Eliza, to settle in Weston-super-Mare. Poor Cousin Eliza was of saintly life, but, subject to a morbid streak which was apt to crop up in her father's family, she had a sad end. Following upon an accident that seemed trifling at the time (entering a room in the dark she collided with a marble mantelpiece cutting an eyebrow) she became completely blind. This she interpreted as an affliction sent by God to punish her for some lack of goodness, and, falling into melancholy, she took her own life.

Aunt Roxburgh lived to be very old, and she never forgot her small namesake. Every birthday I had from her a letter full of good advice and a present (a Bible, a doll, a workbox), and at her death she left me a hundred pounds by which I was enabled to study music for two years in Germany. During her life we children came to know her and to welcome her visits with rejoicing. She had been a Miss Gray, one of the daughters of a family still remembered in Dundee. Her sister, who married my paternal grandfather Dr. Macfarlane, died leaving nine young children. My grandfather's second wife, Miss Telfer-Smollett (a relative of the Admiral and of the novelist) herself childless, had proved unsympathetic as a stepmother. To this situation Aunt Roxburgh had brought so much wisdom, laughter and loving-kindness that my father and the rest came to regard her with more than filial affection. Only one of the nine Macfarlanes – yet another Catherine – had died in youth ('out-grew her strength' was the phrase used) and the eight who survived were unanimous in praise of Aunt Roxburgh if in nothing else. Her descendants are many. One of her grandson doctors introduced a literary element. His father was a cousin of George Macdonald, and his wife is a niece of 'Mark Rutherford'. He also introduced my son into the world, and a son of his own (of much the same age as mine, for Henry married late) is, as I write this, a prisoner of war in Germany after heroic exploits as a paratrooper.

In Hill Street we had had the Synagogue near us. Certain beliefs held with enthusiasm by my mother – less ardently by my father – made the Jews our special concern. She desired that the world should be converted to Christianity with the least possible delay – at all events that Christianity should be preached to all the world so that everybody could know about it and make speedy choice, thus to hasten the second coming of Christ, when all true believers would be 'caught up in the air' to dwell in heaven. From her reading of the Bible she had further ascertained that the gospel was to be offered 'to the Jew first, and afterwards to the Gentiles'. For her there was no disputing Holy Writ. Hence she found that many well-meaning people, more especially in pulpits, were going about the business the wrong way and putting the cart before the horse. She hung up in our dining-room a shiny maroon-coloured card with the words TO THE JEW FIRST embossed upon it in silver letters that caught the eye. And she was sadly puzzled when her ministerial and other Christian friends showed embarrassment or luke-warmness in the face of her gentle but tactless and frequent reminders. Certainly she did her own duty with regard to Israel. Many very poor Jews, mostly Polish, came to Glasgow, to lodge in cheap streets on the south side of the Clyde. They, or some philanthropist for them, had opened a sort of informal club in Abbotsford Place, where at one time rich Glasgow merchants had flaunted their West Indian fortunes. My mother decided that we ought to attend the club, if only to bid the refugees welcome and to help them learn English, of which many knew scarcely a word. I cannot have been more than twelve when I started giving these informal English lessons in Abbotsford Place. I shall never forget the physical atmosphere of that room. The pupils were effusive in their gratitude, but they had travelled across the globe in the clothes they stood up in, and I suppose that few had come by the convenience of a bath since their arrival. For some reason my teaching days did not continue many weeks though the classes were necessarily at night, and it may be that my father forbade them. But in the time I picked up a fair sprinkling of Yiddish. Later, more selective Jews were bidden instead to come to our house, and several of these we came to know well and to like. This, however, was at a later date, and of course long after we left Hill Street.

In the Renfrew Street house (now a large nursing home) while we dominated the western corner the Jesuits reigned in the other, extending far behind the garden walls at the back by way of a training college and nunnery. They, of course, were outside our missionary scope. Were they not already Christians – of a sort?

Our tradition was one of militant protestantism. Not long ago I had for the first time the opportunity of reading my Lewis grandfather's two-volume exposition on *The Bible, the Missal and the Breviary* and he was evidently no bigot, being not only fair-minded towards the sister institution, but urgent that his own might learn much from its greater insistence upon the contemplative aspect of religion. Instructed thus by her admired father, and perhaps because she had been at a French school besides living in Italy, my mother hoped and believed that, when the blissful moment arrived, almost as many Catholics as Protestants would be 'caught up in the air' rejoicing. Jesuits, though, were in a category by themselves. To put it gently they lacked the simplicity of true worship. Thus, from our perches on the back-garden wall, we used to peer across at their windows behind which we felt dark things were planned and done.

Our own contribution to the variety of the street was made by our visitors, who were of every colour and nation – freed negro slaves, Indian rajahs, South Sea Island royalties (my father was on friendly terms with the King and Queen of the Sandwich Islands, where he had spent some time when a young man), Jewish evangelists and all kinds of white missionaries. It was a household full of interest for the young. At least so I found it as a child. I grew to love coloured people, in particular negroes, so that I now have not merely no colour prejudice (few Scots have) but I often find myself wishing that my world was mainly populated by black people and that whites, with their anxious faces, were in a minority. So soothing in their hue, so comfortable in their ways, expressions, smiles and songs, so infectious in their laughter, so touching in their agitations and endearments, so pure in their beliefs are the Africans. I find myself in agreement with Renan when he says that his ideal home would contain a huge, devoted and contented staff of negroes.

My special playmate for a time was an African boy, a Christian convert called Bompole. He and I used to play a football game of our own invention in our vast basement laundry, in a corner of which a bed had been put for him near the fire. He could hold red-hot cinders in his mouth, which I much admired, and when I obeyed his request to pull his hair, a whole curl of black wool would come out in my fingers. This made him shout with laughter, while it mystified and delighted me. He was a well-behaved, merry and truly pious child, far more so than the Glasgow street boys ('keelies') with whom we were also permitted freely to consort. Returning to the Congo, poor Bompole died of sleepy sickness when he was about thirteen. On his account I love all negroes. There was Sophy, too, a negro nurse brought home, strangely enough, from India, in charge of one of our many cousins whose homes were there. I used to sleep with Sophy and to take delight in her affectionate ways. She was dearer to me than any of our long line of nurses save one Highland woman called Kate. Sophy died of consumption. She cannot have been much more than eighteen when she died. She was very pretty and always lovably laughing. Not that we were invariably so lucky with our Africans. There was Nero, a big buck nigger, an eloquent preacher and powerful in prayer and praise, but a bigamist of the most flagrant sort and a great pocketer of collections. But he came too late to affect my amiable predilection.

Perhaps the sort of hospitality we practised had some connexion with a fact that used to puzzle me, namely, that we ourselves always felt alien in Glasgow. Though my mother's paternal grandfather (the soldier with the shop) had settled there, his sons had left in youth never to return. And though my father, returning to Scotland from the West Indies, had become prominent as a Glasgow merchant, a citizen and, in time, a town councillor, so that for us children it was our native place, we never had a relative in Glasgow after the departure of the Roxburghs, and we had no sense of roots in the Glasgow soil. The early associations of both my parents were with the environs of Edinburgh, where we still had vast numbers of relatives; with England, or with foreign parts. My father's dearest friendships had been formed in America. While he had a wide business, philanthropic, and religious acquaintance in Glasgow, he found but one or two close congenial friends among them. And, though he never said so, being strictly loyal to those he worked with, he felt, I am now sure, very lonely in Glasgow.

My mother was frank in declaring that she took no pleasure in Glasgow society, though she was on cordial terms with a few women, mostly older than herself, and rarely Glasgow born. Glasgow ways were not her ways. Admittedly her ways were sometimes peculiar. Heaven was her home, and that can be awkward. But next to heaven she would have felt herself at ease in Italy, in France, or perhaps in Ireland, where she had relations in Wexford of whom she spoke with affection, but we never made their acquaintance. As things were, she certainly felt less of an exile in Edinburgh than in Glasgow. If it may be said without offence, both my parents were of aristocratic, or at least of county tradition, outlook and habits, and their preoccupation, beginning early in life, with evangelical and social effort, cut them off from those of their fellow citizens who were of their own kind. The small number of Glasgow people in whose company they could have felt at home were apt to be religiously indifferent or socially irresponsible. There were, of course, notable exceptions, such as Henry Drummond and his mother, Professor Denny, Professor

Lindsey, Principal Douglas and others. But my father was intellectual, and my mother maladroit, which tended to turn them yet further in upon themselves, upon their manifold activities, upon family life and upon God, who was never far from their thoughts. They accepted this and never uttered any complaint. I once asked why Mr. X, like most of the leading Glasgow evangelicals who came to our house, was 'so awful'. My mother shook her head in wistful reproof. 'Not many rich,' she quoted, 'not many noble, are called to the Kingdom of God.'

CHAPTER THREE

In My Father's House

SUNDAY clothes, lozenge pattern, discomfort.

Drugget on floor for parties.

Decorative efforts. Fairy lights.

Crimson carpet in drawing-room. Salmon-coloured watered silk effect panelled in white and gold on walls.

Father's foreign travels. Chinese sword and helmet. Maltese lace collar.

Grey fur-edged boots.

✻

It is a little strange, when one comes to think of it, what a large place houses and rooms occupy in any human life, how much these insentient things mean to our emotions (so that some would even deny them insentience and give them ghosts of men and women preferring their walls to heaven or escaping from hell to cling to the stones they lived among when on earth), and how they persist and show new creation in our dreams. Most of us who have lived a while and have moved about at all, have a vast gallery of interiors and elevations with which our most memorable emotions are inextricably bound up. If we include hotels, inns, lodgings and the houses of friends, we should have enough to make a city of many mansions. What would novelists do without them? There was something about the bombed homes of the war that made an animal appeal when one passed them in the street and saw the fireplace, the cupboard, the bookshelf exposed; and flapping in the draught a tattered strip of wallpaper once put there after serious choice and admired by the assembled family. But other people's description of the house where they were born demands some patience in those who cannot readily extend their architectural sympathies beyond their own experience, and I do not intend to enlarge on my own. Enough to say that houses – at least buildings where I have slept, eaten, lived, not always with desirable results, have meant as much to me as to anybody. Derelict, neglected, or hopeless houses are hard for me to resist. Houses we pass on the road – in a trice we have lived whole lives in them ourselves.

Homes of which the drawbacks have crystallized character and stimulated idiosyncrasy.

*

It might never be worth enquiring what proportion of writers (including poets), painters and lovers of the arts in general have come from homes in which none of the arts were much regarded. Musicians – at least composers and executants – are in a class apart. So are actors. Learning of the more scholarly sort is often either inherited or induced by early culture. But writers and painters? How many came of fathers or begat sons, of their kind? Not many, I should say.

We were, as can be seen, a simple and Philistine family. How came it then, that lacking all exemplars and encouragement in the home, all four of us turned our enthusiasm to the arts as to the sun? I have no explanation.

I'm bound to say that my father practically confined himself to the newspaper. He enjoyed listening to Dickens read aloud and he sang and recited comic ballads, some of which were to be found in a gilt-edged, red morocco-covered book in the drawing-room. But I never remember seeing him with a book in his hand other than the Bible, and that he handled twice daily.

When I say that we had, except for Scott's, no novels in the house, I omit the presence of one. This was a small, fat, small-printed volume, bound in ornamental red and black, which was kept mysteriously locked in the middle part of my mother's wardrobe.[1]

The revelation of discovering the existence of the arts in a household like ours – no cultured household can know it. Religion we had from the start – with the matchless poetry of the Bible. Nothing else.

*

There was the Lobby Box: there was Grandpapa's Cabinet: there was Grandpapa's Bookcase. The Box is a large dower chest of dark oak, carved on the front and sides, ridged along its double-sloped top which had been polished by years of contact with four young bottoms as it stood in the entrance hall of each house we inhabited. The Cabinet, now robbed of its crowning bust of the Reverend Doctor Candlish in white marble, was a slim-railed and layered stand of red mahogany with a neat hidden compartment at the back for holding unused leaves of the big dining-room table. How we used to enjoy slipping these heavy leaves in and out from their sweetly set baize compartments! But it was Grandpapa's bookcase that counted most, and it was also the most beautiful and lastingly original of the three. The rarest as a piece of furniture, it was the fullest repository of family feeling, so I shall give myself the pleasure of a description in some detail.

Grandpapa's Bookcase, which now looks smaller than I remember it, is none the less an erection not wanting in massive dignity. The glossy timber from which it is made, strongly red in colour and richly grained, is of a kind that Scotland imported in her palmy days, perhaps from Jamaica. Its lines are decidedly architectural. Two substantial round pillars make a doorway, as to a temple, of the upper part, which has the shelves concealed by a criss-cross casement of brass with a small rose cast in the metal at each crossing. The old lining of pleated crimson silk which I remember is gone. It may have rotted away (already in my youth it was brittle) or it

1. From one of the author's notes it seems that this mysterious volume was a copy of Richardson's *Pamela*.

may have been considered out of date. All the books I remember are gone too, and the shelves are now used to display valuable china. Below a narrow shelf and a drawer with fittings for writing materials, is a deep lower cupboard, also furnished with pillars. This cupboard used to be filled by a movable chest fitted with drawers, each drawer having small square compartments full of stones. My maternal grandfather combined sermons with stones, and if he kept his sermons in the drawer midway and his theological sources in the upper temple, he had filled every division of the lower drawers with specimens of quartz, lava and the rest. Among these the most valuable was probably an oyster shell containing several incipient pearls, and one of considerable size that had matured and come away from its parent. I never tired of handling the specimens and of trying to read the tiny labels adhering to them. I even went so far as to make a collection of my own for some time, going about with a hammer when we were in the country. But though I like collecting, I have never had any capacity for keeping a collection in order, and mine have long vanished together with all grandpapa's specimens and the chest he had caused to be made for them.

✻

What the small Elizabethan children must have suffered judging by the costumes in their portraits makes my skin prickle even now with sympathetic sadness. The clothes of the Victorian child were less constraining, but they left much to be desired. We wore in winter heavy woollen combinations and over that a substantial long cloth chemise stretching from neck to knee and with prickly Swiss trimming round neck and armholes; then a wadded stay-belt with buttons at intervals to which other garments had to be attached. Long, thick stockings of black cashmere were joined to the stays by elastic: white long-cloth knickers (also trimmed Swiss) were buttoned to it. Over them a scalloped white flannel bodiced petticoat, and last of all a complicated high-necked dress – and for school a holland apron over the dress. On Sunday for some reason, the dress was made far more complicated and abounding in discomforts. In one of these – it was patterned with lozenges, the shape of which has ever since made me feel slightly ill – I suffered so acutely and continuously that I had bilious attacks. It was a misery which increased when a coat was added and I had to sit still for nearly two hours in church without having the coat removed. By the time we emerged, unless I had mercifully fallen asleep, I was like a fish on land gasping for air at every pore. Yet all this was as nothing compared to what we wore when we became young ladies and put up our hair.

When we were verging on our teens, my sister and I, in scorn of young ladies, vowed to each other (1) that we would never wear 'real stays with bones in them,' and (2) that we should never carry a parasol. We did not keep our vows. At eighteen I wore the same garments as at eight – except that they were longer and the top petticoat was a divided affair, white camisole above and frilled silk or stout mohair as to skirt. The straight padded band of our stays became confining and stiff with steel fronts. The neckbands of the dresses were fortified with whalebones and the lined bodices also. The skirt, also lined, and reaching to the ground in front and at the back, had braid all round inside the hem which came constantly unstitched as it caught in the wearer's heel. Our hair was rolled up over a pad on top, to which pad a hat was precariously pinned and a veil adjusted. Gloves were a necessity, and usually an umbrella or parasol. With one hand, while out walking, the back of the skirt had to be held clear of the pavement in such a manner as just to show an edge of petticoat but no stocking or ankle. This involved many backward and downward glances. The other hand was usually occupied in grasping the hat brim and frantically adjusting the veil – both subject to the least breath of wind. The umbrella or parasol being on the hat arm it was hard to assume an unconcerned smile. At fifteen or so I had more or less reorganised my costume, discarding much below and removing neckbands above, and at all times in the country or by the sea we went about anyhow, often in trousers or jerseys. But when my skirts grew long and I was corseted, I succumbed for a time to overpowering convention.

*

There are two rivers in the city where I was born. One is a romantically genteel stream with high banks along which nursemaids wheel prams. Upon the other – of which this stream is a feeder – the prosperity of the place has been built up. Poems and songs – none of them good – have been written about the stream, none, so far as I know, about the river. Our living was derived from the river, whence my father sent ships and merchandise to the West Indies, but we rarely saw it. We lived – latterly – on the banks of the stream and in the region to which it gave its name.

We did know the river farther down where it grew salt and turned into the lochs upon which we spent part of our summer holidays, and we saw it farther up. The Clyde in Glasgow itself we scarcely thought about.

Money was a subject I never remember as a topic of conversation at home during my youth. Such things as the rent of our town house or the cost of country lodgings for holidays, or even the prices of clothes, food or household articles never came up in talk. Father, of course, went off on foot each morning (after kissing us all round the breakfast table and being assisted with his coat and hat in the lobby and waved after till out of sight) to 'make money' for us; and he returned each evening a little tired after having presumably made enough for our needs. He came home also for his midday meal, after which he lay down on the long red-leather-covered sofa where, covered by us with a huge tartan shawl and undisturbed by the continued family life about him he immediately slept. After some twenty minutes he sprang up refreshed and fit for a renewal of his money-making.

The building where these daily efforts were made bore an appropriate resemblance to a money-box – one of those early money-boxes that were known as 'savings banks'. These were of cast metal painted black, square in shape, elaborately corniced with a slot in the roof for the entrance of pennies. It was in West Regent Street, and we entered it only on special occasions. As we drew near to its pseudo-Gothic portals we became silent: as we ascended the wide but dirty stone staircase awe fell upon us. My father was, I believe, a commission agent. He negotiated in particular the shipping and sale of textiles to the West Indies. Some of the ships concerned were built for, and for a time at least owned by, him. One of these, a steamship named the *Claudine*, I launched from its slips on the Clyde when I was perhaps thirteen years old, and we all took part proprietorially in her trial trip down the river. Another of his ships, the *Collessie* – a sailing vessel named after the village where part of his childhood was spent – my sister Fanny launched. The *Claudine* was wrecked on her first voyage, the *Collessie*, under a different name, came to figure in Robert Louis Stevenson's tale *The Wrecker*. It would seem that father was not lucky with ships, and looking back I seem to know now what was then never apparent to me, that he was frequently unlucky in business undertakings which were much in the nature of commercial gambling. I remember once his bringing home to show us a yard or two of printed cotton – yellow corn stalks in full ear effectively set against a background of turkey red. Some of this, he told us, had been sent 'on spec' to the Sandwich Islands, and it had so pleased the islanders that the more prosperous took to riding about on horseback with streamers of the fabric fluttering from their shoulders. To such a pitch did this emulation in display develop that he had a request for a repeat order of many bales – possibly the hold of the *Claudine* was filled with them.

But such exotic hints had little or no connexion in my mind with the making of money by my father. I had a vague idea that consequent upon certain mysterious ceremonies enacted before his large desk, of which he was sole master, coins in sufficient quantity insinuated themselves through a hole in the office roof. I have said we were awed when we went there. Father in these surroundings became for us a different being – more distant and impressive because of the numerous respectful underlings through whom we had to pass to reach him. There was, for example, Mr. Andrew McCrindell. But of him I will not write now. And there might be a young male cousin whom for a time he had taken in as an experimental charity (or a charitable experiment).

While Mr. McCrindell remained year after year like the office furniture, these cousins, after a short stay, took wing for Africa, India, or the United States.

Of the money father made we each had a penny a week in pocket money. Much thought and choice was expended each Saturday on the laying out of this penny that father had made and given to us. In those days, especially in a small shop in— Street, a penny seemed to go a very long way. You could buy a wooden box of sherbet for a halfpenny (with a wooden spoon in it to eat from delicately), and the other halfpenny could be laid out in a more permanent possession, such as a rubber balloon, or one of those contraptions at the end of a long string, which by a process of suction could fish up something desirable from the deepest street area, if lowered between the iron bars on pavement level. I have even on occasion fished up another penny, thus increasing my weekly allowance by 100 per cent. At a more advanced age we began to receive a threepenny piece each Saturday, and when this was raised to sixpence, maturity was announced.

Coins counted to us, not money. This persists with me even now. With a half-crown to finger in my pocket, I feel far removed from destitution. As a petty trader I take some beating. But money in its larger sense has always remained a mystery, with me as an uncomprehending outsider. It is something that is made in larger or smaller quantities. If I were to pick up piles of stones in his field for a farmer I should demand and value the sixpence paid for each pile. But I cannot see myself as 'earning' money.

With guidance and encouragement I should have made a good counterfeit coiner.

✳

Thirteen, to one of my upbringing, was a serious age, and I was, at least during the midnight hours, serious, nay ethical. By that age, for at least eight years, I had heard two sermons every Sunday, had often accompanied my parents to the Wednesday night prayer meetings. I had been taken to revival and other religious gatherings. At least once I had been moved to hold up my hand as a signal to Messrs. Torrey and Alexander – or was it Gipsy Smith? – that here was a soul convicted of sin and anxious to repent. I calculate that I had heard with attention near one thousand carefully prepared exhortations, many of them appealing to the mind, others effectively addressed to the emotions. In addition I had hearkened, more or less since I could remember, to the converse of missionaries, and had twice daily participated – about six thousand times – in family prayers, which with us involved reading the Bible, verse and verse about, from beginning to end, over and over again, as the years proceeded. I knew most of the psalms and many hymns by heart. I could recite my Shorter Catechism, and chapters from the Old and New Testaments. I won a Bible at my Sunday school for the most word-perfect and intelligent rendering of the twelfth chapter of Romans. I had read and enjoyed a number of godly books, including the *Pilgrim's Progress* and *Foxe's Book of Martyrs* (this last my favourite Sabbath reading when still of a tender age). Pious stories intended for the young had struck me as either tedious or namby-pamby – with the exception of Maria Edgeworth's *The Parent's Assistant*, which I read more than twice with relish. Dr. Whyte of Edinburgh had sent me some of his own *Lives of the Saints*. Until I came as it were by chance upon the classics of English fiction, tears had been shed by me, and sacrificial yearnings instilled, during the perusal of works by 'A.L.O.E.', Edna Lyell, and other mistresses of the current craft. I remember our all weeping uncontrollably together over a story by 'A.L.O.E.' which my mother read aloud to us in a breaking voice one afternoon when my sister and I were both in bed with colds.

At the age of thirteen, I had, I think, put such tales aside (except for occasional lachrymose dips into Mrs. Humphry Ward), in favour of sterner stuff . . . I began to flirt with heresy. To the sorrow of our parents my sister and I became occasional frequenters of Doctor Hunter's church, which to their minds belied its name of Trinity, being little more than a Unitarian conventicle.

Now let me confess that nothing of all this had yet bored me. Church had many a time lulled me to sleep against a parent's welcoming shoulder. From some discourses my imagination had taken flight into fantasies of its own. Upon occasion I had been oppressed – Sunday clothes could make me feel physically ill. But unlike Herbert Spencer at the same age, I did not feel any disgust or surfeit at hearing familiar scripture phrases or Hebrew prayers and songs. These retained for me, and indeed still retain, their startling beauty, and not as familiar spells alone, but as words to be pondered over for their unfathomable wisdom and enduring poetry.

But other things, and I myself were being transformed. The halcyon season of childhood was past. New suns had risen and new shadows fallen.

For one thing – though of this I did not know the facts until much later – my father had suffered financial reverses. Twice he was swindled by partners, both Englishmen, one the husband of his favourite sister Jemima. My father had concealed his financial troubles from her as from us children, and she died without knowing of it. He kept equal silence over unfortunate experiences with the various nephews whom he had taken into his business by way of starting them in life.

By nature as simple as he was upright – far simpler than my mother, with whose innocence much peasant guile was mixed – he was, I must think, a poor judge of character, and anything like deceit found him as it left him, unprepared. He was not so much angered by it as bewildered. He was silent and he readily forgave, but he was saddened.

He had other reverses. I remember his taking us all 'by way of a treat' to Edinburgh to sit through a case before the Court of Session in which he was involved. He had bought and sent upon a voyage a ship that proved to be unseaworthy. Hitherto Hengler's Circus at Christmas time and a recital by Grossmith *père* at the Queen's Rooms had been the nearest we had come to witnessing a theatre. But no play could have entertained or impressed us more than this drama of the Law Courts in which our father was a protagonist. Breathless with excitement, confident of his triumph yet unconscious of how much was at stake, we hung upon every word, estimated every gesture. I forget now who sat upon the bench, but Salveson, then a young man not long married to Lord Trayner's daughter, was one of my father's counsel, and I remember that he had a habit of blushing furiously. He was very blond, and this weakness was obvious to everybody when all else in his demeanour was calculated to conceal chagrin or wrath. No doubt by the time he too became a Lord of Session he had ceased to redden. The case having been taken to *avizandum*, we went off to have a meal, secure in the belief that our father had won. In fact, though he was personally exonerated from all blame, the judgement went against him, and this entailed a heavy loss of money.

A point had been reached in his finances, as I learned long afterwards, at which he was advised to go bankrupt. With my mother's heartfelt support he refused. Given time, he would pay all his creditors in full. He did so, and in addition recovered a fair degree of prosperity. We were never told of all this. Life for us went on much as usual. Fanny and I went to the same schools. But there was a subtle change. This and that about which there had formerly been no question, became 'too expensive'. Mount Quharrie was given up. Though money was never referred to, my mother pored more anxiously over her little account books, and no longer chose the best stuffs when we needed new clothes. My brothers have told me that they were early oppressed by injunctions of economy. Perhaps because I had been used so long to freedom from such thoughts, I felt the change rather as an inevitable development of life, and, occupied with other thoughts I accepted this without troubling to examine its particularity. I remained a dreamer while the substance of my dreams underwent a change quite unconnected with economic circumstances.

Yet these, I dare say, all unknown to us had some bearing upon an ardour which seized upon us to 'make money'. We sang in the streets – I disguised as a boy, Fanny carrying a fiddle on which she played badly. Our performance of rounds and catches for voices only brought people to their lighted windows, and we collected quite a number of coppers and even sixpences; we went from house to house (both disguised as elderly women) taking orders for patent linen stampers, but tired of that before we had delivered them; we addressed envelopes and worked out schemes for making fortunes. Perhaps such efforts were due to ancestral trading instincts. Again, though we regarded them as pranks, it may be that the other explanation accounted for them.

I cannot say for certain how often during these years my father indulged in the sort of speculative business gamble which I think was attractive to his temperament so long as it involved no conscious fraud. But I think that he did. His face grew paler and he became often grave and anxious. At times he looked exhausted, and, though never out of temper, more abstracted and silent than he had used to be. The favourite sister died and he came back from England with a look of deep sadness on his face. When Aunt Roxburgh died and her body was brought from Clifton to be buried from St. John's Church, he was as white as paper and unable to speak. I was at the service, and his face as he staggered up the aisle with five other powerful men, shouldering the terrific weight of the coffin, struck at my heart.

He looked suddenly old. In the street he had often to sit down on any wall or railing for what he called 'vertigo', and though he made light of it I knew it was no trifle.

✳

For my mother the sky was full of angels.

I would set down, if I can, what our religion was, not so much in its formalities, which are sufficiently well known, but in the operative underlying beliefs which have been, it seems to me, far more subject to travesty and miscomprehension (even by serious historians) than to a proper appreciation. Calvinism, Presbyterianism, even Puritanism, have in my experience and my reading been too often wholly misjudged, judged not by their effects upon the living and the faculties of those who lived under their doctrines, but by certain excrescences and exaggerations for which the said doctrines appeared to be responsible, though in fact the main responsibility lay elsewhere.

Predestination: some aspects we regarded with Calvin as an *otiosa curiositas*. On the whole we did say with Locke, 'I cannot have a clearer perception of anything than that I am free, yet I cannot make freedom in man consistent with omnipotence and omniscience in God, though I am most fully persuaded of both as of any truth I most firmly assent to; and therefore I have long since given off consideration of that question, resolving all into the short conclusion that if it be possible for God to make a free agent, then man is free, though I see not the way of it.'

We avoided extravagance. We were orthodox. While we held that our utmost efforts after righteousness were 'as filthy rags' – and hence no ground for 'justification' – we yet strove hard after good deeds. We accepted 'justification by faith' as a general principle, but declined to speculate on its niceties. We were practical, sentimental, orthodox.

I submit that so far as doctrine is concerned we had the sinews both of Catholic and Protestant in an integral blend. From the first the superstition was omitted (with its sensual beauties), from the second its harsh complacency.

We greatly hoped (and my mother inclined to believe) that we in Britain were closely allied to the sons of Judah in being ourselves descended from Abraham. Many eminent persons are of that belief, and at our house some of the more distinguished callers – retired soldiers of high rank, engineers, and other men of action (as, for example, the builder of the great Nile dam) were all convinced British Israelites who had written books upon the subject, nay, had caused these books to be printed and circulated at their own expense.

My mother was 'in love with heaven and heavenly things', as Thomas White urges that Lady Katherine White should strive to be. My mother's striving had rather to be to love earthly things.

My mother's prayers unavailing – except that they sometimes brought sleep while she was still on her knees.

*

My mother's pure and poetic Christianity, as of an early Christian, was awkward for ministers. Sooner or later she felt bound to call upon her pastor with a pressing query and return with a disappointing reply. The worst of it was that her question was of the most orthodox kind concerning the Christian creed, in which belief is declared that Christ not only rose from the dead, but will again appear in person to judge both the quick and the dead and to welcome all believers to everlasting bliss. 'You remind us,' she would say, 'and rightly, of our Lord's suffering and of his death and resurrection. But all the year round we never hear you speak of his second coming, which has been promised to us, and for which we eagerly wait. How is this?'

I was brought up in two securities which, while they conflicted when considered in the light of reason, combined in fact to give confidence. I had been born into a world that was at once stable and rapidly improving. That was the first security – everywhere in the air I breathed and implicit rather than mentioned. True, some of the changes were regarded with distrust and even alarm. But one realised that this was something that could be dismissed as having existed in every age. What counted was that everybody believed in our general advance. Scientific discoveries were exquisitely new and promising for mankind. The social evils that we saw only too clearly, and greatly deplored, were being attacked with a good will, with energy, with every belief in their demolition. My father represented in himself both the stability and the steady amelioration of this world. So did all his friends and acquaintances without exception. They were unsparing of their energy and never lacked sureness of hope, no matter how they might debate details of method. On the other hand, he shared in some degree my mother's very different and almost mediæval sense of security which regarded all the world of man, nature and appearances as a painted veil, a vale of tears, a short season of trial, a school, something that might at any moment, and would certainly some day, be 'rolled up like a scroll' to reveal the abiding world of heaven or spirit, while we ourselves would 'be changed'. Things were not what they seemed. There was a great scheme of which we were a part, and in which we were privileged, if we would, to take a part, but we could never understand it because it was God's mystery. We could only feel it, bow to it, further it by our attitude, faith, readiness.

For wars we were, it follows, admirably prepared. Were they not foretold – with horrors akin to the warfare of 1939 onwards – as precursors to the coming of Christ, which might (my mother hoped) not be long delayed? We could get along nicely without gas, electricity, bathrooms, tap water, indoor lavatories, restaurants, luxuries, hot-water bottles – in a word, in an Arran cottage or a remote Perthshire farmhouse. Like my father I was naturally a good shot and I was skilled at climbing and ambuscades. I should, I believe, have made a good guerrilla fighter and (not having yet made Tolstoi's acquaintance) I should have picked out the country's enemies with satisfaction unmixed with remorse of a pacific nature. It is the custom now to attribute to the Victorians a sort of bland and blind security. On the contrary, we were ready for everything, and though our background was ample and settled we (especially we evangelicals) were instructed twice on weekdays and thrice on Sundays that ours was no abiding city, that all we saw was but an elusive and passing scene, that enjoying the best we must constantly be prepared for the worst.

One thing we were not prepared for, and it is difficult to see how this could have been done without the greatest immediate disadvantages – though perhaps such a proviso is open to argument. We were not prepared for crossness, ill temper, sarcasm or deceit in our fellows. Somewhere in his letters – in, I think, a letter to Georges Sand – Flaubert condemns his own happy childhood. He grew up in an amiable family circle. When he came to see and know humanity outside that circle, his horror and disillusionment was such, that he says he believes it would have been happier for him had he been harshly, even cruelly, reared. I understand but cannot agree with him in this. The unhappiness of a child brought up in fear and without love is apt, I should say (unless the individual is of unusual strength and balance), to create as much weakness as strength. There is a folly that is valuable just as there is a caution that is disastrous. It is well to have some secure ground to stand upon besides one's own integrity, strength, cunning or what not – all of which may break down or not be there. One might as well say that an ill-fed army goes better equipped into war on hard tack or short commons. I can, if need be, do a day's hard physical work on a bowl of oatmeal or rice thickened with water, and a draught of water that has stood on apple peels and cores. But I have the memory in me, and the results, of a lavish, varied and regular series of meals, for each of which God was thanked as for a special favour.

✳

All slightly ridiculous? Perhaps: but we did not feel it to be so – at least I did not. Looking back I have no serious regrets as to my religious upbringing. My parents being kind-hearted themselves, softened the idea of hell, and we were subjected to no such inhuman terrorism as that practised by the Catholic mother of Leopardi. Nature was admitted, suffering and deformity were deplored, as God was our father, and our father would never have sent his worst enemy to hell, let alone his children. We felt fairly sure that God was keeping one of his many mansions for us, and that if our behaviour 'grieved' him we should not have to expect much worse than a scolding before crossing the mansion's threshold. It was nice to feel that God took so much interest in our little doings, that no matter what happened, 'underneath were the everlasting arms'. Then, after all, though it may seem less rational to regard this world as a period of trial, error and discipline rather than as a place in which primarily to enjoy oneself, how much less disappointing when one comes to know what the world is like!

CHAPTER FOUR

Mount Quharrie

SOCIAL shortcomings in Glasgow, though never mentioned and, I daresay, not clearly envisaged by my parents, may have had some bearing on a step my father took which made a profound and lasting difference to my life.

He bought, no doubt at small expense, a seven-year lease of a deserted farm in Perthshire. Throughout that time it was our alternative and, to me at least, preferable home. To the four of us still alive, the place is dear in memory. But the early ages of my brothers during our leasehold (the elder my junior by three years, the younger by five) and the distaste for country life and country things evinced by my sister to this day, confirm my belief that, as among us children, I was the one most affected.

I am not so sure of the significance to my mother. The house was isolated, the conditions primitive. The long journeys to and fro with a young family must have been exacting. With the nearest village over three miles away, the roads rough and steep, and no visiting tradesmen, catering cannot have been easy. During summer months our household there was often increased by young cousins, older relatives, and humble friends from Glasgow who were recovering from illness. Housekeeping in any conditions irked my mother, the more that she felt it on her conscience to discharge every domestic duty with complicated perfection. Not that she was fussy or house-proud. Far from it. I think she would gladly have lived in a tent. But as a wife she felt bound to maintain the convention of her husband's condition, and she held strong principles concerning the health and happiness of a household which included children and servants. She insisted, for example, that a summer month by the sea was essential to our well-being in addition to a country holiday.

Servants, whom my father was generous in providing so long as he could, only added to her cares, because their lives, too, became her responsibility. At the same time the things she most longed to be doing were undomestic, and though she was the soul of hospitality she was not a good hostess. Stupid with her hands, slow, and subject to mental confusion and exhaustion, she found everything difficult. Household accounts, which she indefatigably entered in a series of small railway time-tables, were a nightly agony to her, and she would fall asleep on her knees praying for the ability to cope with their complicated entries. Neither punctuality nor precision was in her nature, strive as she did after both. Her gifts were naked faith, hope and charity, unaided by practical accomplishment. Only now do I comprehend something of what her never-ending struggle must have cost, and with what unfailing gallantry she carried it on. Because she never grumbled, scolded, nor so much as once looked cross. All the complaints were on our side as we grew older and saw her, unaccountably as we thought, holding up some expedition in which we wished her to join, or when, having got her started at last, we saw her fall asleep at the first opportunity. My sister, once complaining of her to my father, received his grave reply: 'Your mother is pure gold'. Fortunate it was for her and for us that he was invariably sweet-tempered, patient, practical, blithe and ready to help; and fortunate too, that she, being country bred, could savour the escape from Glasgow streets and ways. Gardening was a joy to her, especially the tending of delicate or ailing plants in which she had skill, just as she had skill to perfection in a child's sick-room.

Mount Quharrie, the place was called. It was set alone, a plain, square, whitewashed house (we once re-washed it ourselves when both our parents were away in Italy), some three miles from the Perthshire hamlet of Abernethy, and rather farther from the Fife villages of Strathmiglo, Auchtermuchty, and from Collessie where my father had passed his own childhood. At one time it had been owned by his grandfather, concerning whom I know nothing. Perhaps he was a farmer. I know only that, with the surrounding country, it had intimate associations for my father. It is the more surprising that he never spoke of these to us, and that in all the long walks we had with him he never once took us to the village of Collessie with its charming manse and surprising horned church on a pointed hill. Yet there he had been a boy and his father had preached.

This reticence, contrasting sharply with the frequent pictures my mother painted for us of her childhood, may have been natural in him. But I think it was due also to the comparative unhappiness of his early years, about which I did not come to know till much later, and never from him. His father was a cold, silent man of extreme good looks, but no distinction either of heart or head. He believed in corporal punishment, and a day rarely passed without one of his nine motherless children receiving heavy castigation. Having chosen a new wife of considerable social pretensions (a niece to Lord Lennox) he presented his bride without any warning in the hall of the Collessie manse, thus effectively barring comment with confidence. John, the eldest boy, ran away when he was fifteen, never to return. Catherine, who like myself was named after Aunt Roxburgh, died of 'a decline' when still in her teens. My father, showing signs of a similar delicacy before he was twenty, was shipped out to Trinidad, and his early manhood was passed there, in America, and in the West Indies, after which he returned by way of China, Japan and India to settle in Scotland. He talked gaily of his travels and adventures, and our drawing-room cabinet was full of trophies of his travels which I never wearied of examining. But of his childhood I knew nothing except that he once had a pet monkey who brushed its teeth up a tree, and that for years a dwarf, who had escaped from a travelling circus in which he was cruelly treated, had become a beloved inmate of the Collessie manse till my grandfather turned him out alleging that the small refugee was ill-tempered. It must be that, with all its disadvantages, my mother's nature provided a balm to his spirit, and that he found deep satisfaction in his home to which he made such handsome contribution by banishing repression and reducing punishment to a merciful minimum. If God, as we were told, was like our father, we need have no fear of Him, for our father was a leader and a presider over laughter. We laughed at everything and at nothing, most of all we laughed at my mother who was an inexhaustible source of mirth. Having no sense of humour but a great love of fun, she was ready to join in, and her singularly fresh voice rang out above the rest.

The original old thatched house had been destroyed by fire long before our time, and another built in what was considered to be a modern manner. All was strong, sound, airy, clean. A bath was fed with cold water by a pipe from the reed-shrouded, heron-haunted 'upper pond' on the hill behind; and small frogs, tadpoles, newts and leeches arrived, to our joy, with the bath water. Nothing else was changed. The rambling out-houses, forming three sides of a square round the yard and dung-heap, still stood half-sunk in earth and grass by the 'lower pond', their vast, low-sweeping roofs of curly red tiles coming so near the level of the ground that a child could run to the top, and so along. They were roomy with stables, byres, duck- and hen-houses and a big barn on two levels. Beside them the wooden mill-shank of antique fashion could still be turned by a couple of horses yoked under its iron crooks; and it was still connected with the cumbrous machinery within, so that once each year we ground the modest harvest from our own fields. The stream, which ran in pools between the barn and the moor, beneath the uneven patch of grass named 'the lawn' in front of the house, still contained abundance of trout, mostly small but sweet. I soon learned from a neighbouring farm boy – Bob Grieve of Catochal across the hill, who became my instructor in many things – how to catch fish without a rod by 'guddling' them, and we used to fry them on hot stones where we were. The old well was still deep, so that we drew from it our drinking water – ice-cold and delicious. The thatched cottage, which served as a lodge half-way up our 'avenue' from the main road, was unchanged from its first building. The same old fruit-trees high in our unwalled, wild, garden had continued to bear, and the scented yellow tea roses to bloom. Above and surrounding all, was the moor with its patches of wood, rock, mosses, bogs, heather, flowers, berries, grasses, birds, beasts – ever explorable, never wholly known, showing a different face to each hour and each season, but unresponsive to the centuries and to cultivation. Roadless except for some bewildering shepherd tracks, it breathed the honeyed airs of the yellow whin, the broom, heath, heather and bog-myrtle, with here and there clumps of wild white raspberries which throve untended. The cotton flower flew its argent banners over the quagmires. Companies of veined harebells trembled under its pale lichened rocks. Blackberries ripened in profusion. It was an uplifted world, a sky, waters, woods, all our own. There was not another house in sight.

My father bought a strong cob and a stanhope to hold us all, a pony and dogcart for speedier driving, a cow, hens and ducks, a retriever dog. (Sometimes it was a spaniel. We had a long succession.) He bought a gun, a croquet set. He hired a stableboy from Ireland – Paddy Mulhern, who taught us to ride by putting us on bareback, attaching a driving rein to the bit, lashing the beast round in circles with a carriage whip and making us remount after each fall. From this we went on to leaping ditches. I became an inelegant but enthusiastic rider able to go far afield alone. My sister had small disposition for it, so the pony, Judy, was practically made over to me and I soon learned to saddle, groom and water her.

In the cottage an old couple were installed to bake for us, make butter and grow vegetables. From the man I learned to milk. But we had no duties, no tasks, no prohibitions. I can recall no single rule, injunction nor warning. A big brass bell was rung on the lawn to announce meals. Otherwise, except on Sundays, we followed our own devices. No matter how torn, bruised or muddy we might return we were subjected to none but helpful, immediately practical questioning. Scoldings and smacks were unknown, punishments rare and without spite. Neither in town nor in the country can I remember a single instance of ill-temper. It was a shock in after-life to find that people otherwise well conditioned should get angry over trifles.

The first time we arrived, early in the summer of my seventh year, I knew that here for me was paradise. What is more remarkable is, that on revisiting the place not long ago, these early impressions were confirmed. There had been neglect. The house had become an abode for pauper imbeciles, which was perhaps a little depressing for all but the inmates. But everything else was as wild and as beautiful, obdurate to every transgression of human progress, tractable only by the seasons, yet without gloom or oppressive grandeur.

I shall not forget our first coming there. It was a sunny evening. Leaving Glasgow by an early train for the long journey to Perth, we had transferred ourselves and our vast baggage – strapped tin baths, laundry baskets, trunks and holdalls, packed by my father who prided himself on getting more into a box than any other person alive – into the little single line for Abernethy. From there we embarked by horse and 'machine' up the long hill road, being often forced to get out and push from behind. At length, tired but exultant, we attained the roughest, steepest corner, where we must diverge from the main road that would have taken us to the Howe of Fife. Pausing, we received the announcement that this was our 'avenue'.

Sweat poured from my father's triumphant face as he braced us for a final effort. My mother in her grey alpaca dustcloak beamed wearily from the box seat, encumbered by the two boys, the younger little more than a year old, while she steadied the large cage containing our green parrot, who was to benefit with us from the country air. Filled with a biblical desire to strew an oblation before the cavalcade, I ran on in front.

Along one side of the road fields ran up beyond a high, bare bank. But on the other, below which a stream gurgled, many gracious trees arched across our way with a burden of leaf and blossom such as I had never before seen or even dreamed of. In Glasgow, grass hardly grew, and the soot-grimed trees and shrubs were rotted by chemicals which belched from 'Tennant's lum' and the other tall stalks. What I saw, smelt and breathed in that sun-illumined moment was a revelation. It culminated in the miracle of many laburnums, heavy just then with clear gold.

Small as I was, many of the laden branches were within

my reach. In a transport I slid my fingers along the tassels, stripped them of their bright hoof-shaped buds, and cast them before the straining horse. So, past the cottage, round one more corner, and we drew up before the calm, white, waiting house.

I could describe, and rarely be at a loss for detail, most of the many interiors in which I have lived. Yet, though I passed innumerable hours throughout seven impressionable years in Mount Quharrie house, I remember almost nothing about its rooms. This is the more curious because the house was neither large nor intricate. Indeed it is a mystery how many of us found, as we did, accommodation there without crowding. I cannot even recall the presence of servants, though these there must have been.

I suppose that my father had taken over with the lease such simple furniture as was already in the house and that we added nothing but what was strictly utilitarian. There were no pictures, ornaments or books, no decorative draperies, household gods, luxuries. All was bleached, worn, pale, cleanly; neither ugly nor beautiful, it yet achieved an unpremeditated effect, so that when I first saw pictures of interiors by Chirico I thought, 'Why, this is Mount Quharrie!' I do remember how great shafts of coloured light – amber, green, red – poured down from panes in a tall staircase window to furnish or to obliterate where they came to rest, and to delight our eyes as we came from the dazzle outside through the front door that stood open all day. It would not have surprised me if a Chirico horse had galloped down one of these shafts.

I remember, too, that the oil-cloth on the empty upper landing was patterned alternately with the head of a goat and the head of a helmeted Roman soldier – devices which I studied with profound aesthetic approval. I even took laborious tracings of them lying on my stomach on wet days. But mostly I was too soaked with the brilliant outer air, and too intent upon the images received outside, to note anything within walls where we did little but eat, sleep and pray.

Our fare, though ample and honest, was so simple that visitors from the Glasgow slums turned from it in disgust.

They longed so much for their pastries, fish-and-chips, and ice-creams, that I have known visits cut short on this account. My father had a passion for rice-and-milk soup; served in a gigantic tureen, the rice boiled in salted milk containing chopped parsley and onion. Often this would be our main dish. But he was a good shot and, when he was there with us, we would eat the game he brought in. There was tremendous excitement once when he arrived from Glasgow bringing with him specimens of two fruits we had never seen before. One was a tomato, the other a banana.

Our clothes were equally simplified. In town we were dressed with care and expense, and – to me at least, for I did not well tolerate the slightest constriction – sometimes with acute malaise, especially on Sundays. Twice in the year we spent long, weary hours at the dressmaker, my mother having to be awakened at intervals, while my sister took the lead in choosing styles, colours, embroideries. It is difficult to reconcile this with my mother's unworldly views. No doubt she felt that my father's condition called for certain proprieties. Choosing anything for herself was a torment to her and, like me, she was with difficulty persuaded to put on a new dress. I was not without sartorial vanities even at an early age, but these did not lie in display so much as in the gratification of a struggling æsthetic taste combined with comfort. Till much later my sister was the moving spirit at the dressmakers.

But at Mount Quharrie, except on Sundays, we discarded our mass of starched, frilled underclothes, and wore old sailor suits or check gingham frocks so that we might climb and scramble without damage except to our skins. The resumption of town clothes, especially of shoes and stockings, used to cause me an affliction almost past bearing. For some weeks I felt trapped, harnessed, desperate; and the pavements hurt my feet. But a price had to be paid for the months of wild glory. Besides, when one grew accustomed to it again, Glasgow was not without its peculiar attractions which, if sordid, were possibly more conducive to mental development and to knowledge of the human world.

At Mount Quharrie we made few social calls upon our widely scattered neighbours of the landed sort, local farmers apart. On Sundays, after the exacting service in Abernethy church (we sat to sing the Psalms conducted by a tuning-fork from the precentor's box, stood during the lengthy prayers, and made what we could of a sermon with fifteen points) we would go to an old stone house in a garden to be refreshed by raspberry vinegar and cake. On those Sundays when my father conducted an open-air service on a hillside near the village (New Testament in style) we were all given dinner instead of cake. Two ancient but lively maiden ladies – suitably named the Misses Greenhill – were our hostesses. Both adored my father and responded with gaiety to the affectionate gallantry which he always displayed to old women, for whom indeed he had a real fondness. The elder Miss Greenhill wore her own white hair. The younger, who must have been approaching the age of eighty, sported a wig of luxuriant black curls. 'The rest of us grow older, Miss Euphemia,' my father would say, 'but I never see a grey hair in your head.' Often as this simple jest was repeated it never failed of delighted laughter, most of all from Miss Euphemia herself. These were days when, under the pressure of Calvinism, laughter came easily.

Sometimes, as a great treat, we would drive in to Perth, nearly ten miles away, row on the Tay, and then call upon the Mellis family. Mr. Mellis, a minister, had married one of Aunt Roxburgh's daughters, and they had a boy and a girl only a little older than ourselves. And at least once I remember driving to Ayton, a big old manor house in a park with huge trees, shrubberies and walled gardens, near Newburgh, on the Perth road. The only child of this house, a boy, born in the same year as I, impressed me very much. After a long and royal game of sliding down damp slopes I was taken by him to the ripe raspberry canes, there so to gorge ourselves on the noblest berries I ever saw that I began to throw them up from sheer satiety. Robert Seton-Watson, my handsome entertainer was called, later to become famous as an authority on Central Europe. His father was an expert on heraldry, and on the homeward

journey I gathered that this topic had provided most of
the adult conversation for which my sister had remained
indoors. But if I were to meet Robert Seton-Watson today,
I should think of bushy declivities, of giant raspberries, and
of the seat of my clean white drawers which, when bedtime
came, was found to have changed to dark green with the
consistency of cardboard.

If there was one thing I loved above all at Mount Quharrie
and missed in Glasgow, it was the trees. As I have said, those
few even in the West End Park, where we were taken for
gritty walks by our nurses, were as stunted and stricken as
anything of human growth in our east end streets. Hence
I had not before seen healthy, mature beeches or oaks nor
even a larch or birch. At Mount Quharrie I not only saw
them growing in woods or companies in splendid variety,
and singly in magnificent length of years, cleanliness and
perfection; I climbed them. And who that has not climbed
trees can claim to know them?

Even in childhood one lives many lives. One of mine
was lived in trees. Long-armed and very light, so that I
could trust my passing weight to a twig, I dared to go into
the topmost parts. Suspended between earth and sky, with
no more thought in my head than there was in the clouds
floating above. I spent unreckoned hours absorbed into the
life and growth of some tree, pressed against its trunk in
such nearness that I knew the strength of the roots and
the certainty of the sap. The branches entangling segments
of sky, the leafage receiving and giving forth airs – these
formed for the time my existence.

Certain huge, pale-limbed old beeches growing apart
by the stream I came to know best of all, by embrace,
contention, constant visiting. These were in particular my
dear yet dreaded familiars. Sometimes I climbed them with
boy friends. My early friends were all boys. But though this
was fun it was not like climbing alone. Besides I never
found a boy who was not a clumsy climber. They broke
twigs, shouted, and even sometimes fell. At such times my
trees withdrew their magic as if insulted. No, I liked to play
with boys, but it was best to climb alone. Soulless as yet and
mindless (not till later did I acquire these difficult travelling

companions) if I had died then, I should, I think, have merited a place in the arboreal limbo which we may hope is reserved for those of our ape ancestors who were well behaved. On all hands it is recorded that I was a singularly well-behaved child. I have sometimes thought it a pity that I did not have the added 'grace to die young'.

CHAPTER FIVE

Holidays

APART from times spent at Mount Quharrie each year, and besides visits to relatives mostly in the neighbourhood of Edinburgh, we had always, as I have said, a summer month by the sea. Our life was full of holidays, and I remember no year without its water season; without at least four shining or soaking weeks, when we played from early morning to the tardy northern dusk on sea verges, or climbed the rocky hills above our salt lochs to discover smaller and more secret fresh waters above. We sailed, rowed, swam, waded the pools for treasures inexhaustible. We spent all night with the herring fishers, or deep-sea catching by ourselves, to return through the black phosphorescent water, singing as we rowed and laden with far more fish than we could eat. We traced streams to their sources and dipped naked under their falls.

Our unanimous taste was for the quietest, most remote places. Should there be an esplanade or a populous sea front, these we shunned. The only exception was the harbour of some fishing village, oftener to be found on the east than on the west coast. Once, when for some reason connected with business, we were taken to Southport, we got feverish amusement out of nigger minstrels and trips on those ships on wheels called 'Flying Dutchmen'. But we felt degraded, and we refused with scorn to admit that this was the sea or those crowded flats the shore. If our parents did not share (though I believe they did) this predilection or affectation due to some romantic bent, they happily indulged it. Possibly they found in it some economic convenience. I say, happily, because to it so many holidays, especially on the Continent, were later due when they would otherwise have been impossible to the family purse. How often at French watering-places,

Italian villages and indeed English ones, have I found quarters that would not have been considered by more fastidious travellers who, sooner than not go to regular hotels or tourist rooms, preferred to remain at home 'when longen folk to goon on pilgrimages'.

Most often it was to one or other of the Clyde lochs that we went, or to the Ayrshire coast, so that my father could travel to us from Glasgow as often as possible. Still the high light of our day was when we assembled on the small pier, or at the ferry jetty, in welcome of the tall figure which could be distinguished from afar waving to us from a steamer deck. At that time there were two lines of Clyde paddle steamers which raced each evening, and from the moment the rival smoke plumes showed on the horizon, excitement grew as to whether the yellow or the red-and-black funnel would win. I was an ardent yellow-funneller and was prepared to wager my whole week's pocket money on the *Duchess of Hamilton* beating the *Lord of the Isles*. As our great-great-grandfather, Patrick Miller of Dalswinton, had invented the paddle steamer and claimed to be the first man to apply steam to navigation, we affected a nice judgement of marine engines; and when we went, as we often did, on summer cruises, we spent much time below with engineers and stokers, happily inhaling the oily breath of pistons. Fanny having launched a sailing ship, and I a steamship, we had long debates over the comparative merits of steam and sail.

As a rule, especially in Arran, of which we came to know every bay, mountain and stream, we had a cottage – the more primitive the more to our liking, because we found holiday charm in earth closets and curtained wall beds. But sometimes we had to make the best of a modern, roomy, water-supplied, hideous villa. Always we had at least one rowing-boat and, as the boys grew older, a boat with a lug-sail and jib. We never acquired a yacht, though some of our friends did. I never liked yachting as a guest. Nor can I enjoy for any length of time passive contemplation of the sea. I am not a deck-chair subject.

We spent whole days in small boats, fishing with passion, rowing till we were worn out and covered with blisters (it is no joke to row all round Arran as we did), going for picnics on distant rocks loud with gulls, communing with lighthouse keepers, or merely fooling about near the shore. We became so adept or so daring that we were more than once in real danger.

One evening in particular, caught by a heavy squall many miles from home, returning from the Isle of May to the Berwick coast, we expected to founder. Our unseaworthy sailing craft and the small boat she had in tow were both half filled with water – especially the small boat, in which my place was, as it was dragged through rather than over the towering waves.

Our mother, for a wonder, had come with us on this trip. And it was she who had insisted that the old, one-legged owner of the boats should be of the party when we had set out in a light breeze on a morning which had promised well. We had to leave the tiller to him, but his comments, when the storm blew up, were full of Celtic gloom.

Helplessly alive to our situation, but smiling in the face of wind and wave, our mother bade us join our voices with hers in *Pull for the Shore, Sailors* and then in *Abide with Me*, to the rhythms of which we baled. When, after some hours, we came safe into harbour in the drenching, pitch-dark night, we were told that it was more than we deserved, that the sail-boat had long been condemned, that it should never have put out to sea at all, that the harbour watchers had given us up as lost. The old cripple had been unable to resist the ten shillings we had offered.

While at no time fat, my mother was heavy and inept in her movements, ever seeming to be puzzled by the impediment of her body which she often longed to 'put off'. 'And we shall be changed' was for her a cherished promise. She looked eagerly for the day when the earth would be 'rolled up like a scroll', when Christ would appear in the clouds, when we should all be 'snatched up' and when she would be given 'a heavenly body' instead of the clumsy envelope which baffled her ardour to serve, and offended her keen if untrained æsthetic sense. She took great joy in physical grace and material beauty. I think the thorn of her own flesh fostered a solicitude on our behalf which may appear contrary to her unworldly principles, so that she sent us as mere babies to a class where we should learn action songs, had us taught swimming at the baths in Glasgow and, later, took our side against my father when we demanded dancing lessons.

She herself had never been able to learn either to dance or to swim. She was, none the less, an enthusiastic bather and taught us early to float 'by trusting the water as we trust to God's arms'. Suiting action to words she would throw herself backwards on the waves, arms outspread and seraphic eyes gazing at the sky. Once she missed her step while passing from one boat to another in a deep harbour. No other grown-up person was near, and seeing at first only what was comic in the mishap, we all four doubled up in idiot laughter. But when she disappeared under the surface, bonnet and all, clutching in her hand a large bunch of wild flowers, consternation seized us. Upon her reappearance, still grasping her bouquet, shaking her head and smiling encouragement, we recovered enough presence of mind to tow her safely to the landing-stage. She was not in the least alarmed or upset by the experience, merely puzzled by our renewed laughter as we escorted her processionally home.

Two other incidents, though no less trifling, which belong far later, occur to me now as shedding light on her unusual quality – or absence of certain usual qualities.

Long after my father's death she came to make a first visit in London to the home of Fanny and her husband, Herbert Oppenheimer. Herbert had never before met anybody resembling his mother-in-law, and he responded with a sort of astonished affection. But, brilliant, competitive and full of ambition, he regarded her views as childish absurdities. Already he was beginning to make his way as a solicitor, and he arranged a small dinner to which he invited six of the most important and presentable people of his acquaintance. Dinner was announced, but the mother-in-law failed to appear. The host's face clouded. Fanny suggested that they should all sit down and begin. The soup was being handed round when the door opened and the guest of honour, who had been warned that Herbert could not bear unpunctuality, came in with a shy smile carrying as her excuse the lavatory chain. 'I'm so sorry,' she said, 'but it is this that has detained me. I'm used to a plug, not to one of these new-fangled chains. It came off in my hand and I was trying to fasten it again. But as you see, I couldn't manage it.'

The other story that found a place in the family annals belongs to a still later time. My mother had gone to visit her still older cousin, Minnie (Cousin Minnie was only just short of a hundred when she died in full possession of her always sharp faculties, among which humour was not the least sharp). The two widowed ladies had been inspecting the interior of an old church, where no doubt the stone memorials had inclined their thoughts to genealogy. They emerged into the sunshine of the outer graveyard, where some fine specimens of sheep were cropping the long grass. Passing by the ladies, another couple, man and wife, stood for a moment looking. 'What magnificent rams those are,' the gentleman remarked to his companion. My mother wheeled upon him with her beaming, ingenuous smile. 'My great-aunt and my favourite aunt were both Rams,' she announced gently, seeking his response, which was to raise his hat and hasten away. The next day, if Cousin Minnie may be believed, she was with my mother in a bookshop of the town, when she recognised the churchyard couple among other customers. The man also recognised them. He nudged his wife and, in a fearful undertone, murmured, 'Look, there's the lady whose great-aunt and favourite aunt were both rams.' When the story reached us at home and, in my mother's presence we laughed at her expense, she looked a little pained. 'But they *were* both Rams, dears, they *were*. I'm not ashamed of it either. I'm proud of it; and I can't see anything to laugh at.'

The anecdote, which reached and delighted George Moore through some Irish friends, calls for no explanation, but perhaps allows of a note upon the Ram family with which my mother was so pleased to be connected, apart from her deep and lasting affection for her Aunt Fanny, after whom both my sister and one of hers were named.

Its founder was an excellent young Englishman, truly pious and passionately fond of music, who accompanied the

Earl of Essex to Ireland in 1599 as private chaplain. Faring better than his master the Lord Deputy, he remained in Ireland, laboured in a poor parish till it became prosperous, was made a bishop, and had a long line of descendants distinguished in the church and the law. Their home was at Gorey in Wexford, where they intermarried with their neighbours, the Stopfords of Courtown. It was one of the Stopfords who was the 'dear Jim' for whom Dean Swift went to so much trouble more than once. And it was a drunken coachman of one of the Rams who nearly killed the young Swift and his travelling companion, Thomas Sheridan, D.D., when driving them through Gorey:

> England's hope and Ireland's glory,
> Tipp'd in the ditch by the Ram of Gorey,

– as Sheridan wrote in the second number of the *Intelligencer* in 1728.

Mary Anne Ram, after whom my mother and grandmother were named, was a daughter of Colonel Abel Ram, M.P., and Elizabeth Stopford, niece of the first Earl of Courtown. She married Thomas Miller, a younger son of old Patrick Miller of Dalswinton, and we used to have letters[1] written from her brother William on board the *Victory* (he was killed at Trafalgar and is one of the officers mentioned by name in Hardy's *The Dynasts*). In the next generation my mother's best loved uncle, Surgeon-General John Miller, married Frances Anne Ram, who was the daughter of Canon Abel John Ram and Jane Stopford, daughter of the third Earl of Courtown. This Fanny lived until 1924 and seems to have inspired devotion in every person who knew her.

So much for the somewhat tenuous connexion which yet had its influence on our childhood. It is good to know that the Ram family is still going strong: equally it is strange to be almost quite ignorant of how the large Miller family has fared. Yet two were Lords of Session; another sat in parliament and married a daughter of the first Earl of Lisburne; a daughter became Countess of

---

1. We still have. [J.C.]

Mar; and a younger son earned a hero's monument which still stands near the field of Waterloo. They must have many descendants. But I remember meeting only one, Leslie Miller, my mother's cousin, for whom she had a deep regard. He had been so chivalrous as to marry his native mistress in Java, and he came to see us in Glasgow to consult my father about finding positions for his four or five half-caste sons. This my father readily and, I believe, successfully, undertook. Leslie, who had been, as I afterwards learned by chance, extremely popular among his countrymen in Java, was completely ostracised upon his marriage. But my parents approved, and my mother said it was 'just like a Miller to be chivalrous'.

After this long divagation I return to our early holidays.

There were summers, even before my father first took Fanny and me to London or on 'the grand tour of Europe', when we went farther afield than the Clyde. We became acquainted with the Hebrides (sailing all the way from the Broomielaw), and with some of the northern lochs. Once we passed a month of unbroken sunshine on Loch Sween, where we were, I think, lent a house by the Malcolms of Poltalloch, who were related to our Wyld cousins. Young Malcolm had married the daughter of Lily Langtry. Rumour said that King Edward was the bride's father. Be that as it may, a daughter of this marriage was noted recently as one of the two leading beauties among presented debutantes, the other being a half-French great-great-granddaughter of our old Aunt Roxburgh.

One summer, during the period when my father was a Glasgow town councillor, the vast old white house on Loch Katrine for which the councillors held an annual ballot, fell to us, and we then came to know the countryside where our paternal ancestors had lifted their neighbours' cattle when not engaged in fighting the English. 'The mune is the Macfarlanes' lantern' and 'The Macfarlane geese are aye tough' (from being driven so far) were still proverbs thereabouts. And there on their lonely, pine-shaded island, beside their ruined keep, our thieving forebears lay buried – undistinguished, but having bestowed upon us a proprietary right in the moon.

Indeed we had good holidays, unfettered but for the mandates of that never unkindly religion by which our parents lived.

Often and often, when I was no more than ten, I would set off unquestioned and with not a penny in my pocket, to wander alone till nightfall, walking as much as fifteen or eighteen miles before I reached home again. Or I would slip from the house, before the others were awake, with my special friend and cousin, Brian Palmer, who often came to stay with us. Brian's mother, the handsomest of several handsome sisters of my father, had been followed home in the streets of London by a gentleman named Reynolds Palmer, and there had been an impulsive marriage. He was a clergyman of good family (descended from Sir Joshua Reynolds) and he later became chaplain to the Duke of Buccleuch. But his moral character was poor, and she was left by him with four children and no money. Having some literary aptitude (she was a correspondent of Thomas Carlyle's) she tried to earn by her pen, and she had published some articles when she was attacked by tuberculosis of the spine. I saw her only once, lying on a sofa at Eskbank, in the house of her only unmarried sister, Aunt Jane, who had adopted all the children. A vivacious black-haired shadow of a woman, I thought she looked like a Spaniard.

Brian, the youngest, who was my age, unlike some of the boy friends of my earlier school days, became my friend. We had amicably arranged a marriage in which he would be a sailor, I a stewardess on the same ship. Our affection was undisturbed by emotion, and I remember how puzzled we were when I heard Aunt Jane telling my mother that we were getting too old to sleep together. Though as I slept with my brothers and with my father, why not with Brian? This bar increased our daytime devotion. He was a handsome boy; not clever (I had to teach him his Sunday hymn, and it was hard work), but sweet-tempered, honest-hearted, innocent and endowed with a lovely singing voice. He never could pass an examination. But he is now a minister of no known denomination with a church of his own, adored by a scattered congregation in the backwoods of Australia.

He and I, even if we took nothing to eat with us, could

always count on a meal at any cottage. Hospitality was still the rule throughout the Scottish countryside, and we felt not the faintest disgust if the good wife spread the butter on new-baked scones with her thumb sooner than bother with a knife. Germs for us existed only in laboratories and in books. In our absence of physical disgusts and our ignorance of science we were savages. I still find the microbe difficult to accept as an article of faith.

Not that our parents had any pet theories. We did include some homeopathic remedies in the home pharmacopœia. (For a time I became a secret addict to aconite, liking its green taste, so that I took furtive sips or sucked a pilule – without ill effect.) But we were duly vaccinated, and for more than a slight illness the doctor was summoned. My mother, with cheerful efficiency – indeed with zest – nursed Fanny through scarlet fever in the house, and the rest of us remained immune. 'Consult the doctor, but use your common sense', was a maxim of hers.

She had, to her great disappointment been unable to suckle any of us, so we were reared on milk brought to the door in battered beakers of brass-tipped iron, which today would be condemned as unhygienic. As for the milk itself my mother would as soon have poured it out of the window as let it be robbed of its 'natural raw vigour' by having it sterilised.

Such details of nurture are stated, not recommended here. I do suggest, however, that exhibitions of parental fastidiousness, whether based on adult delicacy or scientific fact, may possibly harm a growing child.

Back in Glasgow from the country or the sea, life was different. But it abounded in incident and interests.

Even in town we were allowed the utmost freedom in almost every direction, and I cannot remember a time when we did not play in the streets as and with whom we pleased, so long as our comings and goings did not impinge on the simple home routine of meals, lessons, prayers and bedtime. We made our forays unburdened by warnings, moral instructions or questioning. So we were usually ready to babble of our doings. Glasgow, often known as 'the second city of the empire', might have been our village of Abernethy for all the nervousness displayed in trusting us to the life of the pavements.

In permitting such liberty as a matter of course, and in confiding in our decent behaviour, our parents followed a fashion of life once common but already discarded by those who prided themselves on gentility. Many, I think most, of the families in our acquaintance forbade their children the streets as a playground. We were sorry (I still am) for these guarded children. They missed endless fun. And how we despised their parents.

We did not only play at tops, marbles, 'peever', hoop-running (insisting upon iron hoops and hooks to match those of our street boy friends), ball, and road games, each in their season and correct circumstance; we fought in gangs with peashooters and catapults, rode madly on a tricycle horse, tore about on roller skates or trundling a cane 'mail-cart' crammed with passengers; we coasted the steep hills on wheels or sledges. We fished down gratings for queer objects; we scoured waste lands, dodged policemen, hung on to the back rails of horse trams, four-wheelers and lorries in the traffic of Sauchiehall Street. There were, of course, no motor vehicles, but the traffic was brisk. We followed with mimicry and absurd gestures any passer-by who appeared to us over-dressed or 'stuck-up'. I still feel this impulse come over me at times in fashionable surroundings. Though we returned often with torn clothes and broken knees, and always with dirty faces, we never came by any serious accident. Nor did we ever choose to go farther than a quarter of a mile or so in any direction from our own doorstep. My own habit was to rush home at intervals, ring the front-door bell, inquire of the housemaid who opened it, 'Is Mother in?'– and being told that she was – to run off again, as often as not without entering the house.

Later on, when we moved to a house in a west-end square with large railinged 'gardens' in the middle, I felt no desire to seek amusement in the formal and cultured space thus provided. True, by that time I was at school most of the day and was turning to pursuits other than play in spare hours. But in town at any age I preferred the streets to gardens or parks, as I still do. Even in the country, though I appreciate

gardens and have had several of my own which I have loved,
I always breathe more happily when I leave them for the
common road or the open fields and woods. Perhaps this is
why the semi-privacy of neat and pretty suburban gardens
causes me to feel oppressed when I walk down a suburban
road, no matter how convenient or pleasing; and why the
war-time removal of walls and railings has given me relief.
The only exception to this is the very high wall having in it
a small, closed as it were secret door which leads abruptly
from the public roadway to private grounds – the kind
of entrance that is to be found in full perfection in Italy.
But lacking an Italian villa or palace I like to pass without
gradation between the freedom of my own four walls and
the freedom of the world at large.

So far as the street playing went, I must say that my
parents were justified in their trustingness. We were often
rude, and our companions, who were mostly boys and girls
we should not otherwise have met, were as often both rude
and rough. We trespassed, we came sometimes into conflict
with the police. We fought pitched battles, encountered
crude facts, learned to be wary. But there must have been
far more vice, both flagrant and insidious, in my sister's
expensive and 'select' Edinburgh boarding school, by her
accounts, than in the maze of somewhat low thoroughfares
and the very dark closes round Renfrew Street. What there
was had no effect, sliding easily off our consciousness and
finding no place in our imaginations. This was furthered
by the complete absence of questioning at home. I can
recall a single incident of indecency as childish as it was
absurd. A rather weakly little boy of my own age – round
about seven – invited me to go with him into one of the dark
closes (doorless entrances to tenement houses) and there
suggested that he should make water under my dress. This I
rejected with contumely, but I waited till my companion had
relieved himself in the normal manner, to which I was used
in my brothers by dealing with troublesome trouser buttons.
Thereupon we rejoined our other playmates. My complete
ignorance of what are called the facts of life, so far as human
beings were concerned, my familiarity with the processes of
wild and farmyard animals, and with the structure of small

boys, and my dreams of romantic love ran separate and parallel. This may be good or bad. It does, I fancy, tend less to the condition of childish confusion or unchildish preoccupation which can so easily be induced by adult information which comes untimely into the inexperienced and fantastic realm of a child's thought. Already at six years old I had conceived more than one romantic passion, chiefly for grown-up cousins and for seldom seen male acquaintances. And although I now realise that these were accompanied by strong physical reactions, they scarcely encroached upon my full and active existence; nor had I at any time the faintest sexual curiosity. Though most of the objects of my passion were grown men, some were grown women, and I was able to cherish a number of fervent preferences at the same time, being easily inflamed by the turn of a face, by movements, smiles, ways of talking and of moving which overwhelmed by their individual charm.

Not long after I could read I went to Miss Semple one day in the nursery with a newspaper to ask her about an item of news which puzzled me. 'Look,' I said, 'it says here that a girl of fifteen who wasn't married, has a baby. It can't be true, can it?' She looked at me gravely over her spectacles. 'Aye, dearie,' she said, 'there's many and many a poor girl who becomes a mother without ever having a husband.'

Pondering upon this, I concluded that those powerful feelings which assaulted my breast and the pit of my stomach when I indulged in romantic dreams of being kissed or caressed by one of my idols of the moment, might any day cause me to become a mother. At the same time this failed to check my indulgence. At the same time too, when Fanny and I played at 'having babies', as we sometimes did when lying in bed, we always threw our dolls up to the ceiling so that we might receive them 'from God' in a commonsense manner to be suitably clothed and cared for. Like most children I tolerated paradoxes without the least difficulty. My only tests for the admission of a truth were the tone and expression of the speaker. As in these respects both mother and Miss Semple were beyond suspicion, both had to be accepted. Life was full of contradictions quite as strange, and my mind was receptive and practical, rather than passive.

Most memorable of our street fights was a long campaign sporadically conducted against a family of boys who lived not far away. They were the sons of the headmaster of the Glasgow High School, which we regarded with snobbish contempt as a low seat of learning. Our foes were big, husky youths, our superiors in age and strength, who had the further advantage of inhabiting a house that was highly terraced up from pavement-level by a castellated wall from which they hurled their ammunition with derisive yells as we passed below. How we hated them, and what a variety of plots and ingenious weapons we planned for their discomfiture, not neglecting the derisive epithet! For a time we never went out without concealing ginger-beer bottles filled with water in the turn-ups of the fishwife costumes we wore at that time, our intent being to replenish the squirts with which we might souse an unwary sentry.

Yet once, when we encountered these same boys in conventional festive attire at a curious children's party, I meekly danced with one of them after another, and no reference was made on either side to our prolonged street feud. There was a tacit admission that the street was in a separate category. We behaved like perfect ladies and gentlemen, resumed our hostilities next day with unabated vigour, and continued them until they dwindled into an inconclusive peace. I believe that several of the boys distinguished themselves in later life.

I mentioned a curious children's party. So it was, with an atmosphere different from other parties, which has made it stay clear where others have faded as being all alike. Not that we went to many parties. We usually gave one a year ourselves, and we attended the few given by families with children in my parents' acquaintance, and later, by some of the friends we made at school. Either children's parties are everywhere and at all times the same, or there is a remarkable time lag with respect to them between Dublin and Glasgow. I say this because, though Elizabeth Bowen belongs to a younger generation, the descriptions of parties during her Dublin childhood in her book, *Seven Winters*,

apply in every detail to those we went to. Nor could I
hope to improve on her recording. Certainly for me the
preliminaries were far more enjoyable than the parties
themselves, which I found always disappointing as a
whole and often painful in their particulars. At home
I would labour hard and joyously at every preparation,
helping with passion to arrange the drawing-room, the
flowers, the plates of pretty and unusual foods. Our fairy
lights, concealed in roses with porcelain petals, which we
disposed among trails of maidenhair and asparagus fern,
were to my eye so superlatively festive that in spite of past
experiences anticipations of delight were not to be resisted.
When completed our drawing-room, with its vast crimson
carpet, its pannelled walls papered with shot salmon pink,
its cabinets, fans and nick-nacks tastefully displayed, its gilt
clock with the figure of David shown reclining after his battle
with Goliath, and its picture by Uncle Frank of an Italian
peasant driving sheep through a ruined archway (this on a
large easel in one corner, with a drapery so arranged over
one side of the frame so as to suggest that the masterpiece
was still in the process of creation) – everything there and
in the dining-room filled me with family pride and struck
me with that generous awe which we feel when confronted
by æsthetic perfection. Surely this time I should have a part
in a gaiety that would harmonise with such a setting. But
alas! judged by the noise, laughter and appetite of hosts and
of guests, each party was a great success, and yet I suffered
almost invariably from bitter, secret disillusionment and
was glad when the end was reached. As far back as my
memory goes faces have been my aliment, and my only
consolation for the failure of each party would be in the
memory of some individual face, some figure, even some
single feature which had held my attention and inflamed
my imagination. Most of the human components struck
me as mere blots, and myself as the worst blot of all.
Once indeed I overheard or was later told of a remark
made about me by one of the grown-ups present, 'that
child is like a gazelle'. I treasured the remark. None the
less I always felt painfully shy, awkward and despicable,
even as I felt my party clothes to be as unbecoming as they

were uncomfortable. I suppose the trouble was that parties were both too disciplined and too noisy for my enjoyment. A few grown-ups were invited, ostensibly to assist, really to dragoon us. I harboured hatred for weeks towards the two Miss Mavors – aunts of the playwright James Bridie – who kept lecturing me at intervals on the duties of hostesses when they found me – exhausted as I felt from serving our guests – snatching surreptitiously at my first meringue lest I should get nothing at all.

But to return to the curious party. This was given by a mysterious lady who had taken part of a furnished house almost opposite to ours, but in a row which catered for the theatrical and foreign birds of passage. She was alone with a small girl of our own age, whom she introduced to us as her niece and sent out to join us in our play. The child, called 'Dodo', was entirely different from any of the children we had met. It was not so much that she was pretty, though she was a beautiful little creature. Many of our friends and cousins had notably good looks. It was that she carried about with her an atmosphere like a perfume which was new in our bourgeois air. Even her clothes, her movements, the soft modulations of her speech, marked her off, though she was dressed with the utmost simplicity and was free from affectation as from self-consciousness. She was not apparently clever, original, or particularly lively. We never advanced to any degree of intimacy. But Dodo provided me with my first ideal of perfect style and I watched her with earnest ardour, even if she were doing no more than going up or down the steps of her temporary home. When she said one day by chance that her aunt had been an actress and that she would probably go on the stage herself, a new charm was added. We were never taken to a theatre, and heads were shaken over all that savoured of the stage: more in sorrow than in anger, but none the less with disapproval, as over some unfortunate social illness. Yet when the aunt, a Miss Farmsworth, invited us and all the others within reach to Dodo's party, and although unkind rumour about the lady had already been at work, my mother gravely decided that it would be at once discourteous and uncharitable to refuse.

Miss Farmsworth, a graceful and amusing woman no longer young, was distinguished by her made-up face, dyed hair, and smart, unusual style in dress. She proved herself to be an ideal hostess, neither shepherding nor organising us, but treating us as respected adult guests at a conventional dance for which music, printed programmes with pencils, and refreshments were provided. To our amazement we were regaled with wine, 'the mocker', which we then saw for the first time outside the church on Communion Sunday. True, it was in the form of claret cup, but it savoured to us of the devil's own brew. Members all of the Young Abstainers' Union, we broke by universal assent and without hesitation our pledges, and for once I rejoiced in assembly as a guest surely should. This in spite of being able only to join in polkas, country dances and the schottische, which, never having been to a dancing class, we had learned from the servants. It must, I think, have been from this occasion and from our chagrin at being unable to waltz, that Fanny put up a fight at home, so that in time we became enthusiastic pupils at the Queen's Rooms where the famous, fashionable, Mr. Webster conferred upon Glasgow a sense of elegance. We came just too late to be taught by D'Albert, father of the famous pianist whom I came later to hear often and to meet sometimes in Germany. But Mr. Webster was efficient and stylish in the extreme after a classical mode.

A small incident of the Farmsworth party remains vivid in memory. It must have taken place after I was eight, because we had then met the sister of our High School enemies, having begun to attend the leading girls' day school when I was that age. Jessie was not in my class nor in Fanny's, and we never came to know her, what with our former contempt and because her nose was always running – or so we said. She was without doubt at an unattractive stage. Poor Jessie! When she caught sight of the ruby wine she raised an outcry. 'Mother made me promise,' she said, 'that if we were offered anything like wine I was not to touch it.' Our hostess urged her, smiling. We renegades (including the wicked brother who was my supper escort) all raised and drained our glasses. She allowed herself to be persuaded. But, clumsy with misery after a sip or two, she let the glass fall, spilling the claret over her white frock. As she howled with despair I led her to the bathroom and there spent a long time sponging the stain, trying to cheer her and advising her, with all the eloquence I had, to say not a word at home unless she was directly asked. Her brothers swore secrecy. What happened I never heard. We proclaimed on reaching home that we had drunk real claret. My father smiled indulgently. 'There's nothing I like better myself,' he said, 'than a glass of good wine. It was meant for our enjoyment. But I should be ashamed to go among the poor Glasgow drunkards as I do if I were to have my own decanter at home. Besides if you sign a pledge you ought not to break it.'

'There's nothing *I* enjoy more than a glass of home-brewed ale,' said my mother, shaking her head, 'but with Glasgow as it is, we must deny ourselves.'

We agreed that we would renew and keep our pledges and went up to bed feeling noble. I kept mine till I came of age. As the Farmsworths, who were birds of passage, soon left Glasgow we were not again subjected to temptation. But the word, wine, assumed a radiant character for us, and one day, visiting the new panorama of Bannockburn in Sauchiehall Street *en famille*, as we were going out past the buffet, my father carrying Grant in his arms, my mother noticed with disapproval that the place was licensed to sell wines and spirits. She called my father's attention to this. Grant caught the magic word and declared in a loud voice, 'I want wine!' The more he was hushed and hurried towards the outer door, the louder he bawled his demand, till he was in a frenzy of tears and balked desire. The bystanders laughed and tried to coax the boy's parents to 'let him have a drop'. They were adamant, and bore off the child, who wailed all the way up the long hill.

CHAPTER SIX

Town and Country

FOR many years now, no matter how poor I have been, I have steadfastly maintained two homes, one in the country, the other in town. I have found the benefit incomputable, the effort many times repaid.

I have sometimes wondered whether those bigamists, of whose discovery we sometimes read with regret in the newspapers, are not unconscious followers of this Horatian wisdom. Usually railroad hands or commercial travellers, they have, till unfortunately discovered, led double lives without hurting anybody, while maintaining equable spirits and lively interest in themselves. Knowing by instinct that with only one home they would mope or inflict mopery, they find an inoffensive satisfaction between two hearths. One man, I remember (an engine driver or fireman) kept a diary, which served the double purpose of preventing *faux pas* by himself and of demonstrating his mild, humane disposition. Like so many persons tinged with melancholy, he was absent-minded when off duty. So, while his journal was helpful in the matter of his children's names and characteristics on his crossing either threshold, he was apt to leave it exposed to uninformed eyes. One of his wives, in a passing frenzy – excusable but to be lamented – informed upon him. When she saw her mistake, it was too late, and neither her own public protestations of happiness, nor those of the other wife, which were added, availed to restore the *status quo*.

By country things I mean all rural sights, sounds, textures, smells: the invincible slowness, the immemorial leisure of every procedure, the indifferences, the punctualities.

As in the countryside all that is most sordid in existence

is rendered gracious, so in the city streets our utmost of elegance, efficiency or pomp betrays underlying corruption. Then also in the less careful parts of any town both our human shame and our shining worth lie open, one against the other. I relish equally both the slow pace and the urgency, the simple roughness and the complex veneer, even to the faults and disadvantages of both. Being by nature excitable, enthusiastic, easily fatigued and melancholic, I need each in alternation. But I must have a true double residence. Week-ends in either town or country are worse to me than living in a suburb. The inconveniences of this are evident. By slow degrees, considerable efforts and much cogitation I have fulfilled my main need, which is a sort of oscillation between one rhythm and another. For nearly forty years a Londoner I have yet contrived, though on the most modest scale, my Sabine farm.

I lived in old Hampstead, mostly in charming old houses near the Heath, for about twenty-eight years. I might have grown old there – all passion spent – a gentle Hampstead old age, notwithstanding public and personal disasters. Others have done so. I sometimes go up to see them in the well-loved little streets.

But Hampstead is all reminiscence, beautifully and tenderly preserved, preserved as it were under a glass case. The Heath often looks like an old, well-tended tapestry. Perhaps it was this preserved, exclusive exquisiteness that put Lawrence into a sudden resentful rage against Hampstead, when for a time he lived there. He could not fit his flaming life into its nostalgic scene, nor rejoice in moving, himself so painfully alive, in a souvenir. He felt the past too keenly to lay upon it a wreath of immortelles.

I was to grow old in Camden Town, and I have come to be glad of this. In Camden Town, gritty, shabby, untidy; in Camden Town, as full of poetic and literary memories as Hampstead, but without the sunset glow; in Camden Town of splendid outlines of masonry if one can look past the crumbling details of neglect; in Camden Town, full of Jews, foreigners of every sort, babies in every shade of coffee, hordes of grubby children and multitudes of old waifs among whom I range myself with satisfaction, and endless entertainment mixed with profound melancholy.

Full of hard-trotting, wise little horses, market trained. Full of thieves and toughs. The Bedford. Acrobats. Celebrities: Tennyson, Shelley, Dickens, Dibdin, Keane, Sickert, Dr. Crippen.

Verlaine and Rimbaud. 8 Gt. College Street. May 25, 1873. 'A very gay district; one might be in Brussels.'

Waking in winter I hear the traffic, I know that the red and brown omnibuses with their upper decks scarcely below the level of my windows are carrying the men and women who work in town to their offices and workrooms. Their faces are pale with the cold, the fingers with which they strike matches or unfold their newspapers are awkward and chilly.

As I walk down P[arkway] the first time some mornings, the lives from each side extrude upon me, and their pressure, scarcely endurable, is at the same time exhilarating, like the first waves when one goes into the sea to bathe.

The wood shop – my enjoyment in visiting partly because of the things they sell there, partly because of the people – always in numbers and mostly men – who by their quiet carriage, their intentness upon the exact fitness of each small purchase and their particular way of looking and of speaking proclaim themselves to be crafty of hand but dreamers all.

Sept. 25 [1943?]. Early this morning young man on bicycle called with long slender ladder which he substituted for the heavy one to serve attic in case of incendiaries. Mrs. W. called, full of talk, nervous and overwrought . . . wrote a few letters and washed clothes . . . after lunch at home, went out . . . Went to sup at F.'s and E.'s flat away at Malvern Court. Extremely grand, impressive, etc. Excellent meal with claret. Pleasant evening, tho' I talked too much. Getting to like E. whom I did not at first take to. She's a niece of Ethel Smythe (her companion on the Greek tour) and an astronomer. We talked of social problems, language and the difficulty of getting jam made. . . . Bed long after midnight.

Can hear from my bed the exasperated cries of the lions on a warm night.

❋

Essex rolls in its highlands, but it is all open, fresh, full of air that comes over unimpeded from the sea, yet it is no low-lying marsh, like the Rye marshes, nor mere flats, like Lincolnshire, which can be beautiful, but are apt to be sad or stern. Nothing wistful about the highlands of East Anglia, also nothing romantic or 'picturesque', but none the less a painter's country.

The threshing is over for the year (it costs, says Mr. Metson, the price of one of his four stacks). Today, when I was again at the water-butts covered in mud, the lorry passed carrying a trussed-up load of straw the size of a London house. The men shouted, waved, kissed their hands. How they got it safe under the line of dragging trees I don't know. It was a masterpiece and those men are kings. They look it too, and know it.

I called for a chat in the Metsons' living-room just as Mr. Metson had come in from finishing his job to sit down by the fire and have his morning cup of tea at 11 a.m. Small, dark, unshaven, untidy, but beautifully knitted together and triumphant.

English sunshine. Times in the late summer and autumn when towards evening the air seems so saturated with sunshine that it can hold no more and one expects the particles to drop out of solution on the earth. One looks for gold pieces to fall on the fields from that overcharged air. If we could get a little way away from the earth should we not see England in summer steaming faintly in the sun, her outlines hidden in a gold haze?

❋

The clouds like brushed wool. Patches of blue growing smaller and smaller till they become mere dimples of a darker grey in the overspreading quilt of cloud.

Autumn sunset – bars of cold greenish-yellow behind high trees from which all the lower leaves had fallen.

The colour of a bramble-leaf green, so dark a green, with untermixed a purplish shade coming from the stems. Here and there a scarlet leaf, here and there one with workings like tortoise-shell, held up to the flame of the sun. Feeling of walking on the top of the world. Feeling of darkness, here and there a sordidness, but passionate, stimulating – a hardness. The rustling, withered bell heather, some sprays having one or two red blooming bells still at the top. The little birds flying silently in and out of the tussocks like mice.

The bird flying against the breeze, only now and then making a movement with its wings, like a word spoken.

On the bare treetops they looked like a few black leaves left from the summer before. They did not twitter nor whistle but perched silently, each one facing in the easterly direction whence the wind came.

Another time they filled a clump of trees and remained still as before but not all facing one way (there was no wind), and the noise coming from them was like the squeaking and creaking of thin ice when it is bent and broken.

The flock in the field looked like vermin moving about there, such a dense flock of small black, actively moving objects. The sound of their flight when the whole flock rose – so determined and rushing – one realised the marvellous strength of each pair of small wings contributing to it.

There had been hoar frost and where the shadows lay of trees or hedges the hoar still remained. Everywhere else it was melted. Grey shadows in sunlight.

There was no wind that could be felt, nor did the clouds move across the sky. Each separate cloud stayed in its place and seemed very slowly, as if by its own thoughtful volition, to change its shape.

The snow lay scattered like heavenly manna on the dark brown fields.

It was a bright airy morning – airy rather than windy. Every branch was in gentle movement and sounds as of water falling and rushing came from every place where trees were grouped considerably together. It was as if the air were in movement from mere superabundance. There seemed too much air in the world for stillness. Yet not wind. Just a gay, buoyant jostling – one body of air against another. The birds seemed to feel the delight of it. In the swaying stirring branches of the pines the smaller birds went flying, fluttering, running about like mice. Among the great shafts which looked as if they had been red-hot and were now cool, but coloured, the chaffinches looked tiny till one saw a blue-tailed tit. And the tits looked as small, as light, as neat as any bird could be till there came a light-brown wren. In the middle distance lower down the slope there was a rookery, and the rooks in the sky, planing, veering, floating on the moving airs, were like the scraps of charred paper from a huge bonfire. It was their sport that the air should sport with them as it would.

> Now I am old, but once I was new-born
> In March, this maddest month of all the year.
> To her rough tunes the blush mounts to the thorn,
> Spring has her heart though she sports winter's gear.
> I'm still her child. I cannot walk demurely
> While her impenitent blackbird airs his soul,
> While on black boughs her raindrops insecurely
> Mock all that's sober with their drunken roll.
> She and her blackbird are the first to guess
> What the antique fields will presently be saying,
> 'Age is a myth. Bring out my gala dress.
> Wrinkles are honours. Who will go a-Maying?'
> Indiscreet March! With mop and pail she races
> Till April saunters in and lifts all faces.

The oak trees in spring open their leaves last at the top. The transparent leaf is like a butterfly, brown, red and yellow spotted against the sun. Heath, flowering whin and heather so close set that the flowers were pressed against one another.

What is wrong with the vegetarians is lack of æsthetic ears and eyes. Who can maintain that a raw quacking duck or cackling hen sounds better than a plucked sizzling one being taken from the oven? Or that a pig is pleasanter to look at coated with mud in its sty than with well browned crackling on the table?

Having an extra amount of writing to get off today I dug up some horseradish roots . . . by the time I had got them up, removing a few weeds from the plot, and roughly washed them in several waters, more than an hour had passed. Who that eats the sauce made from them will guess that it cost me a couple of guineas?

No man could look so wicked as an old billy-goat can look. But no child could compete either in innocence or in innocent looks with a goat kid.

No old goat could look so wicked as a man can be.

When the turkey-cock is doing his tail business it is as if God had said to himself, 'Let's see if we can make a being compounded out of vanity alone.' No wonder Mrs. H. laughed and stayed fascinated watching the first live turkey-cock she had ever seen. 'He's so vain he won't eat,' she said. It was true. He scorned to do more than snatch at a few grains when he thought nobody was looking. And when he was not tail-spreading, he was not alive.

The flights of autumnal birds are like a cast of seed flung high into the air, all separate yet all belonging, coming from the same hand and dropping to the same patch of field.

Drive to town. The walk in the morning under gilded skies . . . The women passengers by the wayside dressed for town with their hostesses still wearing curling pins as they see them off and turn back to wash the breakfast things.

PART II
AUTOBIOGRAPHY

CHAPTER SEVEN

The Zoo: The Dream

I HAD to do something. For more than a week out of sorts, possessed by melancholy, afflicted by strange pains and by that lassitude which is in itself a pain, I could neither rest nor concentrate. Though equable by nature and, for the most part, able to nourish cheerfulness from a dozen familiar sources should the day's routine fail in providing any, I have all my life been subject to such attacks. Their onslaught has in it something of the violence of an epileptic seizure. At least, as with the victims of epilepsy, the malady has a way of following with precipitance upon a state of equally unaccountable well-being. After a day in which all one's fountains have played to the sky; a day in which the common ills of life, and even one's own particular sorrows, are shown by irrefutable clairvoyance to be needful dissonances only waiting their time to be resolved in a universal music; a day in which love, truth and worth, no matter how ill-bestowed or unrecompensed, stand beyond question as eternal verities; after such a day, all in a moment, the solid-seeming structure melts into mud leaving the spirit homeless. Then the mildest sunshine, the blossoming trees of spring itself afford no relief. The foundations of life and the incentives for maintaining it are gone. But why attempt to describe an affliction so well known even in better times than those we now endure?

The only comfort in this condition is to have near one a familiar, loving human being in whose smiling 'there, there!' one can take refuge till the cloud goes. I have had this best of all possessions. I have it no longer. So I thought I would walk in the sunshine, following the vast, unending, drab crowd of my fellows who were bound for the Zoo.

I had not been to the Zoo for over thirty years, though it lies not far from where I live now. When I last went it was on a Fellows' day to meet in the then Galsworthian fashion a lover and friend and teacher who is now dead. I was young and had made my toilette with care. On the farther side of the Gardens lay the region of pictorial art into which I had deliriously dipped upon first coming to London. On the nearer side lay marriage, a long history of work, motherhood, success of a sort, friends, tragic and sudden deaths, a penniless condition, the war. The air had used to sparkle with magic. Yesterday, though the sun shone and the air was mild there was nothing of sparkle and less of magic. I drifted as part of the dingy procession zoo-wards and was possessed by sick loathing and melancholy.

Inside the grounds there was hardly moving room. I had glimpses of imprisoned animals and wondered at the beauty of their coats – especially the red dingoes and bright brown wolves. Then by some chance of shifting I found myself in front of a giggling, inquisitive crowd and close to the bars before an outdoor prison of small monkeys. THESE ANIMALS ARE DANGEROUS. I read the printed sign. I held out my finger. The little ape held it and we looked into one another's eyes. 'No trees,' he seemed to say, and he let my finger go. I looked at the horrible contraption of blackened sticks – mockery of a tree – in his cage, which, with the bars was all our provision for two agile geniuses. 'No trees,' said his melancholic eyes, 'but at least *you* can remember them. I have not so much as the memory of trees. I do not even know that that distant greenness in the park outside is made by trees.'

'There there!' I murmured as I turned away. I dragged myself home determined never again to visit the Zoo.

As a child I adored all animals and greatly longed to have a monkey, but my wish was not realised. My father, as a boy in the Fife manse, had a monkey about which I was never tired of hearing. It had escaped, he told us, from a travelling circus in the company of a dwarf. Both had arrived at Collessie manse by night, and for years afterwards they had formed part of the household. The monkey grew uppish. He used to steal a tumbler and tooth-brush, ran up a tree with them, and brush his teeth conceitedly. The dwarf, quite an old man, had, like so many dwarfs, a sour temper. But the children loved him, and they were sad when their parents decided that the little man must go. What his end was I never heard.

In our local Pet Stores in Camden Town I was once tempted to buy a chimpanzee. Almost as tall as I, but 'tame and gentle,' I was assured, 'well behaved, he will give no trouble.' 'Buy me!' his eyes pleaded. But his price was £50, and would he not eat me out of house and home during war-time? Besides I have no trees. Guiltily I shook my head. The chimpanzee followed me to the door as far as his chain would allow. More practicable, I thought, would be this goose in a cage on the pavement – an unusual bird; she had three legs. I might tour the country with her, charging a penny admittance, and I could live on the eggs she laid. Fortunately for me, next day both chimpanzee and goose were gone.

Returning more dejected than when I had set out I repented of my visit. But next day I was glad I went, because the dream I had in the night afterwards, though it still might have been of the sort which carries its peculiar sense of pleasure far into the subsequent hours of daylight, and might so have restored something of the magic my daylight hours lacked, could hardly have been of the same substance and circumstance.

Unhopeful of conveying its ecstatic quality I shall yet try to set it down now.

I walked, in my dream, along a narrow path which skirted a steep hillside. Sloping up on our right through patches of woodland to the summit, and down on our left to a stream which meandered through clumps of bushes and reeds, the place put me in mind of a short-cut at Mount Quharrie, known in the district as the Fairy Path, and used by us to avoid a stretch of hard road when going on foot to or from the village.

I say 'our', because several of us walked there, both young and old, I being one of the children of the company. I did not identify any of the others till I found myself clinging to the front of an upright piano which threatened to fall forward upon me as I stood on its closed keyboard holding by the candle-brackets. Then I saw my father. He was reclining fully dressed on a bed on the other side of the path from me and the toppling piano. Unperturbed by my peril he leaned on his elbow and smiled across at me. 'Help me!' I cried. 'The piano is falling on me!' 'Jump!' he said, still smiling, and he moved a little back to make room for me on the counterpane, patting it to encourage my obedience. I jumped and landed in safety. The piano and the bed disappeared. We all went on along the path. Then, looking down to the left, I saw a pool, partly reed-covered, and my attention was held by an agitation within the water. Some hidden life below was covering the surface with gleaming rings. As I watched the head of a red-haired animal emerged, soon followed by its bulky red body, as the creature rose into the sunlight and scrambled on to the bank. There, while it shook a rainbow shower from its pelt, it was joined from the pool by a second, far smaller animal of the same species and ruddy colour, clearly a kid, which also shook itself in the bright, warm sun.

I regarded them with careful, extreme delight. The mother – as an unusually large and clumsy udder showed her to be – was something between a deer, a goat and a large dog in shape and size, but she exactly resembled no beast I ever saw in reality or in picture. Her curiously formed forehead was without horns, her neck was short and thick, her legs awkward. The most beautiful thing about her was her pelt of long and silky hair, like that of a red setter, but falling in irregular swathes about her, reaching in places almost to the grass. Even her udder trailed these long red wisps of hair. Though this was unbeautiful, and though her proportions were somehow wrong and her movements clumsy, so that she struck me as no better adapted for walking on land than for living under water, I felt inexplicable joy and emotion in her aspect.

Followed by her kid, neither of them uttering any sound, she lumbered through a group of birch trees in young leaf bordering the stream and made her way to where there was a stretch of level sward. There, having turned her blunt head as if to summon her young to emulation, she suddenly curved her whole body like a stretched bow, and, in relaxing it, sprang into the air. All was now revealed.

Rapture flooded me. I saw her rise higher and higher in her proper element, threshing with her four thrusting legs and her flexing spine in powerful unison, wingless, yet able to spurn and mount in the air by her own motion. How describe her aerial progress, which was totally unlike that of bird or aeroplane, having a manner, an energy and a satisfaction that were all her own? She rowed her great bulk easily, strongly upwards on a steep line towards the brow of the hill behind, gaining impetus and height together.

What particularly ravished me was the way her swathes of hair, now made alive by the air of her motion, streamed and rippled back all round her, so that they became part of her motion, while at the same time, both transparent to and illumined by the bright sun, they formed an aureole round her. And within the aureole the outline of her body was revealed in its magnificent adaptability to her true element. I cannot express the extreme delight begotten in me by this heavenward canter of the red beast.

Soon she would disappear high over the hill behind. My one intent became to see her kid spring up and follow her. But he showed no sign of taking to the air. He nibbled at the reeds, looked about him, and presently decided to go farther down hill, where I now saw that there were some cottages and even little grass-grown shops far below the level of the stream on the far side. I feared, as he was very pretty, that he would be taken into one of the houses as a pet, and might then never be able to fly and rejoin his mother.

'Come along, child,' said my father who had seen nothing of all this. 'You know we have a train to catch. If you loiter like this we shall miss it.' Here my dream ended and I woke. But all that day, going about, I saw at intervals the flight of the strange mother beast and her emergence from the quivering pool. And though I still felt out of sorts and useless, some of the magic had returned. Each dog and horse I saw in the street had the air of being about to leave the road and to fly over the housetops. It made no difference that I knew they would do no such thing. They none the less reasserted the marvel of their creation. Let it be admitted that without something of this magic and marvel I cannot happily move, breathe, exist. I am neither proud of this nor ashamed, glad nor sorry – though there have been moments of gladness and of sorrow for which it is responsible. It is merely something I have never been able to avoid or discard.

Yes, I know that there is a Freudian interpretation of my dream of the flying red beast; moreover, I think I know how it would run. And the clinical reading may be correct. I have no objection to this. But it does not greatly help me. I have faithfully narrated the dream by way of a pictorial record of what brought with it an access of serenity and joy. It was a dream essentially delightful which had the power to carry delight forward, as have all those of my dreams which involve landscape, sky, colour and strangeness. May I have many such.

CHAPTER EIGHT

Frank: The Boards

MY young friend had invited me to drink tea with him in his pleasant book-room. He is about half my age, emotional, a convert (within the time of our acquaintance) from atheism to high Anglicanism, with a tendency in both phases to regard me as a Mother Confessor. The rôle is one which I neither seek nor like, but when it is assigned I am bad at refusing it without giving painful offence. After all, besides, it is often, if also painfully, instructive.

We had been talking of this and that, when he sprang up, crossed the floor, took some volumes from a shelf, and asked if he might read me some of the poems which had 'meant most to his life'. His tone, his movements, something about the set of his shoulders told me that he was about to display a spiritual self-portrait. I felt for the moment depressed.

A shaft of amusement lightened my gloom as I considered how the years juggle with the implication of such a request when made by a man to a woman. It was like coming to where one has habitually faced a mirror and finding a blank wall; like putting what one thought to be a lighted cigarette between one's lips and closing them on a stick of chalk. A swift adjustment is demanded.

Smiling my assent I assumed a listening attitude with eyes closed in the comfortable knowledge that, if he so much as marked my smiling, he would ascribe it to anticipatory pleasure.

Why, after sufferings innumerable, have I never learned how to evade this kind of ordeal without causing distress? Surely age should help one here, but it does not me. I have a woman friend who would graciously have recollected a home engagement (I had one, but could not summon graciousness in mention of it). I have a sister – Fanny – who would have deployed her seniority to discard graciousness, as indeed she had once deployed her juvenility. I had a great aunt, well named Augusta, who would have delivered a wholesome reproof, begun with the words, 'My poor, dear young man' and ended by laughter from the accused. But my native pusillanimity is such that I only steeled myself yet once again to endure.

Then, of course, I was not decidedly averse to knowing – though I should have preferred to verify my own guess by a brief reference given unconsciously – which poems had influenced the life of my host. Again: if we may learn nothing from our failures except that we learn nothing, what of the other learning which accrues so astonishingly, not as the logical result of failure but in its course? As one whose courses have been rich in irresolute submissions, delusive aims and futile progressions, I declare that there is some comfort here for the too pliant sort; even some instruction, especially in the subject most recommended by sages. 'Self-knowledge is Power.' I saw it printed on the placard of Madame Lilian, an Oxford Street seer. True, if I had been more immediately strong, or less ill-guided and wasteful of energy, I might, in view of natural gifts not despicable, have attained by this time something more nearly resembling success in life. But what if one prefers barely perceptible sidelights and freakish illuminations to the larger effulgence of achievement? What if . . .?

This reverie was interrupted by my friend's voice, modulated to its best and surcharged with emotion. He was reading to me:

I struck the board, and cry'd, No more. I will abroad.

Hearing the poem, a favourite of my own, I did not need to listen. Instead, I began to see inside my eyelids. I saw, not the poet smiting his table as he made his ultimatum to his God, not the paraded portrait of my reading friend (though both of these stood clear in the margin of my vision) but my father's face and some yellow varnished boards. I went abroad, from Scotland to England, for the first time. I tasted Italy. I struck one of the boards – with my head. My cries were soothed by that word, which not to hear is part of the sadness of age. 'Me thoughts I heard one calling, Childe.'

Perhaps I must explain. My maternal grandmother, Mary Anne Lewis, widow of the bookish George, the grocer's son and our only surviving grandparent, lived on the Continent. Now and then my mother went to see her and a younger sister, Ina, who shared the continental home. But the two could never be persuaded to a return visit to their native place; so, for us children, they were merely cherished images, beneficent but remote. My mother's two other sisters, married and also living in Italy, sometimes dared the northern summer, with or without their husbands and children; but never Aunt Ina, nor Grandmamma who was old and had always been frail.

In the summer of 1883, however, my mother announced with a shining face that Ina and Grandmamma were about to venture as far as the south coast of England, where it was hoped they could keep reasonably warm for a month. She and my father would go there, and with them my sister Fanny and myself. Our brothers were not yet born, though the elder one must have been on his way. Fanny was six and a half, I four.

Corridor trains had not then been invented, so we had to prepare for a long spell of hours in the compartment my father had reserved for us. We should travel by night. That we should, all four, be able to lie down at full length, the space between the seats was measured, and our carpenter was asked to cut and polish enough half-inch boards to lay across it forming a solid bridge.

There was immense excitement over these and other preparations for our journey. My mother loved nothing better than to travel – the farther the better once she could be got to start. But starting was fraught with long agonies for her and those near her. Father, as we often told strangers with pride, had been 'round the world'. He travelled easily, if also ingeniously, and it was nothing to him to 'have a run down to the Village', as he called going to London. For mother a trip to Edinburgh was like going to the moon, so complicated were the preliminaries. For nights beforehand she could not be persuaded to undress and, instead of lying

on her bed, would dose uncomfortably in a chair when
overcome by sleep, greatly to my father's vexation. But
all this added to the importance of the adventure in our
eyes. A peak was reached when she produced from its
careful wrappings and shook out the caped garment of
silver grey alpaca, known as her 'dust-cloak' and reserved
for her trips to Italy in summers past. The moment came
for us to help her into it. She was between smiles and tears:
smiles for our eagerness, tears because she felt, in spite of
her heroic efforts, that she was leaving all undone. But our
four-wheeler, with our special cabby, was cracking his whip
at the door, and she was dragged, feebly protesting, down
the front steps and pushed from the mounting stone by
the kerb into the conveyance. Our luggage was already on
its railed roof. The servants waved to us, delighted by the
growing faintness of the mistress's parting injunctions. We
rumbled over the granite setts. The coincidence that we
were going to a place called Lewes, gave the affair a final
touch of importance. I had no doubt but that the English
had so named that part of their realm in my grandmother's
honour.

Thus it is that, to this day, the word 'board' has for me
a special significance. I see again my mother's tearfully
beaming face, and my father's jovial activity as he dressed
the railway carriage and assigned our places to us. I feel
again the violent contacts between these boards and my
person during innumerable later games in the only nursery
I can remember. 'Yes, it is a splendid poem,' I said to my
young friend, opening my eyes, then closing them again
while he renewed his reading, this time with a poem by
Gerard Manley Hopkins. Hopkins, I reflected, spent a
season of his spiritual struggle just round the corner of
our street, in the building we could see from the night
nursery window; the building we examined with fearful
conjectures, because inside it we knew that the Jesuits
were weaving their evil webs. The poet must often have
passed our door.

Of our journey to Lewes or the return journey I have no
memory. I know we cannot have omitted our morning and
evening prayers, nor our blessings before food, observances

even more desirable when travelling than at home. Our
blessing, composed for us by my father, was always the
same except when we were on picnics: 'God, we thank
Thee for Thy food. Bless it to us and us in Thy service.'
Both our parents were seriously troubled when, later, we
tried to substitute the more modish grace, 'For what we are
about to receive . . .' Before a picnic we all sang a verse or
two of *Let us with a Gladsome Mind*, my mother vainly trying
to make us go through the twenty-four verses with repeated
chorus before we fell to. Perhaps the train journey called for
the Miltonic grace, 'Let us blaze His name abroad, For of
gods He is the God.'

I do remember our welcome inside the small hired house
at Lewes, with details recorded as if by a Dutch painter
of interiors. As we ascended from the entrance hall to the
drawing-room landing, I had to master each step with both
feet. I can still see the steep curve, the massive moulding,
the rich, dark gloss of the mahogany banister, higher than
my head as it swept curving upward. And I can see the tall,
young, lanky figure of our aunt doubled over the landing
rail in welcoming encouragement. She wore odd, bright
clothes, with something of striped silk round her long
neck, and a sort of mantilla over her smoothly parted,
dark hair; and her face was the face of a laughing angel.
Her embraces were full of goodness and gaiety. She gave
us, there on the landing, water biscuits to refresh us, and
only laughed when we dropped crumbs. I had a passion
for water biscuits and used sometimes to steal one out
of our silver biscuit box at home to my mother's distress
because she thought them constipating. But ours at home
were round and hardish with baked brown bubbles all over
them. These were square, flaky, melting in the mouth: angel
food. Aunt Ina's way of taking strewed crumbs set her apart
from our father's aunts in Scotland, as did everything else
about her. The kindest of my father's many sisters would
not have countenanced biscuit eating on a landing. The
handsomest of them (four at least were notably handsome)
had none of the seraphic radiance in which Ina Lewis's
maypole body and irregular features seemed to bathe. No
wonder that my mother felt shy, clumsy, puzzled and at

fault when in the company of her sisters-in-law. Ina might have belonged to a different species. I have often heard my mother say that, except for the youngest, Fanny, who died aged sixteen when at school in Jersey, Ina was the flower of their flock. Certainly I have never seen another woman who looked at once so good and so gay, with underneath it all a charming gravity of unconscious innocence.

She ushered us into the sunny little drawing-room where our grandmother was seated in state. The only grandparent I had seen or was to see, she was for all her graciousness, immensely impressive. Straight, slender, upright in her chair, she wore a red chuddar shawl pinned with a large silver brooch. Crisp frills, white as snow, framed her fine thin old face. Her blue gaze was searching. At first meeting it seemed severe. She was extremely gentle. But I felt awe in her presence.

There was nothing awful about Uncle Frank, the third member of the household, even at a first meeting. He was Ina's husband, a Calabrian and a painter, Francesco Santoro: a solid, small, lively man, with prominent eyes, rolling and bloodshot, a blue chin, a fierce moustache and a ready laugh. A great, a perceptible new bliss, which filled that house and affected every visitor, emanated from him and from Ina. My grandmother basked in it. I shared in its warmth with a child's incurious response. But it was not until much later that I learned quite by chance the particulars of the happiness now so many years bygone.

It was not until the summer before I saw the French clock and started trying to write this book. I was obliged to visit the consulting room of a Harley Street specialist as the prelude to an operation and a month in hospital. As I waited alone for the famous woman in whose hands I was to put myself, I examined a large painting which hung over the mantelpiece. It was the portrait of a vigorous, strong-minded old lady of Victorian times. She must, I thought, be Mrs. Martindale, my surgeon's mother. If so, there was reassurance in knowing that, if I must be cut up, it should be by the judgement and the hands of this lady's daughter.

She entered, brisk, small, vivid, and gave me a keen

look. 'Good gracious!' she exclaimed, 'You are the image of your grandmother, old Mrs. Lewis! Yes, I knew her. We were near neighbours at Vevey many years ago when your grandmother and her daughter, Ina, lived there for a time. My mother and your grandmother became great friends. Yes, that's my mother up there. It was she that brought off the marriage between Ina and Santoro – what a good painter he was! – the summer they came to Lewes.'

Thus, only then, I heard the story.

Old Mrs. Lewis, beloved by all who met her, was the weakest, most passive, most indecisive of women. She had nothing against Santoro in himself. She never had anything against anybody. But she feared to lose by marriage her last remaining, joyfully tending daughter. So she gave no countenance to the match. Santoro, however, himself a devotee who never tired of painting portraits of my grandmother, accompanied the two to England. In England he would submit himself and subject my grandmother to a family conclave. Hence our visit.

But at Lewes he found a strong and swift ally in Mrs. Martindale. That shrewd woman took the situation immediately in hand, arranged for a secret wedding at a church in the town, saw the couple through the ceremony, conducted them back to the house with the mahogany banisters, and presented them there as man and wife. As she had foreseen, their union was blessed with tears of joy. Grandmamma, relieved of what she most dreaded in life, a decision, welcoming a strong hand, delighted by happy faces about her, acquired an adoring son-in-law. The three lived harmoniously under one roof in Rome till Ina died in her early forties. During a hard winter she neglected herself helping the poor.

The rest I already knew. Sooner than forsake what was left of the *ménage*, Santoro presently married the 'companion' from Scotland who was found and sent out for Grandmamma by my mother. By the first marriage there were no children, by the second, three. The eldest of them who also had come under Louise Martindale's healing knife, solaced me with her intelligent presence and her books throughout my weeks in hospital. She had repudiated Mussolini from his beginning, acquired British nationality, become a successful bookseller not very far from Lewes.

Uncle Frank, as we called him, set about painting portraits of Fanny and of me. Fanny posed in a yellow straw hat turned up all round her round face with a prune silk lining. I possessed a similar hat, because we were always dressed alike, but was obliged to be painted without it. To console me my dress of crimson stuff was distinguished from Fanny's by a wide 'real lace' collar. The painter joked unceasingly in his imperfect English, sang while he worked and, when we were tired, played to us on his flute or let us try to throw him on the floor by each taking one of his legs. When it was so easy for either of us to lift a single leg, we were mystified by the failure of our united efforts to send him sprawling. There must have been much noise, but nobody complained.

He became my favourite uncle; and I, failing to win avuncular approval in Scotland, his favourite niece. He declared me to be the one who looked like both Ina and Grandmamma, though they bore no likeness to each other that I can trace, nor can I find more than fleeting resemblances to either in myself. I felt profoundly sentimental when he played *My Times are in Thy Hand* on his flute, rolling his red-brown eyes at me as he played. I suspect him of having mastered that dreary tune in his anxiety to qualify as son-in-law in a protestant family. Both my grandfather and his brother had occupied the pulpit of the Scottish Presbyterian church in Rome.

Every Christmas after that, he used to send us a huge basket of figs and dried cherries from his vineyards near Spoleto. Some of the figs were the 'pulled' kind, pale and floury. Others were dark, split, filled with walnut and pressed into the form of a cross. The cherries were black, wrinkled, full of sweetness. These were food, to my palate, not to be adequated in Scotland.

On the draped easel in a corner of our Glasgow drawing-room, stood one of his portraits of grandmamma, sometimes changed for the one of a Roman peasant driving sheep under an arch. We were proud of having a real artist

in the family. Our ignorance and our reverence, where art
was concerned, were equally genuine.

Stuck away in a less honoured room there was another
picture brought to us by Uncle Frank, a small picture in a
frame that didn't fit. It had puzzled my parents, particularly
my father. He liked to bring home in triumph whole sets of
coloured representations of picturesque corners in Venice,
Nuremburg and Bruges, which he had bought already
framed and glazed at some sale. He would tell us that
the skies in all these works of art were executed by a single
expert in skies, the houses by a house expert, the figures by
a specialist in figures. Was not this a most economical and
efficient way of doing it? No painter could be equally good at
everything. It stood to reason. The picture brought by Uncle
Frank was of a common wash-bowl in a three-legged metal
frame, the kind one bought at the ironmonger's for a corner
in a servant's bedroom. 'I no paint that myself,' Uncle Frank
told me. 'It by a boy, a pupil of me. A quite young boy.
But I say now, grey on my head, if I might so paint I die
a happy man.' Often I looked at this canvas, wondered,
looked again. It was filled with clear slanting light that
came from a section of window. The rapid brush-strokes
were joyous in their appreciation of common things –
soap, water, wash-cloth, crumpled towel, enamelled tin,
illumined by the morning sun. Why was it alive when the
Venetian lagoon in the dining-room was dead? I wish I had
that picture now. But it has disappeared, thrown, no doubt,
into the ash-pit.

Once only, Uncle Frank came to visit us in Scotland.
It was over one of our periodic family troubles in Italy.
He came to us in Perthshire in the summer, raved about
the skies, cursed the climate, painted furiously (wrapping
himself in our biggest tartan plaid) and performed on his
flute. My mother found a bottle of whisky under his bed
and remonstrated. But he said he thought highly of 'ze wine
of ze country,' though it was more fiery than the Italian
vintages. His own wine, which he made at Spoleto, was
so strong that, when I was a teetotaler, aged twenty and
travelling alone to Pisa, I became drunk on half a flask of
it, put for me in a lunch basket.

I had visited Uncle Frank, at Spoleto and at Rome, after his second marriage and my grandmother's death. Some of his friends had been affected by his romantic ardour for Scotland and its inhabitants. One of them, a painter called, I think, Caccini, a pale, grey-haired widower who had exchanged not more than a few words with me, enquired if a marriage might be arranged between him and me by writing to Glasgow. But, unlike my mother's three sisters, I was not destined to make an Italian marriage, and I doubt if the letter was written. In Rome Uncle Frank made me sit under a portrait of Ina, a subtle, smiling portrait, his best. Then, in the presence of his wife, he rolled his eyes, moaned, exclaimed, 'Ah, Ina, Ina!' Poor Uncle Frank: I doubt if he was ever so happy again as that time in Lewes and for a few years after it in Rome. His second wife died, and he himself lived to become savagely senile.

We children never saw Ina or our grandmother again, though the old woman lived to be eighty-one. She, Frank, his two wives, and the two old ministers are buried near Keats and Shelley in the little English church graveyard in Rome.

When I was eight, Uncle Frank painted a life-size water-colour head and shoulders of Grandmamma, inscribed my name on it and gave it to me in Perthshire. I often look at it now, and it returns my gaze in such a way that I seem to see myself in her and her in myself. Through letters, reports and self-examination I have come to know her. Devoid of affirmative character, she was yet constant in affection, and no woman was more loved. There exists a furiously irritable, scolding, doting letter, addressed to her by my grandfather before their marriage. He accuses her of shilly-shallying over his proposal and bids her, almost with threats, to make up her mind and take him without more ado. None of her daughters, highly varied as they were, ever spoke of her without fond, glowing pride. I lack her gracious beauty, but I have inherited in large measure her weakness and a cast of feature which conveys a false impression of austerity and strength. I, too, have had devotion lavished on me far beyond my

deserts or my value. 'Yes,' we say to each other, 'I see
through you. I see the timid, indeterminate, puzzled
soul behind that firm front. In forgiving you I must
needs forgive myself. But I have reached the age of
forgiveness.'

Yet I sometimes wonder how you would have fared,
how behaved, how looked in your venerable years, if
you had been compelled to live through them in, say
Camden Town, seventy years later with the world at
war. What if, like Miss S. who once inhabited a castle
in France, you had been obliged to carry heavy loads
of vegetables for the sodden brother with whom you
shared the two top rooms of a rooming house that
provided you with a livelihood? What if you had been the
fine-faced, nameless crone, in her embroidered garment
of out-of-date elegance, who strides always alone, and
with whose piercing eyes I exchange ghostly glances as
we pass? Would your gallant, gentle bearing, attended
ever hand and foot throughout your days, have survived
such tests as theirs have done? For myself, it is as
well that, besides your pliancy and Ina's indiscriminate
benevolence, I have in me some of the frightful energy
of the idea-ridden parvenu you married: some, too, of
the preposterous qualities which made the least worthy
of your daughters a trouble to all who knew her. Weak,
much-loved Mary Anne Miller, my grandmother: if I
am to forgive you, you must also look with forgiveness
on me.

> All things counter, original, spare, strange;
>> Whatever is fickle, freckled (who knows how?)
> With swift, slow; sweet, sour; adazzle, dim;
>> He fathers-forth whose beauty is past change:
>> Praise him.

My young friend was swimming in another familiar
stream of words. He contemplated his self-portrait, I mine
and my grandmother's, with my own view of his clear on
the margin.

'Yes,' I said, rousing, opening my eyes – 'Lovely.
Thank you.'

'How it fills one with humility,' he said. He appeared to me somewhat distended by the influx. 'Yes, indeed,' I agreed. 'But I must be getting home now, or the furnace of my patroness will be out, and it is such a nuisance to re-light.'

CHAPTER NINE

Florence: The Bank[1]

IF I were a novelist instead of being merely the author of two novels, I should be tempted to find in the history of our family in Italy the theme for a work of fiction. I can imagine a treatment, at once amusing and instructive, by Aldous Huxley, who has besides his skill, an acquaintance with the youngest generation in Florence and in Rome. Unfortunately Huxley has become a contemplative in a hut in the deserts of California.

As things are, if the records and account books could be had, a narrative of fact which would not lack social value, might be written. But if such sources exist they are not within my reach, and I cannot think of any other member of my family who, having them, is likely to utilise them. I shall therefore try to set down such an imperfect narrative as may be made from facts I have heard, known, or seen.

It must have been towards the end of the Austrian rule in Florence (Ferdinand died in 1824 to be succeeded by his son Leopold, who was drummed out in the spring of 1859) that young William Haskard and his father arrived from Yorkshire in the City of the Lily to set up there in a modest fashion as English tailors. Already some twenty years before this, James Lewis, younger of the Glasgow grocer's two reverend sons, had built and begun to preach in the first Presbyterian church in Rome. So between them Lewis and the Haskards catered for the outer and inner

1. As the author admits, she did not think her recollections of the Haskard family were likely to be accurate, and her account does in fact contain a number of errors. Details are now given in my additional introductory comments for this edition on page xxii. I am grateful to Sir Cosmo Haskard, the present representative of the family for his amicable help in removing this blemish on the original.

man of Britishers resident in either place. In this pursuit
they covered the period reaching from the memory of
Byron's circle to the actualities of the Brownings, Walter
Savage Landor, William Story, 'Ouida'; and beyond these
to the more recent group of settlers, such as Lord Henry
Somerset, Reggie Turner, and Norman Douglas.

It is not to be thought that many, if any, of these availed
themselves with regularity of the Presbyterian services held
by Dr. MacDougall in Florence or by Dr. James Lewis in
Rome. They may have abstained even from the Anglican
diet of worship which was also provided. But compatriot
clergy of any denomination are found to be of occasional
use in the most free-thinking colonies. They are further
apt to be knowledgeable as to what is said and done
among the laity. Again, though the self-exiled English
poets, painters and romantics were perhaps content to
wear their native clothes long after these had become
shapeless, or to submit their persons to be measured and
redraped by any Italian tailor, there can never have lacked
a dressier type of visitor who endeavoured to maintain the
sartorial styles and standards of Britain. Until the arrival
of the Haskards this type of Englishman in Florence and
in Rome was obliged to travel to London for new clothes
or to suffer dismay.

Whether such calculations had weighed with old Haskard,
or if he had more personal reasons for leaving Yorkshire and
putting up his plate in Florence, is not known. Nor are his
origins or early history, though the name is uncommon and
his grandchildren have, I believe, tried to make enquiries
in Yorkshire.

He had only one leg, and it is handed down that he
stumped on this – literally on one foot – all the way across
the Alps, shortly to be followed by his wife and son, a youth
still under twenty. He took a small shop which was entered
by several steps down from the pavement, lived behind or
above it and sent round his card to British residents. A good
cutter, gifted in addition with a fine knowledge of quality
in cloth and tweed, he soon had a flourishing business.

His son, by the time I knew him, was my Uncle William,
who had married my mother's youngest sister, Maggie

Lewis, produced a family, and established himself in a large Florentine villa. He was by then no longer a tailor, but an outstanding Florentine citizen. As the English banker of Florence he had premises in the Antinori Palace. The shop was no more. But behind and combined with his banking was a wholesale trade in cloth extending through Europe. Russia was one of his big customers for English woven stuffs. It was just such a development as might have happened to an enterprising member of the commune in the Middle Ages.

What had happened was this. When customers came for suits and overcoats they found that they could also be accommodated in matters of cash, English cheques, and Italian exchange. After a time clothes were no longer needed as an excuse for financial dealings, and though the old man clung to his proper trade to the last, William, ambitious and annoyed, waited only for his father's death to eliminate every trace of his beginnings.

He was a very handsome man, rather he had unusual beauty, from top to toe of the type which used to be called aristocratic. Not taking after his father, who has been described to me as an ordinary-looking little Yorkshire mechanic, he struck one as on the verge of decadence from sheer blueness of blood. His features would have been correctly described by certain Victorian novelists as chiselled. His extremely fine, pallid skin was turned to old ivory by the Italian summer suns. His eyes were deep blue, his hair and moustache black and silky (already white when I knew him, which gave a further distinction to pencilled eyebrows and jet lashes). A sudden winning smile revealed his regular teeth. He was tall, slender, graceful, broad-shouldered and of good address. It would have been difficult for any artist in wax figures to model a tailor's dummy more perfectly calculated to set off a Savile Row outfit. It may also be doubted whether such a dummy would have possessed less by way of heart than was ever by anyone discerned in the breast of William.

He was, I suppose, about twenty-five, and was still impeded by his father and the under-pavement-level shop, when he met Maggie Lewis, who was still some years under twenty.

If Ina was the flower of that flock of five, Maggie was the flibbertigibbet. When all were young their father, a little disappointed at having none but girl children, had favoured her as the aptest in receiving the education which he had determined upon for a family of boys. 'Shakespeare and the newspapers' was one of his instructional mottoes. They must learn long stretches of the major poets and the Bible by heart, and they must know how to read newspaper articles aloud and how to comment intelligently upon what they read. My mother read aloud admirably and with evident enjoyment. But she told us that, at one time she had been broken down in health by her unavailing efforts to memorise. Maggie's memory was good, her intelligence quick and her observations original. As she grew older, however, she became excessively flirtatious, fantastic and wild. At sixteen she expressed such modernist notions with regard to the son of a neighbouring farmer at Ormiston who was smitten with her, that it was thought desirable to send her and my mother (her senior by two years) to Italy, while two daughters of James Lewis came to Ormiston instead.

They seem to have spent part of their time in Rome, part in Florence. I have a letter written to Maggie from Ormiston to Rome by her younger sister, Jessie, which must have been the first one she received after leaving Scotland. It is dated, Ormiston Lodge. Monday. Nov. 28th, 1864, when Jessie was fourteen. 'We will enjoy the exchange of sisters very much,' she writes, 'if they are nice girls.' After some home news, mostly about the servants, she continues. 'You must not fall in love with the beautiful eyes of the priests for Papa says the Church of Rome chooses the most handsome men however wicked in order to attract foolish women, so don't you be one of them.'

Apart from asking for a recipe for Johnny cakes, which seem always to have been a breakfast speciality of the Italian Lewises (they were made from maize flour and eaten hot; many a time I have devoured them in Lewis homes at Hampstead, Tunbridge Wells and Edinburgh), Jessie devotes the rest of her letter chiefly to a book which they are reading at the manse. As the passage throws some light on the household reading and on Jessie's power of composition (she being by far the stupidest of the flock) I shall quote it:

> We are reading the travels of an Austrian lady named Madame Pfeiffer, who till she was thirteen was allowed to wear boy's clothes. At sixteen she fell in love with a very nice young man, but her mother would not consent to their union. Some years after, her mother made her marry an advocate, who was so liberal in money matters that his wife had to struggle many years in poverty in consequence. When she had brought up her family and seen them settled in life she was at liberty to accomplish the dream of her girlhood and womanhood, that of travelling. She sailed twice round the world, visiting different places each time. She next visited Iceland, Scandinavia, and the Holy Land. In the volume we are reading she went from London to the Cape of Good Hope, to Borneo, Java, Sumatra, Celebes, California, Peru, and the United States. All this travelling was performed either by sea or on horseback or on foot: she once ran twenty miles on foot with her guide without stopping: all her journeys were accomplished alone with no one but her guide for a companion. Ida Pfeiffer is the greatest lady traveller that ever lived. She was fifty before she set out on her travels. She died at last of a fever brought on by her fatigues and hardships in the year 1856. Papa thinks she must have had an iron constitution, and as for Mama she doesn't believe half, and cannot understand how a *woman* could live, sit and eat with naked men and women.

She ends,

> Adieu – I am your affectionate sister,
>   Jessica Lewis.
> Don't laugh – it is a new name I have taken and is the same as Jessie.

I have an odd feeling that this letter may not have been

without its influence upon Maggie, who cut her hair short soon after reading it. I am positive that she felt in herself a capacity for Madame Pfeiffer's achievements, including the capacity to live, sit and eat with naked men and women of any colour. I have often heard her express her superiority to current custom.

If one might divide this prism of a nineteenth-century family into primary qualities by way of its five daughters, Maggie would represent the century's modernity, fantasy and realism; Jessie its superabundant sentimentality, undiluted and often overflowing into silliness; Ina its balanced radiance; my mother its naïvety and commonsense. Of Fanny, the one who died young, sweetness would seem to have been the most striking attribute. All were alike in being affectionate, vivacious, unworldly. In spite of the many accusations of hypocrisy and oppressive puritanism made by novelists and others against the period, I suggest that it produced in every class innumerable families of an equally innocent, cheerful and harmless character. It may be that the more brilliant writers found them uninteresting as subject-matter and that they are most truthfully dealt with by contemporary authors of inferior art whose works have accordingly perished.

Maggie, though she can never have been William Haskard's female counterpart in good looks, must have been an uncommonly attractive girl with something of boyish dash about her. Even as an old woman she had a vital presence, made an interesting impression of reckless intensity and possessed memorable eyes, of which, however, she was rather too conscious. She talked well if often too much, without timeliness and with intent to shock.

Poor William, primmest, chilliest and most conventional of men, with a mind which, outside his business, made one feel as if one had dived into a lake of apparent blue depths only to bump one's crown immediately below the surface on a concrete bottom – I suppose he never thought she meant anything she said! The trouble was not only that she did, but that she was always prepared to translate her wildest remarks into acts, no matter at what inconvenience. He could scarcely have chosen a less suitable mate. Nor could she have selected one more fitted to drive her to the extremes of which she was so capable.

She was eighteen, he, I suppose about twenty-five, when they were married in Rome. Her younger cousin, Alice, who was a bridesmaid and slept with her the night before the wedding, has told me that Maggie cried all night, and that she continued to weep while being dressed for the ceremony, protesting that she did not love William. 'Then why marry him?' asked Alice. 'He says I can help him,' was Maggie's reply. 'And I'm sure I can, especially as I like his father so much. Besides I've said I will, and now I must. He would think it was because I despised him for having a shop.'

There was certainly no parental pressure, though there may have been feelings of parental relief. For William, still impeded by his father and the shop, the alliance was regarded as socially desirable. The couple must have returned to Florence about the same time that Victor Emmanuel made his triumphal entry there and when Florence became, for the next five years, capital of the Kingdom of Italy.

Of their four sons and two daughters, all are still alive except for one boy who accidentally strangled himself in his cot when still a baby. All were sent to boarding schools in England and spent holidays with us in Scotland, we returning their visits by going to Florence. Beatrice, the younger of the daughters, became my greatest friend among girl cousins.

With the elder brother, George, I was for a time more than a little, and I believe for the first time consciously, in love. George was the first Haskard to visit us in Scotland. I was six and he was twenty or near it. George was neither good-looking nor particularly attractive, though he had his father's sudden smile. He was, as I came later to know, rather stupid, and so unamiable that his brothers and sisters failed to get on with him. They never quarrelled, but by tacit consent relegated him to a sort of limbo, which was easy because he was by a good many years the eldest and, except for a short futile attempt to occupy a post in the bank, he made his life in England. I was in love with George because of the way his hair grew off from his forehead. It was straight, longish, fairish hair, still having in it the glint of youthful gold. He parted it at the side and thrust back the longer side in such a manner that it curved in a single wave catching the light. This struck me so much when he was present that I could hardly take my eyes off it, and when he was absent I pictured it with an ardour which I can describe only as amorous excitement. George did not single me out for special notice, but once or twice he took me on his knee, little thinking how much of quivering ecstasy he held there.

It is only now, after all these years as I write this down, that I perceive myself to have been throughout my life highly sensitive to the way in which a person's hair grows off the forehead, as to the shape of the head itself. What victims we can be to some trifling predilection! Happily my passion for George or his hair gave me far more pleasure than pain, and it did not outlast his short visit by more than a day or two. Indeed I was inclined to be thus briefly and pleasurably in love with almost any of our grown-up boy cousins who came to see us, and there were a good many of them, some far handsomer and gayer than George, though I cannot remember one whose hair so fascinated me.

CHAPTER TEN

Music: The Arts

LOOKING back at my life as a whole, I find that it has been most nourished and enhanced by love, by the sky, by what is known as 'the country' and by the arts. Of the arts the one I could now least do without is music in its performance. The others, though I still rejoice in them not less but more than ever, are to some extent rifled and stored for my delectation. If I were never able to enter a picture gallery again nor to open a book, I could still fall back upon my memory (more 'visile' than 'verbile'; verbal) for the plastic arts, and on flavour and my experience for literature. I should thus be impoverished but not quite starved. But flavour in music without repetition is faint for me unless it be simple melody. While I can visualise a score when listening, my musical capacity is not up to anything like full enjoyment in the silent reading of a score, no matter how familiar the composition. I must have performance. And increasingly I want music every day. Hence I should now rather become blind than deaf if I had to make that bitter choice. And hence I thank providence for the timely inventions of radio and gramophone. The disembodied music they provide suits well with my condition. I have been to concerts and operas enough for me now to supply what finesse or fullness of tone may be lacking. And I find these more than made good by the absence of the adventitious excitements inseparable from visual performance visually shared. Many musical people will differ from me in this. But so I find it.

I have just heard Sir Adrian Boult on the air, replying to questions by 'an ordinary concert-goer'. The main question concerned the notable increase of listeners to 'good' music which the war has brought about. Why is it? Will it continue after the war? etc.

I found Sir Adrian's reply unsatisfactory. He believed that in such times of trouble, people wanted their minds taken off things – much the same as to say they liked music as an anodyne. While this applies, no doubt, to the more ephemeral of light and popular music, it does not account for the attention paid to serious and classical music. No, one has only to watch the faces of concert-goers in war-time, or to examine one's own response at any time, to see more in it than this.

The truth, I think, is that music above all the other arts has the capacity at its best of consoling and enlarging our outlook by its declaration of an ordered universe. Without words or intellectual ideas, without touching upon individual joys or sorrows or points of view, it somehow suggests that in the last resort all is a harmony. Dissonances are resolved, or at least they have a meaning of goodness. We feel, while listening to the unfolding miracle of sound that there is a solution of pain, of evil, of all that usually foils our research. It will all come clear, we feel. There is an order, a resolution, an ultimate adding up that will satisfy, explain, repay. So we obtain release and comfort as well as beauty and interest. Poetry treats of feelings and ideas and of the beauties of the earth (though there are some few – very few – great religious poems, chiefly in the Bible, that have the same effect as music). The pictorial arts delight the æsthetic sense and enlarge human experience through the eye. But music speaks straight to the wounded, troubled being, admitting all wounds and all troubles, but with the declaration that all is ultimately well. There is, properly speaking, no sad music.

It has sometimes happened that a great book has been written by accident – *e.g.* Montaigne, Pepys – given a highly intelligent man without, however, any creative gift. Many extremely interesting, if less great books, have in the same way been written even by children and uncultured people of riper years. But the smallest musical composition (if we bar simple, unaccompanied melodies) has never come in this way into being. No symphony, or even sonata, was ever written by accident. Charming pictures are sometimes painted by uninstructed children. Even the young Mozart had to learn the technique of musical composition before he became a composer.

Pictures – good ones – force us to look more closely at the scenes of our earth. They extend our vision by enlarging, intensifying, readjusting and instructing our vision of common things. They enrich us. Prose books do the same on a more intellectual plane, dealing with life, men and women, passions and ideas, besides helping us to observe, fix, remember, by their descriptive passages. Also they teach. They let us have some imaginative under-standing of places, people, ways of life we should otherwise miss. They cultivate and furnish our minds. 'Reading makes a full man'. Poetry expresses us to ourselves and 'nature' to us. It reveals delicately or astonishingly the mind and heart of the poet, with whom we find in ourselves an unpredictable sympathy. But let the word-dealer or the painter try to do what the composers do and they invariably fail. They may be truly 'musical', vividly pictorial, but the words and the pigments are too impure as mediums to compete with sheer sound. Sound alone can lift us out of ourselves and, as it were, above and beyond our world with its limits of personality, character, etc., till we become gathered essences of ourselves and look down upon everything as from a cloud or a high mountain-top through perfectly clear air.

Music assuages rebellious questioning. Not for nothing have men imagined heaven to be a musical state. One can imagine a hell with libraries and picture galleries, but not a hell with music. Discord would reign by way of sound.

I studied music intensively for two years at the Schumann Conservatorium at Frankfort-on-Main, where all students, score in hand, attended every orchestral rehearsal as well as every performance in the town. I suppose I have heard pretty well every great instrumental and vocal soloist of my time in one place or another (from Patti and Sarasate to the latest boy wonder of today), and I have sat a few yards from Joachim and Paderewski (talking with them during intervals in the garden) throughout a week of twice-daily concerts at the Beethoven Festival at Bonn. All this was immensely enjoyable, also instructive. Yet I have learned more about music in the comparatively short time since I became an intensive radio listener – to all kinds of music, classical and modern, severe and swing – than in many years of enthusiastic concert attendance. It is fortunate to have had both sorts of listening, for one helps the other. I can happily fill the intervals of a day building a fugue on some such fetching melody as *How Deep is the Ocean*. But it is the second kind that has come to count most with and has done most for me.

Every time I hear on the radio one of those gay – if not great – pieces by Percy Grainger or by Cyril Scott, I feel a warmth of proprietary pride in the Frankfort Conservatorium, and I see again those two fair heads as I did only once or twice with shy admiration, when I was a talentless student and either of these lads, already having got themselves highly spoken of in the wider world outside, chanced to revisit their music school and masters. What incalculable pleasure their airs and arrangements have given in dark hours since then. Little did we dream of radio circulation in those joyful and leisured but limited days! Old Karl Friedberg is still a leading pianist in New York, while in enemy Germany, Hodapp still reigns magnificently at the piano. But where and how are her teacher and lover, Kwast, and mine, Uzielli? Scarcely happy and safe, unless perchance dead.

Frankfort apart there have been several landmarks in my musical experience.

Until I was twelve classical music was a sealed book to me. We regularly sang hymns and psalms at home and in church. We sang interminably the few popular and comic songs of the day, picked up in the streets or from the servants. My father, who had a pleasant voice and loved to sing, would make us join with him in rounds and catches, which we loved, though I found it hard to keep to my part as my voice was the weakest. We sometimes went to 'Sacred Concerts'.[1] Again, there were charitable occasions in one hall or another where resplendent lady soloists rendered *The Better Land*, and tension was relieved by Mr. Frame in woman's clothes, convulsing the vast audience and ourselves on the platform with *Garibaldi's Chair is Vacant*. As a treat we might attend an organ recital, where I grew extremely sentimental, though the organ is an instrument that has never truly pleased my ear – except once in the Cathedral of Bourges when I by chance heard a solitary musician practising in the empty church on the smaller and older of its two organs. Except for our knowing, and unaccountably despising, many of the Scottish songs, this was all our music.

The piano lessons I had at my first day school, to which I went when I was six for two years, were given me by the younger of the two Miss Watsons who conducted the private establishment for the education of young ladies and gave it their name. She was a handsome, dark, terrifying woman who administered correction by way of a sharp rap on the pupil's knuckles from a stout ebony ruler. She used to bend my fingers back 'to make them supple' till they made cracking sounds at the joints. She never expounded or explained, only exploded, and without once indicating the value of a dotted note – or anything else except the names of the notes on the keyboard and in print – she kept me for a whole dreadful year to a piece called *La Cachuca*. If any musical facility had been mine, I should probably have mastered the thing in spite of her. But my panic and confusion were such that I never got the length of either hearing the tune or grasping the rhythm. I merely

1. Benjamin Broomhall, the Methodist who fought the opium traffic, refused to hear Jenny Lind, though offered a ticket for her farewell concert, because there were some sacred pieces to be sung. 'I have a *very* decided objection to anything of that kind in concerts or oratorios. I am sorry there is such a rage for oratorios: more so that Christians attend them. I think it very wrong. Last night there was one on a grand scale in the Surrey Gardens New Music Hall; a thousand performers – the hall will hold ten thousand persons. There is a very eulogistic account in this day's *Times*. The enthusiasm was at its height when these performers (among whom were many of the principal opera singers), sang *Worthy is the Lamb*. One's heart sickens.' 1856.
[Author's Note.]

plunged through what struck me as a dense undergrowth, hoping feebly for the best, but made aware by the smart action of the ruler on my shrinking hands that the worst was happening. I hope, but I can hardly believe, that 'the young Miss Watson' suffered as much as I did. She was not really very young, but we thus distinguished her from her sister who was 'ancient'. Looking back, and remembering certain hints thrown out at the time but ignored by me, I think the young Miss Watson may have been frustrated in love besides being unendowed with any gift for teaching. At arithmetic she would sometimes give us sums of noughts and ones to add up while she fled from the room, perhaps to weep. It was an expensive school – the most expensive in Glasgow at that time. So much for my first music lessons.

What music really might be, and what counterpoint, was revealed to me through the wall of my bedroom as I lay in bed.

Next door to us lived two maiden sisters with their aged mother. Of the Misses Gilfillan, the elder one had long since settled down into spinsterhood. The younger – generally known to us as 'the pretty one' – was held to be still just marriageable, so that my father used a hopeful gallantry in mention of her. She was dressy and we learned with awe that her elaborately puffed raven hair was dyed and that the red on her cheekbones was something known as rouge (this from the servants, not from my parents who eschewed and discouraged all personal remarks). The Gilfillans had few visitors, and I never remember their entering our house or we theirs, though we exchanged polite greetings on pavement encounters. I doubt if I should ever recall even this much of them had it not been for their inestimable, unconscious gift to my life.

Of a winter evening, when old Mrs. Gilfillan had doubt-less gone to her bed, and I, being still under ten, still lay awake in mine, the two lonely sisters cheered themselves with light music in their drawing-room. Though on the floor lower than that of my bedroom, the piano stood against the party wall, so that sound travelled up and I could hear every note – faintly, with my head on the pillow; clearly, if I listened against the wall by my bedside.

The taste in music next door was not extraordinary. The repertoire was mostly limited to such sentimental ballads of the time as *In the Gloaming, O my Darling, London Bridge, Ora Pro Nobis*, and *True, True, till Death*, the music of which was always carried to evening parties by ladies and gentlemen who could render them. But if the younger Miss Gilfillan sang indifferently well, her sister had attained to a certain bravura as an accompanist.

One night a new air came through my wall. For many nights afterwards there was no difficulty in getting me to bed. The melody was in itself captivating, but what enthralled my ear and penetrated my inmost heart with delight was a passage of six notes on the piano, interposed by way of counterpoint between the two last notes of the refrain. Those who are familiar with the composition – *The Man that Broke the Bank at Monte Carlo* – will remember the passage. It consists of a rising scale of crotchets from the major third to the tonic, while the singer holds the super-tonic as a minim till both are merged. With pulses throbbing and ear pressed against the plaster, I waited for this progression. And when it came – smooth, pearly, mounting through the five planets[1] to meet the last reluctant descending note of the melody in the final effulgence of Venus – I felt that nothing else mattered, that no sorrow on earth after this joy could be too hard to bear. Here was the compensation for all life's griefs. Here was the majesty of music, the miracle of counterpoint, fountains and fields of everlasting refreshment and solace opened to me.

I failed to make any connexion between this starry progression and the identical five-finger exercises of my hated music lessons. I knew nothing of those thirteenth-century Song Schools of my own country which existed to imbue the young with 'musick, meaners and vertu'. I was ignorant that what brought me such delectation had been denounced by Pope John XXII in 1322 as 'voluptuous',

---

1. The ancients identified each note of the scale with a planet. Hence poets correctly make the stars to sing together.
[Author's Note.]

'lascivious', and 'proscribed from the sanctuary', until the Englishman, John of Dunstable, two centuries later, ruled that such 'florid counterpoint' was in order, and that a discord to an unaccented note might properly be solved by step, though not by leap. But I knew that a new heaven had been opened to me, and for some weeks I went about humming the evocative syllables 'Car . . . lo', with secret, extreme rapture.

When scale passages, be they rising or falling, occur, as they often do, in a piece of classical music (as, for example, early in Mozart's[1] E flat Symphony, or soon after the opening of his Overture to *Don Giovanni*, or of Rossini's to *The Barber of Seville*) I still experience a strong access of pleasure. And while I enjoy modern music as much as I do classical, I often wish that the new composers would trust more often to the contrapuntal magic of the diatonic scale. Elgar and Delius seem always to avoid it, with the result that the music of Elgar makes me feel sea-sick very often, even when I appreciate its huge merits, and that of Delius strikes me, for all its wishful beauty, as something sick. On the other hand there are not wanting signs that still younger composers, such as Berners and Medtner (to mention two at random) are rediscovering its irreplaceable uses.

*

Sidereal scales – starriest of composers.

Bach and Handel, to my way of hearing, proliferate as trees in root, branch and twig, as water with its flowing and its playing with light, with harvest fields, with bird-song. Bach is for me the bread and the wine of music. But Mozart takes me to the Milky Way and brings me into the Pleiades and Orion's Belt.

*

1. Wolfgang was unnaturally obedient. He never received any corporal punishment . . . at bed-time he would stand upon a chair and sing with his father.
[Author's Note.]

My first experience of great vocal performance[1] must have been about the same time as the Monte Carlo revelation.

The Jubilee Singers visited Glasgow. Nobody at that date had heard of 'negro spirituals', but as the performance was clearly one of sacred song, we attended. Accustomed as we were only to Presbyterian choral singing (sometimes fortified by a paid quartette of mannered professional vocalists), we sat amazed at what unaccompanied voices could do. Men's voices, like every shade of velvet from *café-au-lait* to deepest black: women's voices of palest satin texture, and all combining in crescendos and diminuendos that seemed as artless as the autumn manœuvring of a cloud of fieldfares. Here again was deep joy.

It cannot have been long afterwards (having between whiles come upon Handel's *Largo*, which I learned to pound out gently and slowly in blissful solitude) that I discovered classical music. Few of my parents' friends in Glasgow possessed more acquaintance with the fine arts than they did themselves, and I had not heard so much as the names of Beethoven or Mozart. It happened, however, that an old business acquaintance of my father's, who had been also his fellow-elder in the first of our churches, and had remained there after we moved to another, had a family of sons and daughters who were genuinely musical. Some sang in the church choir, where they had the training of a remarkably fine organist. One son – an international footballer – played

1. Opera – Many extremely musical people have condemned opera as an 'impure' art (*e.g.* the late Walford Davies). The most musically gifted of my friends has often said to me that she prefers to hear operatic music without seeing the performers or hearing the words of the dialogue . . . Then there are the silly stage shifts, like the swan in *Lohengrin*, that is so apt to stick, and jerks along like a badly made child's toy . . . But I find that opera has its place as the best emotional expression for the mass of ordinary people who need music and find their own lives dramatic, comic, tragic, without finding these things adequately expressed in any other popular form. The experiences like death, falling in love, jealousy, solitary suffering, social rapture . . . cannot be expressed better than in opera. No novelist can give heart-searching speeches to a dying person, nor to friends round a

the violin. One daughter, more seriously, made a study of the piano. Though she went to our school, she was older than we and our families did not visit. But there must have been some chance meeting, now forgotten, when we learned that their minister, John Carroll, a man of quiet mark whose orthodoxy was suspected by my parents, was giving a series of Dante lectures well worth hearing on Sunday evenings. The name of Dante, though we had not read his works, was august to us through our Italian connexions. So we went. And for a whole season of Sundays we sat in the darkened, half-empty church of St. John's in which I had first attended a service, ascending and descending the superb circles of heaven and hell in a sort of trance. To me Dante and Mr. Carroll became one and the same man, and indeed they were not different in spirit. There was, besides, unusual church music.

Then, one weekday, at the home of our new friends, Jessie, heavy-bodied, plain-faced, serious, sat down at the piano and played two successive compositions such as I had not even dreamed could exist, making the piano do things I had never thought possible. She called them 'a prelude' and 'a fugue'. Shaken to the soul I asked for the

---

deathbed. It would be too unrealistic. The poets, unaided by musical accompaniment, have to keep all such things short, telling, memorable . . . Shakespeare has given final and perfect expression to this in the famous passage in *Troilus and Cressida* where he describes the parting of lovers. All is said with heart-rending briefness, as in life itself.

But opera is hampered by no such limitations imposed by reality. It can set the scene, provide words that need not be adequate, and extend a momentary sentiment indefinitely by the musical content. Opera is indeed impure by strict standards; but I think far more people have obtained catharsis from operas than in witnessing the great tragedies of the Greeks or even of Shakespeare . . . Every character in opera is Everyman as he inwardly feels himself to be. There could be no 'Madame Butterfly', no 'Mimi', no 'Pagliacco' except in opera. But these characters are of everyday occurrence in life. The world will never let opera go, no matter what the musical æsthetes may say.
[Author's Note.]

name of the composer. She pointed to the outside sheet of
the music. Bach, I read. It was to me an unknown name,
and I pronounced it 'Batch'. I drew a long breath. 'I shall
learn everything that man has ever written,' I said solemnly.
Jessie smiled. 'That'll take a bit of doing,' she said. I began
to learn and to practise. We started piano lessons with a new
teacher. We bullied our parents into buying us season tickets
for the orchestral concerts, conducted by Henschel. Photo-
graphed portraits of Schumann and Schubert, Beethoven
and Chopin, stood along our bedroom mantelpieces. Later
on I went to the Frankfort Conservatorium. Still later, I even
had some music pupils of my own in Glasgow. Though my
enthusiasm quickly proved to be out of all proportion great
as compared with my talent, I have no regrets for energy
expended. I had passion and some taste – even by way
of execution – but I lacked facility, *i.e.* talent. Compare
the writer.

This, though I am convinced that with equal application
to the art of painting I could have come far nearer to
accomplishment, for there I possessed a natural facility.
If, as very nearly happened – would have happened if I
had not conceived an adolescent passion for my piano
mistress – instead of 'taking up music' I had gone with my
greatest friend straight from school to the Glasgow School
of Art, my life would have taken a different course. I should
have also gone with her later to study in Paris. What then?
Futile speculation, no doubt. But I know that the joy which
overwhelmed me when I first heard Bach played was of a
different order from the conspiratorial delight which filled
me when, equally uncultured and uninformed, I stood alone
among the jeering, sniggering crowd at the first exhibition in
Scotland of the French impressionists. *Here* was something
that was all mine, something in myself, something in which
I could come to take part. But I turned from the idea. If I
could now have a second life on the same terms as the one I
have had, I think I should choose to become deaf and dumb
after some twenty of my years, so that I might devote all
the energy of the remainder, freed from the distractions of
sound, to record a fraction of what has continually claimed
my eye in colour and in form. Having only one life, and

with circumstances as they were, I cannot regret what has brought so many diverting experiences and has become so deep a source of happiness. As an ineffective lover of music I can be perfectly content. To keep the balance between the two truths that everything matters frightfully, and that nothing matters at all – that all I do is eternally important, and that I am not, either now or eternally, of any consequence: in this paradoxical endeavour – which I take to be the secret of a useful life and of individual happiness – music has helped me more than anything else. But to keep it up needs much music. A day without music is for me a blind day.

I doubt if I could have found anything but chagrin as a dilettante painter. To know what is good, and to have to look at or destroy canvases by myself which I knew were indifferent – I could endure almost any failure more easily than that . . . It would come too expensive, would nag at my old vitals . . .

CHAPTER ELEVEN

Letters and Women

Evangelicalism has spoiled both the minds and the bodies of the women of Scotland – there are no women now like my mother.

E. IRVING of Mary Lowther, 1840.

BERNARD SHAW is reported to have said that he felt nowhere so much at home as in the company of the mighty dead – or words to this effect. All lovers of books whose love is pure (*i.e.* whose love has not been diverted into the side channels of specialism which find a living for the journalist and a reputation for the professional literary critic) must often have felt the same. We feel happy and interested and at home with the writers of good books as we do with none of the living, save at moments, and this not only because we feel that we know, understand and love them, but because we flatter ourselves that they would have loved and understood us. We are all misunderstood, injured innocents or social blunderers in some degree. (Hence in great part the hold a man like J. J. Rousseau has on the world.) We long to explain ourselves, to justify ourselves, to share our peculiar hearts and minds by expatiating, but we soon find this to be impracticable, so far as the living are concerned, dearly as we may love them. If we had the power to do it, they have not the patience to listen. When they do, we become conscious of the hopeless barriers caused by our own inadequacy in expression, by their prejudices, by the subtle but overwhelming effect one personality has upon another when physically adjacent, besides which, work, the world and a thousand preoccupations do not cease their clamour and interruption. We cannot go on. When interrupted we cannot take up the thread again where we left off. So friendly gestures such as the pressure of a hand, a kiss, a smile, a hackneyed but significant phrase must serve. We can only signal to our nearest and dearest, or serve them by repeated action or a flow of goodwill. But if we love to occupy ourselves with minds as different as Rousseau's and Samuel Johnson's, we can easily cherish the happy illusion that Rousseau and Johnson would both have conceived a sympathetic liking for ourselves. They would discount or smile away our faults as we discount and smile away theirs. We make no intrusion on their time, energy or patience. When we have had enough of them we can close the book and turn to another without apology. All strictly literary considerations are subsidiary to this in the importance of books in our lives. To say that the writers of books whom we feel to be our friends cannot answer us back is a poor and partial way of expressing their profound convenience and preciousness. The fact is rather that they never cease to reply to us, correct us, remain with us when most of what they say is verbally forgotten. They probe our weak spots, hurt our consciences, stimulate our efforts, correct our mistakes. But they do it without alienating us or permitting us to annoy them to our own confusion and humiliation.

. . . I had been reading a new slim volume by a woman writer which attempted to narrate in the brief manner of verse a love episode which had ended sadly for the narrator. The thing was delicately done; it was sincere; it did not lack charm; it induced some degree of sympathy and a greater degree of liking for the writer and the woman lover. But – and now we reach the subject of our discussion – it half induced in me a feeling of discomfort a little resembling the distress one feels at the sight of exhibitionism or at the hearing of a certain kind of rude story (no matter how essentially funny) when an otherwise correct woman is the moving actor. You may say this was because the narration was not successful, not well enough done. No doubt in this particular case this was true. But it is not the point we stumbled upon. The point was this. Had it been no better done by a man writer, would it have created the same discomfort? Should we not have discussed it and dismissed it on grounds that were purely literary? Again, had it been a compelling work of art, and still by a woman who told her love story directly, personally, intimately, would those feelings of discomfort have been absent?

Do we as English readers feel perfectly comfortable when we read the love poems of the Brontës, or Christina Rossetti, or Mrs. Browning, or the prose love confessions of a Marie Bashkirtseff, the married confessions of a Sophie Tolstoi? It is to be noted that neither of the prose confessions, though taken at random, are by an Englishwoman, for the reason that none stand out.

To begin with the question seems a simple one. Is a woman writer fundamentally handicapped in a whole important sphere of verbal expression? If so, why? It was agreed that this looked like the real snag. The man can give himself (and others) away passionately, wittily, blatantly, imperfectly, coarsely, neurotically, without the reader feeling that his effort or his achievement was unsuitable to a man. Without liking or commending the autobiographer's character one can read and judge of what he wrote: Rousseau can say anything: so can George Moore: so can Keats in his letters, and a thousand others, English or not English, without offending any reader save on moral grounds; and morality here does not enter, because be the woman never so moral, she can still offend by the mere intimacy of her confession. Is there here a marked, an essential disparity between men and women? The woman, because she is a woman, must as an artist suppress what the man as artist or as man is entitled to reveal.

Writing of a book of poems by Charlotte Mew, T. E. Lawrence says:

> All the women who ever wrote original stuff could have been strangled at birth and the history of English literature (and my bookshelves) would be unchanged.

Note the spite of this and the unfairness. Women writing anything have never set up as rivals to men writers. They, like men, have written because they wanted to find expression in words. Their contribution, as it happens, has not been negligible. But even such original writers as

Jane Austen, George Eliot, the Brontës, Christina Rossetti
and others, whose work could not have been done except
by women, never made any claims that I know of to
exceeding, or even to equal excellence, with men writers.
Virginia Woolf is a possible exception, but there have been
men writers also of overweening vanity. What one would
like to ask T. E. Lawrence is, how much literature, even
on his shelves, would suffer if God had made this a male
world. Women figure one way or another in the origins
of literature as in those of life. The point, not disclosed
and perhaps scarcely conscious, in his comment, is that
he resents this, just as he resents the presence of women in
his cottage and their being the wives or beloveds of his men
friends. He not only wished no women in his life (except his
mother whom he could not quite annul, or a few wives of
friends who unobtrusively made those friends happy) – he
resented the fact that women could trouble the emotions of
any man. Yet Lawrence, forcing himself to share a mess and
sleeping quarters with common soldiers, deludes himself
into believing that he understands and sympathises with
common men. He lives with his head in the desert sand.
Into these sands he blasphemes against the ordinances of
nature and of man's conception of God.

*

My preference is for the direct style, a page that looks at first
sight empty, or at least full of space. My theme demands a
crowded page and the tortuous style that belongs to nature
rather than to art. My skill is not equal to a more artful
way. The impulse is to contrive that one page should be
superimposed on another, as they will not properly follow.
Tiresome for me and unamenable to the material of words.
The method will, I fear, cause exasperation to the reader:
as there may not be a reader, I shall forget about him.

Suddenly, with no practice worthy of the name, I became
dramatic critic on a famous daily newspaper.[1]

Knocked – more properly cudgelled into shape as a

---

1. *Glasgow Herald*. [J. C.]

journalist, luckily I wrote easily and without much self-criticism (a thing I have never attained to since). I had an emotional response to the theatre that was both clear and strong; and I had the faculty of communicating interest. It never occurred to me that one ought to be either witty or learned – (just as well perhaps for I was neither). These embellishments did not occur to me till long afterwards. I had not even read the work of other critics with attention, still less with intent to emulate. I attacked the matter in hand with superb disregard for models. I have long ago destroyed all my cuttings and have no desire to see them now. Still, I must have achieved at least some success, because, while diligently read by those on whose behalf I wrote, William Archer, in a London journal, asked (rhetorically), who 'this man' could be who was writing dramatic criticism in a Scottish newspaper that was equal if not superior to anything the London critics were doing just then. I rather think that just then London dramatic criticism was in one of the troughs . . .

Writing – for women. Inherent difficulties. Easy early writing. Increasing agony, as if one had never before formed a sentence.

Vanity a cause. Suffering is extreme.

In a man there is nothing ridiculous, certainly nothing disgraceful here. In a woman there tends to be something of both. Jane Austen hid her MSS.

I am weak. Any strength I may have acquired has come by my refusal to calculate beforehand either on my strength or on my lack of it. I have acted at all only by trusting that strength would come to me out of the air. So far the air has not done badly.

In practical matters I usually think quickly and effectively. I do so without putting the thing into words, even to myself.

In all that requires the spoken or the written word (with the exception of letter-writing, which I do easily) I have almost no faculty. Talk, mere talk, is no problem – to keep silent is the difficulty. I flow at a hint – or without one and without being invariably able to stem the tide as it flows out of my mouth past my ears. But for the exact reply, I cannot compass it impromptu. I *know* as often as not, but am deflected and cannot say. In writing I have to begin anyhow and rarely write a first line without crossing it out and starting a dozen times. Everything has to be repetitively, slowly, painfully worked out.

I am good at concentrating on the thing I am not doing.

A day rarely passes without my determining – upon waking or soon afterwards – that I shall go to bed in decent time. An evening *never* passes without my becoming deeply interested about eleven o'clock in something that cannot exhaust my interest for a couple of hours. There are some occasions when at that hour I find I search for some activity without any particular interest, attaching to it my sense of duty, dormant all day.

Work. Conscientious objection to. I have gone to the ant and considered its ways. I don't feel it would be wise of me to emulate it. I prefer to consider the lilies of the field. I stand by the New Testament in this.

Gospel of work. Curse of modern life. Enforced retirement. No reason why an individual should not indulge a secret vice.

The contempt of the hard worker for the idler is as nothing compared to the contempt of the idler for the hard worker. Both are justified.

It's a great shame and a mystery that I am driven by so strong an urge to intellectual and literary pursuits for which I am ill-fitted (so that I am always trying to escape them) and that I cannot give myself up to some kind of manual work at which I am by nature apt enough and in doing which I could give rein to my inveterate disposition to dream and to think without trying to find words for my thoughts.

It has been my lot to work always under a disadvantage

and with inferior tools, more especially handicapped by my own poor intellectual outfit. The gifts which I believe are naturally mine – of a certain understanding, insight, enthusiasm and love of perfection – have been confronted by my bad memory, rapid exhaustion, and incapacity for all kinds of discipline except for perseverance in grinding hard labour. I have had to work like a mediæval craftsman – not because I chose so to work, but because I could never understand or achieve the use of civilised methods.

I am not built for hard work. Possibly few people are – either men or women. By hard work I mean sustained efforts demanding concentration whether of the body or the intellect. I hate work, but so desire its results, which I have found can be obtained in no other way, that I have worked, one way and another, pretty hard, if also desultorily. True, I have – or it always seems to me that I have – to work twice as hard as the next person to get an equal effect. So I set myself to work three or four times as hard as the next person would need to do.

*

All men of genius in this world are innocents abroad. They have this in common, for without innocence I have never known genius. Innocence, of course, does not exclude wickedness. It excludes only fundamental sophistication, and – though I may be wrong in this – fundamental narcissism.

Artists are those who give their bodies and spirits to the vivisectionist that is newness of life. The reward that comes of this is for those who sneer at the contortions made by the artist in his pain.

Dante is a good example of the horrible revelations made in a noble soul by suffering. Yet his value lies as much in this as in his power to rise in pure sweetness and abnegation.

Those who succeed in hiding their own ugliness from themselves are those who have never deeply suffered.

*

Those who shrink from ugliness have never known beauty.

When the wife of an artist, painter, singer or what not, goes about saying she 'doesn't understand anything about her husband's particular art', you may be sure that he is not very good in his line. Many women have no understanding of the arts, but all women know talent when they share a bed with it.

Some men become book scholars to avoid learning about people. This is wise of them as men, but it makes their books less good.

If [D. H.] Lawrence had lived to be sixty, he would have been admirably dry and moderate. But he would have repudiated nothing except the small mistakes of his past.

The historians of single life, like the historians of an epoch, may select incidents and influences to form a coherent narrative. This makes interesting, possibly also instructive, reading. But how much of the true past life is in it? It is a good game, a useful convention, an opportunity for a new sort of creation.

The recognition – pleased and personal – of a fine piece of art – no matter of what kind – is the purest and one of the keenest joys of life.

How know that it is a masterpiece and recognised as such by oneself? By this. In that blessed space of time the world and all life becomes perfectly good. The work makes a harmony, an acceptable necessity of everything outside of itself, of all existence without which it could not have come into being. Pain, suffering, misfortunes, sin, imperfections which at other times we deplore or rebel against are somehow soothed into a scheme. Not otherwise could this miracle have achieved existence. Now, here it is appealing to our senses, our minds, our emotions, itself unpredictable and beyond explanation. Outside, perhaps, of what we can term comprehension in its originality and sufficiency, it conveys in itself direct delight. But the finer it be, the more is its quality proclaimed by its conveyance of something besides itself. By this keenness with which one becomes sensible to this side issue, this by-product or background in one's pleasure, one can, I believe, surely distinguish what is first-rate from what is merely effective, interesting, amusing, quaint and the rest. A second-rate effort may make a strong appeal; especially at first it may carry one away. But it does not carry with it and illumine the separate world. What I am trying to express has nothing to do with interpretation, still less with illustration. There is no deliberate connexion. The reaction comes about. That is all. Some people may not be conscious of it save by a sort of heightened delight. Others may not recognise it so described. With me it is invariably the same and invariably the hallmark of the genuinely great work.

I never can see why, especially in the arts, a love of the best should exclude a love of the second or third best, nor why in almost everything appreciation of quality should debar one from the appreciation of qualities. Pure gold is pure gold. But there are times when it is more interesting to look over a handful of the precious stuff mixed with dross or cunningly combined with baser metals to form a new amalgam.

The pulpit has put a soft pedal on the sin theme. 'Heart deceitful and desperately wicked.' Tells us (instead) what nobility we can achieve.

But has the old 'conviction of sin' transferred itself from theology to fiction?

✳

To be sure dirt is a drawback. But come to think of it, St. Augustine, Montaigne, Mr. Pepys, if we glance down the ages, must have found personal cleanliness as difficult to maintain (given the desire to maintain it) as any basement dweller in Camden or in Kentish Town. Dirt has not been inimical to literature.

*

I can truly see only when alone. The most congenial companion takes the edge off my seeing.

Things happen in life and in a mind suddenly with a minute, scarcely noticeable explosion – like the tiny but decisive 'pop' one may or may not hear when a spill of paper, after lying for some moments in a dull fire, decides to ignite into flame.

Process of unconscious thought. In a piece of work, for example. Never thinking consciously of it, it develops, sorts itself out, comes clear for next approach. The artist, does he think?

I remember the aroma of a sentence, the flavour of a sequence of words, but have to search long for a single word.

If to have expressive words and balanced phrases ringing in one's head is to be a writer, then I am one.

CHAPTER TWELVE

Men and Women

Love, the most generous passion of the mind;

That cordial-drop heaven in our cups has thrown,
To make the nauseous draught of life go down!

I HAVE noticed that the best autobiographies written by married people devote almost no space to the incident of marriage. The marriage is recorded and references are later made to the husband or the wife. But the marital picture is not filled in. This may seem strange at first sight, but there are good reasons for it, some of which make themselves apparent in those less good autobiographies by married people who dwell at length upon the happiness or unhappiness of their married state. This dwelling may have a great interest of its own, but it upsets the balance. Marriage is at once too important and too inessential to be contained with any circumstance in the proper account of a single life. It queers the pitch. Let us therefore – say the best narrators of their own lives – dismiss it with a mere mention. As a reader I must confess I have found the method unsatisfactory.

It is hard for me, very hard, to begin this part of my story; avoiding it I have written the preceding parts, but at last I am brought face to face with it. But away with weakness: what one could live through, one must have the strength to remember. – *Alexander Herzen.*

Since I remember I have more than anything else wanted to be deeply loved. At first it was a blind, instinctive desire – to be entirely loved by an individual. The desire to be popular was never mine. As I came to something resembling maturity and a degree of self-knowledge – both with me slow processes – I realised two things which had not before occurred to me. One was that such love as I needed, rare in itself, was especially unlikely in my life. It might easily not be for me. The other was that I should indeed need a love of the entire and indestructible kind, as my faults of nature were so great, and my general make-up so unsatisfactory. I had to tell myself in all soberness that I must write off the desire as a dream. I cannot say that I succeeded wholly in doing this. I succeeded partly. I could put an end to expectation, never quite to hope. Now that I am old, I never lose my astonishment that my pretentious obstinate hope met with complete fulfilment. During the interim, various offers of love were made to me, encouraging more to my rational effort to abandon a dream than to the irrational persisting dream itself. My first marriage as the result of one such offer may have seemed the extreme of irrationality to those who looked on. It in fact did, as I was made fully aware. I made what may truly be called a rash and foolish marriage to a man I scarcely knew. In reality – the reality that is oneself in so far as this at any moment can be termed real – it was a desperately rational act, and though of course informed by hope, it did not partake of that hope which I have mentioned.

The result was what may fitly be called in the appropriate connexion a disaster, and it did not take long to happen. Through nobody's fault I was thrown up on the shore of a single life again, returned home to my mother and bore a girl child.

When, after some fairly adventurous years – embarkation as a journalist being among the adventures – I was able to marry again, it was by a devotion and persuasion that did not convince me of my ability either to hold and increase such devotion or to experience it myself. I did, however, marry a man who for years had both revealed many difficult idiosyncrasies of character – some of them obvious weaknesses – but a man who over a long period of years had shown himself to be the staunchest of friends. Our decision was not, however, so simple as it may sound. Is any such commitment simple as between a man and a woman? We both entered it with illusions – illusions dissipated in the course of twenty-five years of close and constant, almost hourly, companionship, marriage, parenthood. On his part, shortly before our marriage, he said once, as if to cheer my despondency, 'My love for you is not a physical one. I shall not trouble you greatly on that side of things.' On my side, I was able to say, with what I took to be bitter truth, that I had come to regard myself as 'one who could not inspire a lasting passion.' I don't know what impression my warning words made on him. His to me caused a foreboding chill, not an immediate shock alone. It may seem strange that there were no signs of coldness in our courting, but that is the truth. Then, as our silver wedding drew near, he repeated what I had grown used to hearing and to having no reason not to believe, that beginning with passion his love had only become more passionate with the years. He of all people knew my bad sides, my faults, my ineradicable and maddening failings. Yet it was so between us. My foregone hope had been amply fulfilled. Did I fully appreciate my marvellous good fortune? I think I did. I know also that I relied on it and lived by it. Conscious appreciation was delayed until that which I had so heavily relied on, and so richly lived by, was taken from me without warning and in a single moment, without the space to make it known in words or deeds.

It may be, and indeed I think it must be that each one of us in love is born with an ineradicable disposition inclining us to belong to a particular period and sentiment. No matter how unpunctual each birth – premature or out of date – to that period we belong: rational, sensual, romantic, sentimental, mystical, frivolous, sceptical, ruthless, self-sacrificing, affectionate, possessive, magnanimous. Elements of some or all these qualities may be present in our loving. But one conception will dominate the others, or two beat equal war. The most widely accepted view of our own time will overlie our natural disposition, may seem to obliterate it, doubtless will have a certain modifying effect in action and in effort. We may ourselves believe that we accept the current ruling. But when and if love comes to us, we are discovered through suffering and by our actions – so often against our will – that we do not fit with the convention to which we believed ourselves at least amenable. Then, with or without our comprehension, we are apt to get into serious trouble, and confusion. We have deceived ourselves and others. Profoundly romantic and with an exalted idea of fidelity, we have proceeded as might a character in a Shaw play. Disillusioned or ribald at heart, disbelieving the importance of love, or possessed by a fundamental physical disgust, we take as to the manner born the rôle of the sentimentalist.

Philosophies the same; we do not choose among them. They choose us. All, no matter how exploded, stand for truths and values peculiar to individuals far more than as representatives of the particular era and society which enabled them to be set forth in their logical forms. The same is true of theological doctrines, and of heresies, even if we allow for the phenomenon of conversion. The Roman Catholic communion contains innumerable Protestants who never leave their native church. Many Protestants are, save in outward and superficial mannerisms, profoundly submissive to Catholic tradition, yet they do not reach the point of secession. But in love there is no escape.

'We suffer far more from the feelings we inspire than from those we experience,' says the Abbé de Voisenon in the mouth of his character Thémidor. May we say that we enjoy the feelings we inspire more than those we experience?

> Almendore had another equally dangerous talent, that of being amusing, and it is something one cannot guard against . . . Have no fear of men who are really in love: there is nothing so lugubrious as your man in love . . . but beware of those who . . . are not too sentimental to use their wit . . . These are the men who understand the art of seduction . . . They arrange their course accordingly and the woman's head is turned before her hand is kissed [says Zélamire].

Of all sufferings in love, perhaps in life, the bitterest is to see the change in face, voice, eyes, movements, from affection to indifference or boredom or hostility in another. It dwells like a cancer in the system. And what a panic and a gap it creates within, so that we are unable to do or say anything right in their company! We live up to the new image.

Suppressed disapproval on a face that once proclaimed indulgent love can cause panic in the heart, and this, suppressed, brings about a temporary insanity in the mind. A crash, a lapse, a covering smile. The moment has been saved – but at some immediate and more future cost. It will be paid in compound interest during wakeful hours of the night.

Chemical (?) *agitation* of one's entire surface which affects the whole, though some people more than others can retain a small and shrunken retreat which is unaffected – a sort of gas- and bomb-proof shelter to which they scurry at the alarm sound of the social siren.

It has been noted that we do not meet ourselves. What is queerer is that we do not see other people, being deprived of meeting[1] them in their solitudes, and that other people cannot meet us except in so far as the reaction of two agitated surfaces is concerned.

The thing known as love is our attempt to overcome this disability. We have a vision of and a passion for the loved one's being in solitude. It is unfortunate that love so often makes us long to intrude or to possess instead of merely worshipping.

*

There may have been women cynics. I have neither known nor heard of any. Women, whether by inclination or obligation, spend much time and energy in serving the needs of others, even if they serve as servants or as prostitutes for their living. Their lack of cynicism bears out the doctrine that service induces happiness.

If women could cease to have husbands and children, if

---

1. 'See' alternative not deleted in MS. [J.C.]

they could have absolute leisure and be released from the daily duties (even the duty of self-decoration) they would produce as many cynics as men.

Note Ben Johnson's remark that if one woman be dispraised other women resent it as meant for them all, but that if the whole sex be praised we take it personally.

In our greatest givings and takings there is never anything to show.

Women are not such good wives as men are husbands.

Men can and often *do* love their wives but not the women their wives are.

It is a more fatal step for a man to commit himself consciously to a woman than the other way about. Marriage, even for a man, is an easy step compared with that flight.

Why are men so much more afraid than women of losing their identities? Does nature provide for the more striking physical changes through which every normal woman has to pass – i.e. when she bears a child? How would men tolerate the change in their very shape? Although the shape is restored (more or less) after childbirth, the woman has had her lesson that nothing is static, including herself. With men the illusion of their own firmness persists much longer – indeed until destroyed by age. Herein may lie yet another explanation of the greater longevity of women. They are less brittle than men to the assault of change. It would be interesting to know if, on the whole, women submit more easily to the last change. But too many other elements enter here for statistics to be useful.

In my life I have met only two men who did not wish women to treat them essentially as children. I have found that men, in all other ways admirable, have insisted upon flattery, upon extreme tact, upon suppression of opinion, in short, upon the sort of extreme and conscious consideration one shows to children or to persons suffering from nervous ailments.

Men ask to be deceived: women, more foolish, ask not to be. Yet is it in the end more foolish? Men get what they ask. Women don't. But in time men will give us the truth, while we will go on deceiving men even when they ask to be undeceived.

To show that women are less vain than men – a woman can receive no greater compliment from a man than that he should manifestly take her in hand to improve her. Or does it show that women are consciously inferior?

Benson (I always forget if the one I mean is C. F. or A. C.) is right when he says that women want to alter the men they like. But he doesn't say that women like being altered by the men they like. Women always feel there is room in them for improvement. And they prefer to be improved by the men they like. From man to woman it is a compliment. From woman to man a nuisance and a fear.

It is, I think, not uncommon for women, especially when young, to imitate mannerisms and habits of men they love. I never met with a similar disposition in men, even in the youngest, most love-struck boy.

A man will sooner treat a remarkable woman badly than he will a commonplace woman. By showing the chivalry of a superior to the ordinary woman, he gratifies his sense of honour and stands before his world as a chivalrous gentleman who stands by the weak, be it even at some expense to himself. If he falls in love with a woman whom he discovers to be in her own way his equal, perhaps his superior in gifts, and chivalry is demanded, he is in a different taking. He will be but giving her her due and there is no special credit to him in this. Hence, in such circumstances, the woman is commonly treated far worse than if she had been beneath the man in his estimation as a human being. Either he is afraid of giving himself wholly – as he knows she deserves – and abandoning his self-conceit as a man, or he fears that he will be shown up by comparison. Or he thinks that she, being a superior creature, will find superior consolations for scurvy treatment in love. Men have little imagination as regards women. They seem not to know that in love all women are essentially the same and want the same of their chosen man. Ten to one, in a difficult case, a man faced with the choice of chivalrous or mean behaviour towards a woman of marked gifts, will make his escape by telling her that she is too good for him – as if anybody was ever too good to be loved.

If love transcends anything it transcends the weighing of goodnesses. Nobody is good enough to be loved – or anybody is good enough.

CHAPTER THIRTEEN

Age and Youth

HAVING slept well enough since I stopped reading at 2 a.m., I lay collecting myself, then wondering what time it was. Darkness encircled me. Only an indication of light seeping along the edges of the three heavily curtained windows, more from the most easterly one. It must be after dawn. The end of February, 'winter time', I mused. This meant anything between 8 and 9.30. But birds chirped rather than sang in the gardens. I had missed the dawn roulades. Something indefinable in the sounds of the distant, scanty traffic supported this judgement. In my basement I could know the time of day immediately from the traffic of trains behind and motor-wheels in front. Here, with all that at a faint distance, I have to guess. My own physical sensations corroborated the bird noises. I felt it not absolutely needful to turn over and sleep some more, as I should had I slept much less than eight hours. Without eight hours the day and I both suffer. I need that much but it can't be helped, save in an emergency. Early rising over any considerable period is the only thing that makes me bilious.

The temptation remained nevertheless; I considered with distaste the effort required for me to assault my feebleness, throw off my warm clothes, rise from bed, cross the icy floor of my damp bedroom, draw the curtains, release the blinds, look at the clock and return to my cowering. I felt myself sink towards a familiar coma. It resembles, I imagine, the trance of the opium addict – a peculiar state not unknown to me in youth and in middle age. But there were then a hundred urgent reasons for resistance. Now, more frequent and overpowering than before, it comes with no attendant malisons to aid resistance. Who beside myself will be put to any inconvenience if I yield? I can make up for the lost time by speeding up later in the day. For that matter, what does it matter to me or to anybody else if I don't get out of bed at all? I can think of no fixed engagement for the next twenty-four hours involving another soul. What I had unimportantly planned with myself to do might be done as well tomorrow. The methane flickers its raree-show inside my fallen eyelids. The sweet, loathsome miasma rises in my nostrils. Phrases, gestures, a kaleidoscope of important visions demand my attention. I poise on a merlon, high on battlements overlooking a vast landscape. I am not sleepy: I am somnambulic – wide, wide awake and observant while a million shimmering spider threads bind my nerves, my limbs, with deadly fascinations. In a moment I shall submit myself to the luxury of being devoured, of dropping blessedly extinct into slumber. With affection I murmur the name of Samuel Coleridge, Thomas de Quincey . . . and did not the great Lord Tennyson sometimes sip from the laudanum bottle? But conscience makes convicts of us all. I call on God, on the sainted memory of old Cousin Minnie Mackintosh, on my early-rising Scottish ancestors. Just then my French clock strikes a mid half-hour. The French are up betimes. How I admire that! 'Half past what?' I query. With one spring I am out of bed and victoriously making for the nearest window (not every morning, but this morning victorious). The rings rattle along the rod, citron light pours on my face through the bare trees. 'Half past nine,' I read. Not so bad that it might not be worse. Just bad enough. I creep back to bed, muffle myself in chicken feathers, reach for my thermos of hot liquid, gnaw my bit of bread, begin my morning meditation.

There is a new music in the reflectiveness of age. Often in the past I have longed to be in prison – to be shut within the four small walls of a cell with one small, barred window for my sky, so that I might shut out the torment of new visual impressions, and sort out, consider, gloat over my riches.

In a sort I have this now. Age contracts the room and enlarges the opportunity for meditation. Each morning for a time (perhaps an hour), after drawing the curtains of my curiously shaped room ('Rather like a cell, isn't it,' one visitor remarked), I lie thinking. Two barred windows at delightful angles to my coal cellar door directly face me, that on the left giving ingress to the dawn. I lie watching while the citron glows through the moving twigs of the trees. Or maybe there is rain or fog. No matter.

I think it has been held out as a consolation that age deadens or at least lessens the capacity for pain, particularly pain caused by misfortune in love. I have not found it so, and can scarcely believe myself to be singular in such disappointment. In my own experience, instead of the alleged diminution, years have brought added and more refined tortures, supplying at the same time a lamentably greater capacity for endurance. Neither is there a falling away in any power for self torture. The fact that I am no longer interested in my suffering – far less expect or wish to arouse interest in another – does not help. My cold distaste for the sufferer and my acute ennui at the unrolling of the familiar finished pattern of the torture, do not mollify its effects. Hope for a release by or in life has gone from the scene. Release by death, though more certain, takes on some curious aspects.

Healthy age a cocoon with all its youth rolled safe within its drab exterior. No longer an anxious silkworm subject to a thousand frustrations, but rich and ready for the inevitable shears.

> Unaffected, modest, and thoroughly wise . . . I asked him what kind of cigarette he preferred, eastern or western. He said it didn't matter. He just took whatever came. He didn't care about many things and as soon as he owned something that he had wanted, it ceased to please him.
>
> His age proved to be fifty-two, whereas mine was fifty-eight in May next. He said he *wanted* to be fifty-eight – every year was a conquest. He did *not* envy young people; in fact he felt sorry for them. They might die any day, and if they did die – what a suck-in for them! How much they would have missed – without knowing it.
>
> *Arnold Bennett's Journal. April 7 1925.*

It is a strange and unexpected comfort in the happier hours of old age to find that life itself has become more and more interesting, especially in its material and everyday aspects. The mystery grows and grows. One can just sit and think about everything without feeling the need to grasp at or put anything to persons.

Earnest youth best lays the foundations for a frivolous old age.

As I become less and less desirous to achieve, I appreciate with more and more fullness and delicacy the process of mere being.

I felt that the old were wilfully slow, the middle-aged wilfully stout or cranky. Without thinking it out I felt that experience could be added to youth without youth decaying. There is a halcyon interval when this is true – at least in one's inner feelings. But I'm getting held up here.

In youth we cannot believe we shall grow old. In age we often have to pretend we have ever been young. Each looks with incredulity at the other's condition.

The gates between are overgrown and rusty.

A friend and I were talking – she sitting on the edge of the bed. We discussed the fraud of age. Here we had been looking forward to sitting back and growing older, but no sitting back was allowed. The fight had to be renewed on another front. Even to be a clean, cheerful, unrepulsive old human being – it was going to take some doing. We discussed in detail the incipient moustache, the question of coiffeur. Our mothers were clever to take to caps.

The Old Ladies. Not one seemed, as so many ageing women do today, to be sorrowfully haunted by the ghost of her lost beauty or youth. Rather they seemed to have enjoyed the youth of which it was then the fashion to take an early leave, and to have entered with zest and grace into the new order of being old. This was irrespective of class. Not only the old who were of an elegant way of life, but the many poor old women whom we knew and delighted to visit – for example, old Jeannie, who had nursed my mother – were extraordinarily sunny, full of mischief, abounding in good talk, sometimes sharp of tongue, sometimes downright jolly in their ways and their ready laughter.

Montaigne admits that many bad men made good ends. Malefactors' last speeches are notorious for piety. Not quite fair this, because they *know* and they cannot only mug up their stuff for posterity, but can deliver it while in robust health and full command of their faculties. Many of the best-living men when on their deathbeds are, from a variety of reasons, unable to form a conscious sentence.

Montaigne, like most delightful people, was timid and conventional. No matter how useful or enjoyable we may find it, we should always be on our guard against his wisdom.

He is never more timid, more conventional and, to my finding, more wrong, than in his passage on deathbeds and last words. Here, as in so much, of course, he was merely a man of his time, or rather a sheep of his century.

The circumstances of a deathbed are uncommonly conducive to *esprit d'escalier* – one's parting witticisms or apothegms – no matter how well rehearsed in advance – being often postponed till its begetter finds himself descending or mounting the ethereal staircase.

Misprised love. Agonies. Only sadness in a churchyard the records of early deaths. Otherwise a well-filled churchyard would be one of the most satisfying pleasure gardens on earth.

Persons are sometimes heard to express wonder that old so-and-so should 'cling to life', and to ask whether such tenacity bespeaks old so-and-so's craven fear of death, in the face of the supposed fact that the young meet death readily with a smile. The reply is simple. Old so-and-so clings to life because he thoroughly enjoys it, most likely more than ever before over an extended period.

Not all old people are individually wise, but age itself has a sort of wisdom by necessity, if we could know how to elicit and use it.

Savage tribes well-ruled considered this with good results. 'Tis a suggestion made by nature, scoff at it as some moderns may.

Middle age is the fighting time. The young would fight in pairs or groups, not in wars, if the middle-aged did not egg them on and organise them. A false imputation that the old make wars using the energy of youth. Peace belongs to age.

Women, being more physically conscious, are more apt to square their behaviour with appearance, even while they may endeavour – being the less vain sex – to resort to artificial aids. But few old women who paint and dye are under any real delusion as to the result, which is mainly intended to cheer them for their loss and to bear about an impression of gaiety rather than of gloom. There are, no doubt, silly or sex-ridden women here and there who are incorrigible by age. But for one such I have known six truly intellectual men of great attainment in the world, who have failed to recognise the most obvious signs of years in themselves. One of them – so celebrated for his brain power that I shall not name him – exclaimed to a young woman who had gently rejected his advances, 'Surely it can't be that you think I'm *old*?' She looked at his shrivelled face, his sparse silvery hair, his distended paunch and skinny legs. 'Oh, no,' she replied soothingly, but with wonder in her heart, 'you aren't old at all.' And I have known others, but never a woman, who suffered from this particular blindness. She might pretend blindness: but that is something different.

There is, of course, the question: so long as a man or woman suffers from neither weariness nor disinclination, can he or she be regarded as old? Do mere appearances matter? Most men would say, perhaps, in a woman, yes; in a man, no – at least in the matter of sex attraction. It is a ruling which has not, I dare say, been closely examined, and perhaps it cannot be examined because silence is maintained by too many needful witnesses, especially among women. Old men, making advances to young women, can often, and do sometimes, testify that their age constitutes a positive attraction. The young women are ready with their corroboration, in words or deeds. Nobody sees anything indecorous in this. But older women who receive corresponding advances usually feel called upon to treat them as a joke or to accept them with the utmost discretion. The advances are none the less not at all uncommon, and – contrary to a popular opinion – they are made, not by the woman, who may be in her sixties, but pathologically in all seriousness by the man, who may be any age from twenty to eighty. Does this arouse disgust? I do not see why it should. Love can be of infinite variety yet still delicate in all its manifestations. It can mock at more formidable barriers than the locksmith's, and there are everywhere innumerable obscure Ninons de Lenclos. I do not propose, however, to involve myself by becoming more specific in this complicated if also captivating subject.

One thing seems sure to me. To fight the oncoming of age by denial or by effort is a sad resort. The better strategy is to take time by the forelock and to run out to meet the inevitable with a premature but genuine welcome. If, like Max Beerbohm, a man (or woman) can summon the humour to declare himself (*sc.* oneself) done with youth at forty, one can escape much that is tiresome in middle age, while ensuring a long, sunshiny St. Martin's summer of grateful, scarcely perceptible decline. The rays of the setting sun are more glorious when leisurely enjoyed than when their light is snatched at to illumine some final competitive endeavours. This is to make the best of both worlds. In the disguise of age one can still save to the full all that remains of youth. There is much to be said for it. By ceasing as a worker one can continue usefully and with zest to do those things one does best, even to create for the general good and one's own delectation. Many more people could act thus if they had simpler ideas of living. A mere dole is enough for health and happiness if a mature person has attained sufficient serenity to ignore worldly standards. But each must choose whether to combat or to anticipate old age. Even so we shall each have our private landmarks and signposts.

CHAPTER FOURTEEN

Youth and Age

Born was I to be old.

OLD, as compared with young and middle-aged people, lack guidance. Jesus of Nazareth's earthly experience excluded age no less than sin and remorse. The Psalmist uses us as hoary object-lessons, but spares us his rebukes. Even Saint Paul refrains from advising us for our good. I take this to be no small advantage that we are past reproof, left alone with or to speechless life itself. At last we are free to be under none but our own compulsions or those imposed by conditions of nature within which we may find much play. Neither Socrates (seventy when he died without a word against life) nor Plato (over eighty and equally discreet) seems to have judged that getting into years called for special remark. They both most likely enjoyed good health, as did Cicero, who boasts of increased rather than diminished powers in his last lustrum. Possibly the pursuits of philosophy and oratory make for a green old age. I have heard more than one aged judge of the High Court declare, like the author of *De Senectute*, that he never felt fitter in his life. We have the more explicit Renoir, still painting hard at seventy-one (though scarcely able to move a limb), and saying that, if it were not for ill health, old age would be 'a very happy time, as it has all sorts of pleasures special to itself'. He was properly annoyed at having begotten a child – a form of pleasure he felt entitled to be spared.

Other old men have been known to sport paternity as a singular feather, though old women commonly rejoice as much in cessation of child-bearing as in the status of grandmother. *Autres temps, autres mœurs* is an adage good for other than social application.

Women, however, in spite of their longer-livedness, have

disclosed themselves less than men on the subject of growing old; and their fewer records, mostly to be found in letters, are as contradictory as men's autobiographical data. Georges Sand embraced her old age as heartily as Madame du Deffand detested hers. 'Le jour où j'ai résolûment enterré ma jeunesse,' she wrote to Flaubert when approaching sunny seventies, 'je me rajeunis de vingt ans.' A difference of health or of temperament?

But we have Ben Jonson and Montaigne both declaring that old age is a disease, Montaigne finding in addition that the disease in the vast majority of men begins at thirty (not that this affected his wish to live beyond three score and ten) and Shakespeare presenting the lamentable picture of a being incorrigibly minus. The stone was undoubtedly an ageing evil, and surgeons, dieticians, dentists and oculists of those days were in unconscious conspiracy with what Shakespeare regarded as nature. Yet, even in those days there must have been a fairish number of hale old persons keeping quiet.

If age is indeed a disease, what of infancy and of youth? What of our so-called prime? For entire lack of ease and for hopeless resentment there can be nothing more piteous than a baby wrestling aloud and alone through moments which seem to him eternities, with life's incomprehensible miseries and his own poor adaptability to facts. Yet the mother (forgetting her own infancy) smiles as she picks him up. The child is further surfeited with tediums uncountable, repetitive and none the less painful for being pressed upon him as beneficial, or in the form of enjoyments. The unconscious helpless boredoms of childhood are dreadful. Youth again, though so delightful to the unthinking eye, is the season of green sickness, of ill-assurance, of desperate melancholies, of the agonies of misprised love and irremediable mistakes. It is also subject to physical decay, arrest, death. I have seen a girl of fifteen warped in body and made elderly of soul by a severe form of rheumatism. Middle age, like the others, has its halcyon periods, and these are often happily extended. But it is forced as often to submit to peculiar ills – gnawing cankers of disappointment and failure, the itch of envy, the harsh callosities of success. Bearing the heaviest burdens, inexcused of complaint, it has to contend with malaises, miscarriages, mortifications, secret declines. Ennui can prey upon all three. The helpless boredoms of childhood give place to the guilty boredoms of youth, and then to the corroding, exquisitely conscious, inescapable inflictions of the prime. Yet each condition is normal to us and may be fruitful in its kind – given a future.

The contradictory statements about age by mature persons of integrity can be reconciled only in the conclusion that truth here is as various as in any other department of human existence. One might add that it is easier to utter adequate generalities about childhood or youth than about old age. Seedlings are far more uniform than ancient trees, each one with its different history upon which its form and florescence depend. This, even if pasts were not far harder to read than futures.

Crabbe's pronouncement, when approaching his seventy-fourth birthday, is perhaps as prudent and compendious as any we have. 'I think the state of an old but hale man is the most comfortable and least painful of any stage in life; but it is always liable to infirmities: and this is as it should be. It would not be well to be in love with life when so little of it remains.' A homely rider might be appended in the words of a nameless old woman from Montrose. 'Auld age disna come its lane,' she used to say. 'Gin it bring naething else it brings sweirdness.' Sweirdness – a mingling of weariness with disinclination – and the nearness to death not as a possibility but as a certainty: these are the invariable elements, as they are the distinctive prerogatives of age. They are both to be welcomed, because of their beneficial action upon each other and because together they can work upon the past of every individual to produce a sort of magical blossoming reserved for mellow age alone. Second childhood is no slighting term when it is applied to the unique experience by which we savour afresh but with profound consciousness the primal joys.

To find beneath our worn exterior these astonishing springs purged from all utilitarian uses; to be excused from moral lessons; to escape tiresome demands; to dodge boredoms; delicately to eschew competition and hurry; to jettison inessential cargo from our tested timbers for the last strange voyage, there is a new kind of happiness here. Behind, the known lights of the bay still shine. Before, we have a sure haven.

In what lingering leisure may be afforded, it seems to me that we can enjoy a deeper gaiety than the child's, because we have no future; a more informed tenderness than the youth's because our present is unimportant to our fellows; a purer compassion than belongs to maturity, because our past provides a mythology of mercy. If the bad old person (always a blamer) is worse than the worst young one, the good (always a forgiver) is surely better than the best. Bad or good, we have the huge advantage that we can cock a snook at the world.

Good and bad, we have our differences in being as in growing old. We hold our pasts like worlds between our wondering hands. The young have only the world's past to decipher as best they can after the fashion of the moment, and a tiny puzzling segment of their own. Their moons have not, may never, come to the full harvest. They are claimed by the factitious present, inveigled by the feigning future. They feel pity for us (perhaps envy too, if I may judge from my own youth) because in their eyes we live in or on the unimaginable past. They can level this as a reproach. They are compelled to see it as a weakness.

Is it in truth so? Goethe said it was. 'Wir alle leben vom Vergangenen und gehen am Vergangenen zugrunde,' he said, which has been translated, 'We all live on the past and the past is our ruin'. A sweeping statement which seems to include all ages of men; but as he was nearing his seventy-third birthday when he made it, and was talking to Ulrike von Levetzow who had not reached his nineteenth, it is supposed that he had his own age in mind. He must have believed that his utterance was wise for he noted it down at the time and, a year later, published it as an aphorism in *Aus Kunst und Alterthum*, the periodical he then edited.

What did he mean? With equal truth or more he might have said, 'The past lives on us all and is our making'. Was he making the *amende aimable* to youth – a mere

old-gentlemanly gesture? By the past did he envisage not
the true past, which is for ever unnarrated and unknown,
but the plausible fiction of the historians, or the string of
obsessive personal memories which parade like a stage
army? I suspect that he was giving vent to a blast of
Olympian nonsense. To do so is a perquisite of age.

We cannot know. Since his day both past and present
have become restive. We can neither pin them down nor
keep them apart. The future alone, because always expected
but never there, can be clearly predicated.

Probably, like many old men of any epoch, Goethe saw
the past as a series of static pictures recoverable in and
capable of dominating thought, instead of the shimmering,
shifting, unstable, unpredictable, ambushed thing it surely
is. Even so, it is curious that he did not perceive it to
be, at its simplest, the grand element of time which most
distinguishes us from the brutes.

Each furred, feathered or scaly beast lives in and on the
present. And, their present being more intense than ours,
their speed, smell, taste, hearing, sight keener, they ought
to be happy. But are they? I look often and long at their faces,
into their eyes, and I see that they are puzzled, sad, ashamed.
'Pity us,' they seem to say to me, 'for we cannot remember:
we can only react to repetition or to fear. Pity us, for even
in dream we have no future, only the little overlap of habit
and instinct. Pity us, for, having only the present, we have
no perspective, no vision of the day or night skies, of the
broad seas, of the far landscapes, of our own grace. Hence
we have no story, no words. Pity us, for we have no past by
which we can be either ruined or saved.' I think Goethe can
never have looked into the face of a dog or a lion. I think he
can never have felt the sorrow of an old hound by the fire
without memory of his hunts. He cannot have watched the
dawn in a child's face while his mother recounts an incident
of his lost infancy, nor have seen the fructifying sun mount
in the listening eyes. What the child sees and hears is not
what the narrator sees and hears. But each is a vital image
conjured from our protean past. It teems with potent life.
Figs or thistles may come of it. And the mother cat can
inspire her kittens merely to the catching of mice.

No. Though it is our tragedy that what's done is done, it is our glory that nothing is ever finished. In each present moment we move in an ever changing past. The fabric of our lives – tough yet tenuous, clear to a glance yet flickering defiance under steady observation – is interminably in the weaving between old warp and new weft. At any given time the warp is incomparably the greater. But it comes to light only as the weft plays across it in unforeseen patterns, new refinements, surprising surfaces and textures. As the web advances so does our estimate change. What showed as mistaken or bad when the shuttle first flew over, may later show as good: what seemed fine may be revealed as a flaw. When the shuttle wavers on its last crossing, who knows what fresh play of light may direct us to a different appraisal of the whole? Who knows what unexpected face of the past will confront us when we look upon the face of death? A few kisses, tears, smiles, gestures, these only stay, immutable, fixed stars in the embroidered cloth of each firmament.

But perhaps Goethe meant merely that we are in peril of becoming ossified in age if we dwell on memories, detached and wilful, and therefore perfidious. It may, I suppose, be said that there are two ways of growing old – to ossify or to evanesce. The resolute character tends to contract and harden in form, while the more loosely assembled being tends to evaporate. I am of the nebulous, volatile sort. Even when young, I often felt myself to be composed in difficult proportions of elements which threatened to fly apart. This feeling of immanent dissolution has recurred at intervals. Now I foresee my danger in age to be some sort of senile imbecility: I try to provide against this. Visiting my contemporaries and my seniors, I note their lapses and their triumphs, and later I examine my own speech and conduct in the light of my researches. I even devise disciplinary exercises for myself. At the end of a day I often spend some minutes taking myself to task for failures, inaccuracies, egotisms, blanknesses, verbosities; and at the beginning of a day (when I remember) I lay down certain vetoes. I do not invariably succeed in observing them, but I shall persevere. If these efforts do not avail and I go to pieces, I shall bend what identity remains to becoming a tranquil, not a troublesome old idiot.

*

Like Cousin Kate. My mother's first cousin, Kate, was a daughter of James, the younger of those two Lewis boys who chose books before business; and she became, before she had reached my present age, evanescent in mind. She knew and loved us all. She did not lose her conscious identity nor the remembrance of her name. She carried out the day's unselfish routine in her brother's house at Tunbridge Wells with much of her accustomed efficiency. She was unfailingly kind and good. But she had ceased to have a texture. The warp of her past had dissolved save for a few shreds. 'Yes, I smile,' she said to me once when I was visiting there. 'I grin. I go on grinning because there's no use in making you all miserable. But I am absolutely wretched the whole time.'

Kate had been a great favourite with us all. She had looked after us once at home for some weeks when my mother was in Italy. She had managed us well. My father acknowledged it. My mother, herself constitutionally incapable of mastering the demands of daily life, admitted it. 'Dear Kate,' she would say shaking her head and smiling a little sadly: 'It is she, not I, who should be the mother of a family.' Kate was practical, merry, intelligent. She was a member of the Browning Society and introduced us to the works of 'dear Robert Browning'. (Nobody now speaks of 'dear T. S. Eliot', but we felt affectionate towards our poets in those days.) Yet she dissolved. Stray facts alone remained like reefs half-showing here and there above the sea that submerged her past. 'I like you,' she said, grinning and staring at me with pitiful benevolence. 'I liked you the best. But you never spoke. You were the only child I ever knew that never spoke. Why did you never speak?'

How my early speechlessness changed into loquacity I shall tell later. What poor Cousin Kate remembered best of all in life was her father's interdict against marriage for his four daughters, which only the eldest, Minnie, defied when she went off with yet another minister of the Free

Church of Scotland. I never heard if he forgave her, and whether an equal defiance on Kate's part would have held her together in her later years is impossible to determine. None of us children had seen this Lewis great-uncle. I know only that he quarrelled with my grandfather over money – my grandfather being, we were assured, in the wrong; that the quarrel (a singular and shocking vulgarity in our family history) was eventually composed as between Christians and Disruptionists; that he married into a remarkable East Country family, the Wylds of Gilston and begat four daughters – Minnie, Maggie, Kate, Alice – and one son, George. All these passed much of their youth in Italy.

His wife, whom we children knew only as his elderly widow, Great-aunt Marian, was one of five Wyld girls – 'the five finest female figures in Fife,' as Professor Blackie called them. He married one himself and was known to the family as Uncle Proff. With his beautiful features, picturesque attire, innocent exhibitionism and considerable reputation, Uncle Proff was clearly loved by his nieces and nephews in spite of his habit of always leaving a note for each of them pointing out what faults he had observed when he had been upon a visit to the house.

I knew two others of the Wyld sisters, one who married Lord Trayner, and one who remained a spinster and became a *vierge terrible* as Aunt Augusta, with a whirlwind presence and a habit of discussing audibly in the presence of the victim any personal peculiarities that struck her. 'What *very* red hair he has!' I heard her exclaim once in a penetrating whisper, as we sat in the Tunbridge Wells drawing-room to receive the first visit of a new clergyman, since famous as a preacher. 'Did you ever see such red hair? It's indecently red. You don't think he dyes it, do you?'

Besides the five Wyld girls there was at least one boy, his son being Cecil Wyld, the philologist. Connexions between the Lewis and the Wyld families have been renewed from time to time. One of Cecil's sisters married a grandson of Aunt Marian's. One of his brothers became involved – with equal innocence and scandal – in a divorce case with a sister of my mother's. And more recently, one of Cecil's sons married the niece of my only brother-in-law, a girl of British birth but with an Italian mother and a German father. So it goes on.

Aunt Marian, who ended her days in Edinburgh, was the straightest, nippiest, most exquisite old woman I ever saw. All about and around her was perfectly ordered (in contrast to our Glasgow home). Though we loved to visit her in Dean Park Crescent we had to mind ourselves. For lounging was a thing she did not tolerate. 'Child,' she would say, 'you can't sit like that in my drawing-room.' And with the precision of a drill sergeant she would rap out, 'Head up, chin in, chest out, belly in.' She herself sat always in a straight-backed chair, and even so, did not permit herself to lean back against it. If any of my father's sisters, whom also we visited in Edinburgh, had corrected us for a similar fault we should have felt the bitterest resentment. But there was that about Aunt Marian's acidity which braced and delighted without searing our susceptibilities. We liked, too, her employment of the word belly.

Her eldest daughter, Cousin Minnie, carried on something of her mother's eighteenth-century flavour (all the Wylds lived and died in the grand manner) until her hundredth year, when she reluctantly but neatly died. At ninety-nine she retained all her faculties, including her wit – with the aid of an ear trumpet and an ebony walking-stick, for deafness and rheumatism were Wyld evils. She wore widow's weeds, the plain black gown with its white collar and cuffs (washed and starched afresh for each day) and the crimped cap with its long streamers behind and its row of false white curls in front, became her extremely. She refused the eager offers of her daughters (both married to clergymen of the Church of England) to share their homes, lived alone in furnished rooms with a paid companion-nurse, and to the last never forgot to write a birthday letter of cheer and good counsel to every child, grandchild, great-grandchild, niece, nephew and cousin in her vast connexion.

Like her mother, Minnie never leaned back in chairs or sofas, and – small in stature – she stayed slender and upright, with quick, trim movements which matched her mind. She told with amusement how, alone one dark night, she was followed by a man in the street, she being then over seventy. She allowed him to come level with her; then suggested in her pleasant East Country voice that he should accompany her to the next lamp-post. Under its light she turned to him revealing her quizzical old face with a smile. Left badly off, with four children to educate, she had taken, for many years, pedigreed students into her house in Edinburgh as boarders. She had been obliged to work hard and continuously. 'I could never afford to have such a luxury as a biscuit in the house,' I have heard her say. But, gay of heart as she was stern of principle, she seemed to do everything with a sort of accomplished enjoyment, without any sense of oppression or tinge of resentment. I remember calling one morning at her Bournemouth rooms when she must have been at least eighty. She complained of feeling sleepy. 'Why not have a nap?' I asked. She sprang up and began to walk briskly up and down the little room. 'Nap, at this time of day?' she mocked. 'Nap indeed! Nonsense, child. Life is far too precious to waste in napping.' So she walked herself awake. Spartan though Minnie was, it was she who said to an over-conscientious daughter, 'Don't overdo yourself, my dear. God will get on quite well without you.' A thorough-going evangelical Christian as to creed, she remained unaffected by the emotionalism which was so marked an element in nineteenth-century evangelicalism. Her tart, rational flavour belonged rather to the eighteenth century. There was a touch of Voltaire about her.

Her three unmarried sisters were equally remarkable in their different ways. Maggie – stately, royal, beautiful, welcoming yet reserved – seemed born to stand at the top of a red-carpeted staircase receiving guests. Even severe rheumatism failed to ruffle or upset her perfect serenity. Then came Kate; and much younger, Alice, a darting, golden-haired, piquant-faced girl, who became one of the pioneer workers with Octavia Hill in improving slum properties and conditions in London's East End. Not as a charitable lady visitor but as a professional rent collector, she transformed a district of Hoxton, made a home for herself in one of its back lanes, and was trusted and feared equally by the ducal owner and his tenants. In middle life she abducted her sister Minnie's eldest son (her junior by only ten years) because they loved each other and she saw that he was pining into a nervous wreck in uncongenial office work. With him she set up house in a delectable small house in Sussex, where he displayed a genius for the practical details of country life during the week-ends. And every Monday morning – for many years until they acquired a car – they tramped five miles or so to the nearest railway station for London to labour in Hoxton till Saturday afternoon. Both the ménage and the partnership were entirely successful. They worked on together till, when well on in the seventies, she was stricken with inoperable cancer. Thereupon she went to bed, put on gay wrappers, filled her room with flowers and brightness, and issued invitations to us all to visit her on this 'my first real holiday for fifty years'. This was because she had never wanted holidays from her work, insisting that they made her feel ill. For everybody she had some little carefully considered memento. Her sister, Minnie, I fear, never wholly forgave the theft of her son.

George, the only boy in that family, seemed at times a little overshadowed by his sisters. Yet he had character, and ability. He had gone, when young and penniless, to Australia, founded the first big tea and coffee firm in that Continent, returned with a fortune to operate from London, and retired rather early in life to enjoy tranquillity and tennis (his form was professional) and to maintain the later years of Maggie and Kate in unpretentious elegance at Tunbridge Wells, where many Wylds had congregated. Before leaving England, George had fallen in love and had believed that his love was returned. It was for this that he had made the fortune. Shortly before leaving Australia he went to a dance. There, overhearing a conversation, he learned that his beloved had married. He fainted. I knew him only as a gentle, rather prim old man, who wore a Shetland shawl lest he should take cold. I was, I suppose, about eighteen when I went to stay with this unmarried family of cousins at Broadwater Down. There was talk of a writer called George Meredith, whose name I then heard for the first time. 'Let's put her to the Meredith test,' said somebody smiling at me, and I was led under a double cherry tree in full blossom in the garden, while they stood round regarding me as if part of the landscape. 'Yes, she stands it all right,' said one of them. 'What a thing is youth!'

CHAPTER FIFTEEN

Intimations of Mortality, and of Senility

A CHILD, having once seen a small dead beast or bird, acquires – if I may judge from my own experience – knowledge of death: its helpless immobility, its finality and sadness incurable. For some children a dead flower is enough. I remember once, while I was renewing the spring flowers in a vase for the house, how my son, aged perhaps six and standing by me, picked up a withered daffodil from among those thrown aside. 'What about this one?' he asked me. 'It's dead,' I replied. 'Look, we are putting these lovely fresh ones in, instead.' I have never myself been able to throw away withered flowers or leaves without a pang, and, seeing his clouded and desperate face, I knew we were hearing together the sound of the passing bell, he for the first time. My instinct was to shield it from his ears.

'After all,' I said in a cheerful tone, 'the bulb that daffodil grew from is still alive in the ground, and lots of others will come from the very same bulb.'

He pondered over this, still gazing at the flower in his hand. 'Oh, but *this* daffodil,' he said presently, 'this daffodil will never come again,' and when to that I could find no reply, he wept, knowing all.

From such a moment, which comes early in most lives, we easily see ourselves as dead and can die a thousand deaths in fancy. But not in the wildest imaginings of youth can we see ourselves as ever being old men or women. We shall grow, we know, and change as we see other children do. We shall even – though this appears less possible – grow up. But to become like these slow-moving, peculiar beings whom we call the old. No. We can love, serve, pity, delight in them; we cannot envisage ourselves as ever being them. It may be worth noting that, to the last, we all remain children, or at least ageless, in our dreams.

If only because this is an old woman's record, I shall give myself the pleasure of describing at least some of the many old people, old women in particular, who have figured in my life. They stand out in recollection like beneficent giants, or peer back at me from the undergrowth of the years like wise and kindly pigmies. But for the moment I shall tell only of Miss Semple.

As far back as I can remember and for some ten years thereafter, she sat in our day nursery mending our clothes and minding our doings. Unlike our nurses whom we addressed always by their Christian names, she was spoken of and to as Miss Semple. Not that she was in any degree a governess or of a class superior to the nurses, who were all country girls. She came of village weaver stock from the neighbourhood of Johnstone, and her speech was the broadest Lanarkshire. Of her history I know nothing. I know only that my mother regarded her as 'one of God's saints' deserving of our reverence and as a friend to be treasured and sought for good counsel. I remember my mother once saying that she had 'come through great tribulations'. My mother's own old nurse, affectionately known as 'old Jeanie' and cherished by the family till she died at a great age, had started her womanhood by having an illegitimate child. This we were told at some time without guessing at the implications, though my mother made the characteristic comment, 'God looks gently on the sins of the flesh; it is the sins of the spirit that call forth His wrath,' and Jeanie seems to have upheld this finding in the godly Lewis household where she made herself loved.

Miss Semple must have been over seventy when I first knew her. She was a tiny hunchback, almost a dwarf. But we did not think of her as deformed, we were so used to her sitting all day and every day in the same wicker chair, by the same west window, in front of the same low green pillar table with its wreath of painted ivy leaves in a darker green on which stood her basket of mending. Sometimes we would pass wondering hands over the strange great lump which projected below the grey Shetland shawl she wore summer and winter. But she was as little self-conscious about it as we. We did not connect her with hunchbacks we saw in the streets. With any other shape she would not have been Miss Semple. Her face was long, yellow, seamed, horse-like, discreet, but lighted up sometimes with a smile of the utmost sapience and tolerance. She dressed always in black, with a cap of black cotton lace over her thin grey hair, and her gnarled hands never stopped their work of repair unless they were needed to soothe or bind up some nursery casualty. She spoke seldom, never told us a story, and neither took part nor interfered in our games except when these grew dangerous, when a word from her was enough to reduce us to submission. She never scolded, never suggested. I am sure that she observed and pondered everything. The nurses accepted her as we did, though I think the younger, flightier ones (we often, though not always, had two) went in some fear of her glance. We had no fear. She existed to be appealed to at need and to issue a few routine orders. She was unobtrusive as a piece of nursery furniture, yet we should have felt her absence as one feels the removal of a lighted candle from a room otherwise unillumined. I have no doubt that she reported on us to our mother, but we were never given reason to be aware of this or that she observed us.

She must, of course, often have left her chair. But I can see her only once standing up in the middle of the nursery floor, and this was as a bride wearing a long white muslin veil. My younger brother, Gordon, aged eight, had proposed marriage to her. She had accepted. So we had a wedding full of circumstance. By then my sister, Fanny, by her own urgent wish had gone to a boarding school, so I was sole bridesmaid. My other brother, Grant, aged ten, officiated, using as his pulpit the big square nursery stool upon which he towered over both bridegroom and bride, who were of equal heights. For me this stool had both sacred and secular associations, because on it of a Sunday night I had been stood countless times to sing *Shall we Gather at the River* or *Fair Waved the Golden Corn* while my mother bathed the boys in the tin bath by the fire. It was only the other day that Gordon, being reminded by me of his wedding to Miss Semple, told me that, soon after the ceremony, he had enquired of my mother with some anxiety if she thought they would have a baby 'as married people do'. He says he was on the whole relieved, while puzzled, to learn that considering everything a baby was in the highest degree improbable.

When she died some twelve years or so later, Miss Semple left by her will, to the only husband she ever had, the big silver watch that was her one precious possession.

∗

I cannot have been more than six years old when, one night, I woke in my bed and could not sleep again within the usual minute. The least nervous child has such seasons of wakefulness without pain, terror or other apparent reason, and I, never night-nervous, was much given to them. I lay there at peace filled with a diffused well-being, invaded by that gentle but insistent crescendo of thriving and building which it is given to healthy childhood to feel.

There must have been moonlight or a nightlight in the room, because I held up my two hands and looked at them. I had learned to read (on my sixth birthday I remember the delighted ease with which I galloped through a book called *Susy's Six Birthdays*, which somebody had given me) and I could count at least up to ten. I counted the dimples on my knuckles and wished them away, because my sister had made me cry by calling me Little Dolly Dimples in a voice of scorn, and I thought it babyish to have them. At the same time, with nobody there to jeer at them, and with that insouciant narcissism of children young enough still to enjoy the novelty of their bodies, I found that they looked rather nice in the faint light.

I lay regarding them. Then I remembered Miss Semple's hands, worn with work, deformed with age, stiff with rheumatism. 'If I grow old,' I thought, 'my hands will be like Miss Semple's.' The impossibility of this led me to a logical conclusion. I knew that I was supposed to be delicate. Like so many of the children in the more advanced story books that were read aloud to us, I was going to die young.

Having made this discovery I decided that I ought to impart it to my parents. As I might die before morning there was no time to be lost. I got out of bed, opened the door and, in some trepidation, set about the journey to the dining-room, where I knew my father and mother would be at this time if any lights were still burning. Nothing in daylight, it was something of an expedition in the half-dark. But the occasion called for resolution. Along the nursery landing and down the top flight of stairs – both cold to bare feet. Then the length of the lower, carpeted floor, past the two doors of the silent drawing-room. Then down again, round the wider, circular staircase, till I stood in the tiled entrance hall with its two thick pillars wide apart. I loved and admired these pillars, which were painted to resemble yellow marble, and they looked most beautiful to me just then, as they reflected the multicoloured glass of the ceiling lantern. They were like the portals of heaven which I should so soon enter.

Standing there I could hear through the closed dining-room door the quiet voices of my parents. I crossed the hall and opened the door. I knew they would be seated under the gas chandelier of crystal, drinking their tumblers of milk and eating chunks of the rich, black gingerbread which was always brought to them on a tray before the servants retired (I never see gingerbread of this admirable kind today). My father would be wearing his brown velveteen smoking jacket, for which every evening he changed his surtout of dark grey broad-cloth. On his bald head with longish, fine iron-grey hair round the back, would be his round smoking cap of a sort of brown plush that looked like sealskin. This became his handsome, bearded face exceedingly well to my mind, and it emphasised his extraordinary likeness to Garibaldi, of whom we had a photograph in the family album which we could scarcely believe was not of my father till he insisted, telling us at the same time how he had met, and how greatly he venerated, the Italian patriot.

As I went in, trembling a little in my nightgown from the long, cold descent, he was flicking some crumbs of gingerbread from his beard, and my mother held her glass tilted to drain the last drops of milk from her glass.

'Child, what's the matter?' exclaimed my mother, putting

her tumbler down, taking me in her arms in affectionate concern, and kissing me. 'Is it that tooth again?' asked my father with his jocose smile. 'You should have let me pull it yesterday. Then it would have ceased from troubling and you would have been at rest.' (He indulged in this kind of facetiousness did my father, and dearly loved a pun.) 'No,' I said. 'It's out, Miss Semple tied a bit of pack-thread to it, and we tied the other end to the door-handle, and she made Grant shut the door, and my tooth came out. Look!' I displayed the gap.

'Good old Miss Semple!' said my father. 'What's the new trouble then?' He picked up an antimacassar, wrapped it round me, took me from my mother, and stood me between his big safe knees. 'No fever,' he said, caressing my forehead with his gentle, large hands that always felt dry, warm and smooth. 'A nightmare, perhaps. We all have them sometimes. What was yours?'

'It has come to me,' I said, 'that God is going to take me to Himself. I'm going to die young, perhaps at once, like the boy in *The Story of a Short Life*: you know, the one Mother read us about, who sang *The Sons of God go Forth to War*, and said "Happy is my lot" – only he said it in Latin – "lettuce something mere."'

My parents continued to regard me with solicitude, but my portentous news was somehow invalidated by the smile father sent over his gold-rimmed pince-nez to mother as he lifted me on to his knee. He took my hand and turned my face to the light. 'I think,' he said, 'you'd better get back into your nice warm bed and go to sleep,' and he kissed me. 'We'll see how you feel tomorrow morning.'

My mother restored the antimacassar to its chair, putting round me instead the shawl she was wearing. Then my father carried me upstairs – she walking beside us – put me in bed and left her to tuck me in. 'If it is our Heavenly Father's will, my darling,' she said, fondling me, 'any one of us, young or old, will go to Him any day. It is as He thinks best. We are all in His hands, and all He doeth is good. Never forget that underneath are the everlasting arms. But I think you will be spared to us for many, many years. Now I'll sing you *Hush My Babe*, and you'll soon be fast asleep.' It happened as she said. Death receded to an infinite distance, and with it, age.

My mother's singing of *Hush My Babe* was a rite sacred to bed-time distresses, a fetish that goes farther back than my memory. Its power to soothe lay partly in my mother's rendering – confident, tender, low-voiced; partly in our belief that it was a lullaby peculiar to her family. She had told us how her own mother – one little girl in a family of boys – had used to sing it to her dolls when playing under the great trees in her father's park. It was in none of our hymn books, and when I later discovered it in some compilation of sacred song known to other people, I felt outraged, not by my mother's innocent deception, but by the trespass of the compiler.

'But Hush My Babe is *ours*,' I cried out upon the thief.

In any event – toothache, heartache, nightmare, fever – the words and melody cast a spell never known to fail. When my mother had done all she could to ease our bodies we asked for *Hush My Babe*, and to her singing what remained of pain, fear or grief would yield. She was at her best in the lines, which I quote, perhaps incorrectly, from memory,

> I could give thee thousand kisses,
> Wishing what I most desire,
> With a mother's tenderest wishes
> Which my every thought inspire.

This verse apart, my favourite was,

> Soft and easy is thy cradle,
> Coarse and hard thy Saviour lay,
> For his nursery was a stable,
> And his softest bed was hay.

As I lapsed into slumber I felt that Jesus on the hay, my mother beside me, the holy angels she had summoned to guard my bed, my child grandmother under noble trees, and my grandmother's dolls were all equally sustaining and infinitely precious.

A curious point, and one which encouraged our appropriative stand, was that this was the only tune my mother could perfectly sing. Unlike my father, who was pleasant and frequent in song (we loved it when he rollicked out in *A Southerly Wind and a Cloudy Sky, Proclaim a Hunting Morning!* and often he made us join with him in rounds and catches, some of them in Dog Latin), she had a poor ear and not much of a voice. Yet she had been singing at a harmonium when my father first saw and fell in love with her. This was in Stirling Castle, the same place which had brought her grandfather a wife. But instead of a soldier and a milkmaid the younger lovers had been co-workers in the Lord's Vineyard, stimulated in their labours by Moody and Sankey's Scottish campaign. Entering a room on the Rock my father had seen a face of such radiant goodness and had heard a voice of such naïve sweetness that he had immediately determined to win both for himself. But while the goodness continued to shine, the voice, after the mating period, had wavered and become uncertain. She still loved to teach us hymns and nursery rhymes, and songs like *There were Three Little Kittens, who Lost Their Mittens*; she still took part during church services and our daily family worship in choral praise. But these last efforts in particular met with our united disparagements and the pulling of faces. She excelled only in a single song and in a darkened nursery, with no thought but of the troubled child who listened for comfort.

Since then, to drive out pain or grief, I have tried sometimes to sing *Hush My Babe* to myself. But this, wanting my mother's voice, has not availed.

From the early incident of wakefulness it appears that I was a priggish rather than a prophetic infant. Happily my parents were never bereaved of any of their children. That loss was reserved for me later when I had an only child and was without my parents' jubilant faith. All four of us ('The Awful Four', as we designated ourselves later when we conducted a family magazine) are now at least twenty years older than my father was at that time, and my sister is still full of uncontrollable energy at sixty-eight, the age at which he died.

I had had many other sessions of sleeplessness when, though still young, I was more prescient and less of a prig. But I shall skip all these to describe, if I can, a comparatively recent experience, which is both relevant to the one already described and bearing upon my mother's prediction that I should survive my tender years.

Further, if I can with any adequacy record the experience, I shall be answering a question put to me by the young man upstairs.

He asked me if I could say of any definite time, 'This marked the end of my youth. Today I begin upon my maturity,' or 'From now on I shall be old.' He wished to know if, looking back, one could point to a clear dividing line between one stage and another.

On the drag of the moment, which was unpropitious, I made a vague reply. But the question remained in my mind. It is a question, I imagine, which, if answered truly by a number of different people, would elicit precisely that number of widely differing answers. But among these some would no doubt date the conscious passing from stage to stage by a critical incident, an illness, or a bereavement which altered their outlook on life. Others might say that they slipped unawares across such frontiers, their crises having no connexion with the years. Others, again, would deny any essential inward change at any point. They 'feel no different', they would say, from what they always felt, and it is only to the outside world that they present a changed aspect. Physical changes they brush aside quite sincerely as being irrelevant to their experience.

My own physical consciousness has always been so intense and, on the whole, so pleasurable, that I am unable to divide it from the rest of my being. I certainly do not feel the same now as I did when young, except in that curious, frail thing we term identity. And although I am not always quite sure about even this, I can imagine that it may persist through greater transmutations than those I have known. I do know that if there be a heaven (or a hell) such as my parents believed in, and if I had gone to either at the age of six, the six-year-old immortal would not much resemble what I became at sixty. Yet I can fancy that, if the two could meet, some sort of recognition would be possible.

What happened to me has been something like this. Till fifty I felt no radical change. The world and the people in it had, it is true, come to look in many respects wholly different. Shocks, sorrows, disappointments, and circumstances which had altered at times with violence, had affected my outlook, my thought, my behaviour. But these blows came rather as discoveries than as transfiguring agents. I developed, or I think I did. I suffered. But I was not aware of any essential pressure upon the familiar integrity of my being, which remained in itself as it had existed from the dawn of consciousness. Perhaps an illusion helped by good health and an agile physique, this was none the less my experience.

Then, one night I woke of a sudden from an ordinary sleep to a knowledge that was new and full of acute terror. I had no pain. The cause of my condition was not, I recognised, that worst of all woes which I knew from a thousand sudden wakings hitherto and had painfully learned to combat by a rotation of methods. No; this was something different in kind. It smote not upon heart or conscience, nor with the poisoned weapon of memory. It was the inhuman attack by unconscionable nature upon the core of my small natural being. I had, it seemed, wakened only just in time to detect the secret, furious activity of a myriad tiny energies of demolition, surprising them for a fraction of time at their appointed work. With my waking they had left off, but not immediately. They had scurried away, but not swiftly enough. With indescribable alarm I knew that during sleep my body, which hitherto had served me so well, had become subject to a new metamorphosis, the metamorphosis of dissolution.

The experience may be a common one, but I had never heard or read any expression of it so, to me, it was strange. At first it horrified me. Later, by degrees and as I came to look for its repetition, I became interested. Something of me drew aside to watch. Or it may be that I was driven to form, if it might be, a new core that would serve my time out when the old was quite destroyed.

The process, however, was difficult and slow. To begin with I tried to put off conviction; to attribute the whole thing to fancy or to some irrecoverable dream. But it recurred too often, though not with regularity, for me to mistake its significance. Again and again for at least a whole year I woke to the awareness of disintegration, and to the sense that its creatures had barely escaped my survey. I reckoned that the irregularity was due rather to my lack of vigilance than to theirs. My body – the body that has served me well through the years – was crumbling, infinitesimally crashing, shrinking, falling in, giving way all over the surface of the skin, and by deeper withdrawals. The brain in my skull seemed to join in the widespread treachery and subtle collapse. It was the experience of pregnancy in reverse, and the opposite of that sense of burgeoning which I had felt when I lay awake that other time so long ago.

The sense that familiar formations were giving place to a different, unpredictable outline was so strong that, in the morning afterwards, I would look in my glass, prepared to cry out with the old woman in the nursery rhyme, 'Lawk a mercy on me, This is none of I!' Yet what I saw looked much the same as it had been the day before, and throughout the day I felt no different save in my knowledge.

At length the process seemed to be arrested. At least I stopped waking, no doubt because I had become used to what, on its first onset, had been so remarkable. I ceased fretting over it as over more outward signs. But I did not forget. I entered into a new outpost.

Now I am prepared for further assault, knowing however that my observing faculties may themselves be first insensibly invaded and reduced. So be it, if be it must. I shall try by the dodges of discipline to keep up a running fight, and, while any capacity remains, I shall look full at all I can see of nature's inescapable process. Already in my tissue of blood, bones and brain I have contemplated declension. I can feel the richer, not the sadder, for it. 'Farewell and Hail!'

PART III
FRAGMENTS

Of the fragments which follow, some had been federated by the author under such headings as 'Money', 'Faces', 'People', and 'Houses'; others had no labels at all. Some were probably intended for inclusion in a reflective chapter which was to have been called 'In Rest and Quiet', but no draft of such a chapter has been found. I have therefore thought it best to give them as independent pieces, preserving the author's arrangement (*e.g.* when different fragments were given similar headings) wherever this exists. [J.C.]

FACES. Can think for long stretches of the faces I have known.

Faces like books. Books like faces, fleeting yet permanent glimpses – not recorded verbally, but ocularly, or like a melody or a succession of chords. Looking up the passage.

If only they would not converse. I wish I loved, etc. Endlessly subtle variety – in the country, expressions of actors, Garbo. Stupidity and intelligence, types, album. Patience of wisdom, prettiness, how they write themselves. Animals' unmoving, sad masks.

＊

I attribute none of my own human weaknesses and meannesses to persons who attract me, and it always astonishes me when I find I was mistaken. Sometimes it endears the person more to me, sometimes not. To persons I don't like I have at times attributed faults neither I nor they possess. When I find I have been mistaken I am capable of feeling a sudden rush of love for them and can do fantastic things – even write fantastic, eager letters – on impulse. But this impulse always arises when I am in solitude. I have only to meet the person concerned for me to know that I can't stand them – not if they had all the virtues. The chemical reaction is irresistible.

It is often said, and with some truth, that you have only to meet a person face to face to feel kindly to them. I find the opposite more profoundly true – for me. In solitude I can love everybody, even those I regard as enemies. But when I meet them – superficial accommodations apart – I know that it is no good and that nature made us to be hostile in essence. One need not therefore, of course, be hostile in action. I try not to be, and can usually be magnanimous from solitude without a strain, and without repenting afterwards.

❋

The dreamers are commonly the doers. They incline while dreaming, or perhaps as an excuse or makeweight for their dreaming habit, to make things with their hands while they indulge it. Or it may be the other way about; that liking to work with their hands they find they must dream. The knitters, the cabinet-makers, the embroiderers, perhaps the painters. Dreams are of many sorts, including leisured or impassioned recollection of scenes, faces, tones of voice, colours, lines, textures, atmospheres, incidents. Now and then a thought, or at least an intellectual or practical conclusion, will stand out like a sudden rock in the shifting sea. Here they go in hand for a moment with the thinkers, the philosophers. But they cannot *pursue* the isolated thought further. They can only note it and possibly at some future time link it logically with some other thought which crops up in seeming isolation.

The thinkers do not commonly work with their hands. Thought is a work in itself demanding the full attention of the body as well as the mind.

❋

I am embarrassed by the multiplicity of my interests – of my likings I might add. I am not adept at excluding or concentrating. Those who are so have my admiration if not my envy. I should like to have their capacity. Yet I cannot think I should be happier on the whole and from hour to hour if I exercised it. Perhaps for a woman in particular, and for the savouring of life throughout a lifetime it is better to enjoy much than to concentrate selectively. For the deficiency in achievement and in mastery one has the wider field for speculation, contemplation and delight. I am not sure of this. I have little doubt that for a man with gifts it is happier and more fruitful to concentrate. Even so I am not sure that if I were a man I should not rather be a tramp than a scholar or a specialist.

Most people, I have noticed, pride themselves, perhaps rightly, on their exclusiveness. They can't eat this, they can't stand that, they take no interest in the other. I am inclusively constituted. I like aristocratic people and common people, British people and foreigners. The Jews delight and amuse me and elicit my sympathetic admiration. I enjoy every sort of food and drink that human beings eat, and thrive on it.

*

A scatter-brain is admitted in some degree a crack-brain. Yet I am of the tough not the tender tribe.

Picking up sticks and other street oddments. Sooner that than an office job, far sooner that than a chair and table in the Ministry of Information or in some refined ante-chamber where charm of manner demands its price. Once (and once only) I tried an office job for six months. The pay was five pounds a week, which at that time was pretty good, and hours easy enough. I had to listen sympathetically to disquisitions on his schemes and his ideals delivered by my employer (this took a considerable part of my day), and between whiles I was sent out to interview celebrities. Over these interviews I prefer to draw a veil.

*

This is one of my handicaps in so short a life, that I continue so often to be interested after I am bored. At the same time boredom affects me with great frequency and excruciating results.

Real boredom resembles the attack of a physical malady, and it inflicts physical symptoms. 'Dying' of boredom nicely (or horridly) expresses one's sensations. Worst of all when it is induced by those we are truly fond of, such as old friends. A woman I know intimately said to me that while she was unable to stop loving her husband – even to stop being jealously in love with him – he bored her excruciatingly. Love may cast out fear. It does not necessarily cast out boredom.

*

The papery wasps' nest of egoism – deadliest of demons.

*

Radical divisions: those who'd like to be changed – 'we shall be changed' – and those who say, 'I am I, myself'. The first are people of faith, lovers of heaven, the second of unfaith.

I am that I am, or I am what I am, or I am as I am, or I am I, all of the devil. Permissible and different is I am – a mere statement of being.

*

It is always safe to be kind – in easy ways. Most people play for safety. Therefore kindness – of the easier and more flattering sorts – is common.

Many people who wear no religious habit have none the less taken the veil in life. Finding the problems and diversities of life too much to face they have withdrawn into a regimen of duties and 'good deeds' in which they are as cloistered in spirit as if living in a monastery, but often more dead at heart than any monk or nun. Such people serve a useful purpose, as they can be counted upon for the sort of kindnesses which are their apology to themselves. But they are apt to become more smug than the declared religious who are kind because they love God. And often there is an obverse side to their kindness which is the reverse of attractive.

*

To those who have sanctities it often happens that in the end nothing is sacred but their own vanity.

The Disciples were able to love somebody who made them feel themselves to be wanting. In no other way were they distinguished from their contemporaries. We put a line round the heads of these otherwise commonplace men to mark this little difference.

*

People doing the same small things in what to an unobservant eye is the same way, may be doing these things from a profoundly different source of energy.

The person – and I am now thinking especially of women and of individual women I have known – the person who occupies herself largely and apparently happily in small activities may do so from an overflow or from a poverty of life in herself. Take the woman who possesses some profound satisfaction. It may be in human loving or being loved to the utmost and happiest commitment of her being, or it may be in a spiritual love – a satisfactory religion. She does not need to bother herself about the great thing that fills her being and by which she lives. It is there sustaining, warming and cheering her all the time. Though she may not think much about it all her thinking and feeling and observation refer secretly to it. Perhaps she scarcely mentions it directly. But each small activity she undertakes is made sweet, and energy for doing it is furnished, from the same source, and all are informed by it, and made worth while one after the other. The woman who lacks this central fountain has to go on day after day doing things like everybody else. But she has to do them without any real life-energy. This means she does them as an escape from lack of life and happiness. Very likely she will regard them as duties, and regarding them so, may do them well and with apparent vigour. But they are all separate trickles of energy induced by sheer will or as a relief from the desolation of boredom.

*

Arnold Bennett has an entry in his journal for April 14, 1913 (he was then some years short of fifty), headed 'Advance of Age'. 'I now sit down to brush my hair and put my collar and tie on. I also take a decided pleasure in forming habits and reforming old ones . . . the pleasure of doing the same thing at the same time every day, and savouring it, should be noted.'

Certain things of course have to be done – more or less. They do not always get done by me. I can cut almost anything out incidentally. Almost the only thing I do every day the same is to turn back my bedclothes and open the windows. There are things I do because I must; others that I do if I can. But each day is for me like a new musical composition – not always successful but always different, subject to accident and surprise.

Eating my slice of bread or piece of oatcake, sipping the tea, coffee, cocoa, milk, or water (never the same for many days on end) I had the night before, and thinking.

I can cook, clean, sew, save, for love (while not caring for such activities); I could not write a review save for money. Yet I love, if not writing, having written. Writing interests me more than any other activity.

I have wished that I were more given to the acquirement of habits. Compared with any of my contemporary and senior friends I seem to be ill-adapted to this useful practice which, it has seemed to me, simplifies existence and makes old age easier – to oneself, if not so much to others.

By habits I mean good or at least harmless and useful habits, such as doing certain things regularly at the same time and in the same way. Smoking, for instance, I exclude, because smoking can rather be said to have acquired me than I it. This I term a vice. While I am ashamed of it – in spasms – I continue it.

Smoking. Often drunk, giddy, sick with nicotine.

I am desperately conscientious and idiotically reckless, disorderly but passionately addicted to order, religious of heart but profoundly sceptical in mind, incapable of following up any advantage, contemptuous of striving yet pertinacious to a fault, easily and consciously cheated, helpless before rudeness or coldness, detached yet entirely dependent upon love, faithful yet capable of small treacheries, extremely weak and despairing, always hopeful. I love life, and dislike myself.

Nobody could be much worse equipped for life or much better fortified against its onslaughts.

*

Every important action I have ever taken (important to myself) has been like the first flight of a fledgeling. I can calculate on myself from experience only in the small daily things.

The prudent fledgeling would never fly.

*

Religion is a gesture, a posture, an attitude, a faith, a sovereign guide to the individual life. When it becomes a gesturing, a posturing, an attitudinising, when it is formulated into a creed for more than one human being, it has become something other than religion. It then constricts, bullies, persecutes, turns smug or crazy, militant or morbid. It ossifies into a moral code or rots into emotionalism. Everything, then, that gave it life at first, is preserved by its forms only as a forgotten source, and – as religion cannot die – this remains for the adventurous individual to rediscover by making new tracks back to it. When this individual comes again upon the source, he finds it pristine, unchanged. Yet it is not the same, for he brings to it all he has learned from its modern decay with which he is familiar. Also he brings to it all the new knowledge and experience of the world of his own day, so that he applies fresh tests and wins from it undreamed-of reactions. He may find that the known phrases and the worn gestures he repudiated when he set out on his pilgrimage of rediscovery can still be truthfully applied. For all that his discovery is a perfectly new thing. At least it will be new for a moment. The person is, as we say, 'converted'. Then there are two ways open to him. If he is weak or distrustful, frightened or unduly exalted, he will be persuaded that there is no essential difference between the source and the polluted channel. He will make humble, public confession, and return, shielding his inner illumination as best he can, to the established social religion of his world. If he is none of these things, he will soon betray, even by his use of the familiar phrases and gestures, something that will impel the religious leaders and priests to repudiate him with horror. They will kill him if they can. If tolerance happens to be one of the current tenets, he will merely . . . [*cetera desunt*].

Forgive us our trespasses as we forgive those who trespass against us. May this be a way of saying that, once one has been plunged into hell by the horrifying vision of one's own sins, shortcomings and follies, one is immediately endowed with ease and eagerness in pardoning those of other people. With our eyes upon those who wrong or irritate us, we condemn because we justify ourselves. If we look towards God and, in the light of His eyes strip and confess ourselves, the iniquities and idiocies of our fellows are seen to be trifling in comparison with our own. Forgiveness is then a natural gesture made to save ourselves from total despair.

The conviction without which Christianity is void – that we are miserable sinners – makes it unique. It also makes more play for the hypocrite than any other religion or even code of ethics.

To be morally a hypocrite is distinct from sanctimoniousness of the Christian sort with its false humility; leaves room too for more self-deception. But is it with all its faults worse than what I have sometimes wondered is not the new non-religious and all political code – 'Everybody else is a sinner'?

The need for humility should be discovered, not enjoined. This is the trouble with most truths, particularly religious truths. Preaching falsifies.

*

Suffering refines. It also coarsens.

Strong and coarse natures are purified and made gentler by suffering. Natures that are originally pure and gentle are sometimes hardened unpleasantly by their need for self-protection.

Artists are those who lend themselves naked to the shares of newness.

*

In the future the unknown past waits to beset us and waylay us with surprise.

Who knows what new clarity from the past will present its face when we come face to face with death?

The present is confused, different from both past and future, though inextricably woven from both, and never in our hand or our control as they may at least at times appear to be.

The present does not lend itself to be lived in.

✳

I have always found a peculiar, solacing beauty in the outdoor playing of a good band – preferably playing marches by Sousa – while the evening sky darkens slowly upon a summers day. A good military march gives me the essence of Alfred de Vigny.

✳

In human converse, admissions help, self-disparagement hinders.

✳

I cannot find very lovable persons who have not a good slice of stoicism in their composition. Sensitiveness in some directions is, of course, to be desired. But how disengaging when the possessor once begins to draw to this quality the attention of his fellows with the aim of enlisting sympathy or eliciting admiration. It is always displayed, though perhaps not consciously, as a mark of superiority in its possessor.

✳

All human beings not quite trained have a streak of what we call treachery. An act of treachery can be a vindication of freedom?

✳

Success and failure are equally easy to explain away. They remain, however, success and failure.

✳

'That'll be a lesson to him,' we say. How we hate learning!

*

I should like to have lived in an age of faith. By faith I mean religious faith – faith in a living, sentient God or providential being with a heart who created this world and has a plan for mankind. Failing this I should choose an age – necessarily a future one – of settled non-faith. For me as an individual the worst thing in this unhappy age in which I have grown old is that one was born into a faith which could not, without deceit or strain, be maintained. I am aware that there are still millions of believers in God, self-styled and real. But look at them. Above all, listen to them. They merely add to the sorrow of the general loss. The more they preach of faith the less they leave for the clear-eyed honest soul to believe in. If only they would keep quiet there might be a shred of hope. But their tongues wag in a way that shocks me. I believe that I am of those – if there be such – who are naturally religious. In any event I was imbued with the Christian religion since before I can remember by parents who themselves believed in it and lived accordingly.

To the true believer – let alone the religious martyr or hero – that strong something, that deity outside the self yet able to inform it, is needful for ordinary existence. As my mother, a true believer, used to say, 'I could not get on at all unless I believed in God and His revelation in Christ.' And this was her argument for God's existence as revealed in Christ. Life would be intolerable without it. By living she constituted the proof in herself. In clearer ages of faith, even such a proof was not called for. There was a God, and that was an end of it. You might get on without Him or not. He was there all the same, no matter how opinions might differ as to the nature of His being. He was predicated by the joys no less than by the sorrows of life.

I remember feeling a dreadful pang when my mother advanced her personal feeling as a proof of the existence of God which I had never doubted. Her exclamation touched me, but I now see that it created a doubt in my mind – my first doubt. So long as I was told, God exists; He is

this, that and the other; He loves you; you can trust Him;
I accepted without question. I was ready to believe that
God, having given me breath, having made me out of
nothing, was something upon which I depended wholly.
But it was from *His* end that the dependence was imposed.
I was His creature. Something desperate and sorrowful in
my mother's tone gave me the impression that it was the
other way about – that God was a creation due to her need,
not she to His; that even if, by some dreadful chance, He
wasn't really there, she would have to substitute faith in
faith for faith in Him. But surely faith in faith is not the
same as faith in God.

My father and mother were, I am sure, true believers.
So true that in so far as they passed on to me in early
childhood a strong, unquestioning faith in an all-sustaining,
beneficent and just creator, I shall never be able wholly to
rid myself of that instinctive trust. It has done much for
me. But my parents lived at a time when orthodox faith
was being closely questioned, when modern science was
a new religion, when the first tremblings and differences
were beginning and when uncertainty was in the air. The
era of faith in God was passing into the era when the
choice was between faith in faith and faith in science,
when, desperately, those who would once have believed
in God clung not to God but to a need in themselves which
could create God as a projection of themselves. I believe,
moreover, that this element of dissolution has always been
present in Christ's teaching, as distinct from the teaching
of Jehovah or of Mahomet, or indeed, from the religions
of Greece and Rome. All that about the grains of mustard
seed and about removing mountains shifted the onus of
faith, made of it a psychology, a science, centred on the
believer, not on the divinity.

There is a deeper wisdom than one's nature, and this
wisdom, won, as it were, against one's natural bent, will
open deeper springs than one suspected. Are these also
part of one's nature, or from that outside source we call
God? It does not matter. By means of their nourishment
we are enlarged, even transformed. Like the vast majority

of children of my generation I was born into and reared up in the Christian faith. For better or for worse I shall never be wholly rid of the deeply instilled confidence that 'Underneath are the Everlasting Arms'. The belief is mine no longer. The confidence reasserts itself spasmodically. The emotion remains, and the hope. I am of those who will be glad should they find that a good God exists, even should it be to my confusion.

PART IV
POEMS

The poems range over almost thirty years. Many were destroyed by the author, but a search of magazines published in the last few decades might considerably enlarge the small collection given here. These, however, are all that were left among her papers. They are printed in chronological order of composition, so far as I have been able to establish it. The first three pieces were never finished. [J.C.]

I

Fortunate swan, thrice enviable dove,
Care without love is yours, desire without
Or duty or imagination.
Let fox or kestrel make one cygnet less
You'll lay no nestling feather by
For heavy, cisterned tears to fall upon;
Or, outmatched losing all your season's brood
Will get another every way as good
After brief flurry staying not in mind.

.   .   .

Can live and take another, or can pine
And shortly die without once wondering
How the sweet mate may be, where gone or
    loving whom.

II

I tied my joys in one fine sheaf
I hid my woes away with curses.
But down my years a nimble thief
Slides out his finger and reverses

All that my wasteful heart rehearses [.]
Where was my joy is now my grief.

I bent my strength so to employ
What chance brought in to form a shelter [.]
Here love should dwell and never cloy,
Here escape from mortal welter

III

. . .

Brown breathing furnaces the cattle stand [:]
I watch while old Cornelius brown and slow
Tends them with voice and hand [.]
The mist is clearing. For all men say or do
Old people know a thing or two.

. . .

And when old country people die
Dies also much sagacity.

IV

Gentleman Farmer

Vapours, night-created,
Stand on the barley-field,
Till the bright warmth with quiet awaited
Shines, and I watch them yield
In swift submission to the sun.
Straight they are gone, their life's work done
All sweetly unbelated !

Next come the scythes for reaping,
Labourers to bind,
Order of harvest keeping
As in time out of mind.

Glad on the hill the foreman's shout
Rings as he turns the beasts about
Heavily homeward creeping.

Birds on the barn roof hanging
Seaward at dawn will start.
The snake his girdled coat is changing;
Each knows his place and part.
Bird, beast, mist, seed – here's none will stay
Ignorant, questioning its way,
Save my unpunctual heart.

V

i

In word, in act, this man was slow and faltering,
In gainful deeds feeble while he had breath.
But being swift in love, sure, never altering,
He triumphs and grows eloquent in death.

ii

This man was reckoned wise:
Perhaps he was
Because
To love and suffering he closed his eyes.

iii

He has his faults. Not one of these I'd spare.
They make of him, as Shakespeare says somewhere,
A man for whom one must sincerely care.
It is his virtues that are hard to bear.

iv

To be alive is vulgar, you have said.
And you, my love, are usually right.
But have you thought, my love, that it is quite
As vulgar, if not more so, to be dead.

VI

On the stale platform I saw a porter suddenly dancing.
A station porter clapping his hands and springing.
Soiled, heavy body on small feet retiring advancing
To the music of a weary harmonica and pale soldiers
    singing.

VII

Hands of Soldiers[1]

Crashing rattling banging pounding down the
    metalled road
Which nowhere yields,
Putting nerves and bomb-damaged houses ajar
Comes the lorry load
Closepacked,standing,youngmenfromEastAnglian
    fields,
Italians. Prisoners of war.

Un-Anglian eyes flash. Tuscan tongues gabble in
    mock suit
To the woman on her doorstep alone,
That woman I.
Laughter goes up. Hands frolic the fascist salute
To the English sky.
Then they are gone.

O but I am haunted by the hands of the young man,
Small, vulnerable, bare,
The hands of the soldier everywhere
Since history began,

1. The anatomical drawing of a hand is pinned to the
manuscript of this poem. [J. C.]

At all times the same, in all places.
Skulls vary and faces, armour changes,
Battles are not the same, nor armament.
There are fashions in dread.
But the hand that arranges,
Carries, drags, salutes, props the tired head,
Curls the fingers in death, this is no different.
Hands of the Axis men, hands of the Allies,
Hands on land, at sea, in skies,
Hands of the local warden,
Are the hands of ancient Roman, Spartan, Philistine,
Are the hands of Adam in the garden,
The hands of Jesus in Palestine.

Frail fronds of bone and flesh,
White nerved to each tip, blue veined on tender
    inward of each wrist,
Delicate intricate mesh
That spreads tapering or bunches to a fist:
Naked tendrils, sentient, remote,
Articulate, informed, unguarded, they emerge
From each sleeve of khaki, from the seaman's serge,
From the captive's ugly coat.

To them earth owes each single enterprise,
Without them love herself loses her eyes,
But fashioning with dove-tail skill the Trojan horse
They now press triggers and tap out death in Morse.

O they haunt me the hands of soldiers, the hands
    of the young men.
When will they reach
In good will each to each
Across the world they made, Christ, when?
I shall be dead, but happy, happy those who will live
    then.

VIII

Envoy

It will not be long now, my soul.
Not long,
Till that comes that filled you with fears
These many years,
But now not at all.

I have had children, I have had lovers
I feared to leave.
Now I am alone. I have put all from me,
And have ceased to grieve.

Once, long ago, I was alone,
Before life took me and played with my heart.
Now, again, my solitary fountain
Rises apart.

In joy it rises
From a deeper source than before,
Joy to have lived, and this deeper joy
Soon to live no more.

PART V
LETTERS

Dear Florence

I'm glad you got back all right last Monday. Still more glad if you find things straightened out a bit as a result of our talking them over. When you use such a phrase as feeling – or rather *having* felt, on trying to write the love scenes, as if you were 'stripping naked in public', it shows clearly how hopeless *as a writer* your attitude of mind has been. In a pure autobiography or diary there may possibly and permissibly be something of this feeling, but in an autobiographical novel of the kind you are trying to write nothing is any good until you get somehow a stage *removed* from the self of the story, outside of that self, cool, critical, perhaps even hostile, having exchanged *human* sympathy for that very different commodity artistic or literary sympathy towards your characters. Not till then anyhow will the characters assume that life of their own which they need both to make a book and truly to relieve you. During this process it is true you need to face yourself – if you like to strip naked, but the stripping is between yourself and God, *not* before the public. As a matter of strict truth one gives a reader far more the unpleasant sensation of witnessing such a public exposure when one draws veils, leaves blank canvases and shrouds all up in vagueness, for one then conveys a sense of shame and half-heartedness. It is by facing oneself and by then – if one must and has the impulse – standing off and telling one's story firmly, unfalteringly, as clearly as one can that one retains in absolute secrecy and possession and privacy whatever secret inner truth there may be in one's experience. This is all rather badly put, but I'm sure it is true.

Yours affectionately, *Catherine*.

TO F. MARIAN MCNEILL   *21st February 1927*

. . . But how are you, and is there any word of your being in London these days? Let me have a line some time. We have been up and down and have all had colds but not flu so far. We continue to sink deeper and deeper into debt week by week. Don is putting in for another post (this time his friends are running him for a job he would not have thought of applying for himself), which is anyhow cheering, and of course, we can't help hoping a bit as usual. But it is admittedly only a try as there will be many men senior to him at the Bar who will go for it, and, of course, *their* friends will back them. Anyway he is now beginning the 6th and last of the biographical essays – Andrew Lang, and Sadleir is very enthusiastic so far over the others. Glad to see the Muirs translation of Jew Süss is going so well and is so highly praised too. I *do* hope they get royalties on the sales ! I am toying with the idea of doing a small book on Robert Burns, but please do not mention this *to a soul*. Not that I have started yet or anything like.

Love from us, *Catherine*.

TO F. MARIAN MCNEILL   *27th November 1927*

My dear Florence
I got back on Thursday night feeling tremendously stimulated by my week in Scotland. In Dumfries I was particularly happy and longed to stay on ever so much longer. Now my spirit quails at the work and duties in arrears, so that goodness knows how I'm ever to get under way with R. B. and I'm just straining to be at him though I know it is going to be difficult. Still the *efflatus* is there all right and that's everything. I went twice to Ayr, Mauchline, Tarbolton, saw a lot in Glasgow and had wonderful luck in being allowed special access to Museum MSS. and so on. At Dumfries I fell in love! No more on that head, but it has done me *good*!

Love from *Catherine*.

TO F. MARIAN MCNEILL *12th December 1927*

Dear Florence

I'm having a time of it. Our char still ill and her young daughter substitute not at all efficient. J.P. with a temperature and a violent attack of nettle-rash, my hands partly incapacitated by burns (the oven went on fire last Sunday!). Still I have made a beginning (a tiny one) to the Burns and shall – I hope, get it under way while in the Hartz.

The publisher Murray is so keen on *Brother Scots* that he has asked Don (through Curtis Brown) if he will write a book on Scott's Circle (Sir Walter's) to be ready in 1929, a year or so before the Scott centenary. Don likes the idea so is accepting. Of course the money isn't a living wage but they are willing to put some down *at once* on signing the Contract. This is a great point! We hope to get it for our fares this week. Not sure yet how much. Soon there ought to be a little more from Constables . . . He is also thinking about a play which I feel might turn out really fresh and good. (3 Acts – Scottish.) So much for work.

My librarian at Dumfries thinks highly too of Lewis Spence. I must get his poems.

Don says he did *not* say Scots culture was English with a Scottish accent. He said that Scots culture is an English culture merely as a fact in history, *i.e.* it is not a Celtic culture, though of course it has Celtic elements. It is not English in the narrow political sense, but 'descriptively' it must be called an English culture and has been so ever since Scotland was Scotland.

However no more now. Yes, Dunbar – how does it go: –

> London, thou art the flower of cities all!

So, you see what *he* thought! But, as I say, no more!

We are off – all being well next Sunday as ever is. I shall write you a full, true, and accurate account.

Our love to you, *Catherine*.

TO F. MARIAN MCNEILL   *24th April 1928*

My dear Flos

I wrote a long letter to you and next day decided not to
send it, as I felt the matter could not be helpfully thrashed
out in letters. You needn't have worried as I wasn't a bit
shocked or anything of that sort.

We must have a real long talk some day – though, of
course, one knows by experience that this is not always
helpful either.

I'm determined for your sake as well as for my own,
not to write at length today! Must however say one or
two things as briefly as possible.

I would never dream of suggesting that my way (or
Joanna's[1] which is not identical with mine except in certain
respects) should be indicated as your way . . . or as you put
it 'Everybody's'. My truth is only valuable in that it is mine.
The only point is that Joanna does fashion or find out *some*
way for herself and *some* truth. Whereas — remains vague
and without a clear impulse.

I'm sure your trouble is (and it sticks out in your letter
and in your phraseology and in your habits of thought)
that you are too much given over to *ideas* which have not
sprung straight from your own experience but have been
imported from without by reading, etc. and always through
the intellect first. This is all very well for the undergraduate
stage. Such expressions as 'wild love', 'bitter virginity',
'children for the sake of children', and all the heredity
business or the explanation of one's difficulties by reason
of one's heredity are essentially adolescent expressions.
The time should come when experience and personal,
individual emotion breaks through and transmutes and
crystallises the whole thing. Till that comes, as I see it,
there can be no sense of creation. It is all floundering
in a morass of ready-made ideas which have life only
in so far as they are handled and re-created afresh
by each new soul. Each soul must cut some time or

1. The heroine of her first (and semi-autobiographical)
novel *Open the Door!*.

other the umbilical cord and stand up in its essential integrity, knowing that there is a birth independent of heredity, nation, accident and all else. And if there is not there is no creative soul. There are no valid excuses or explanations. Every individual has enough hereditary difficulties, repulses, etc. – some more than others – and it is not always the most happily dowered who succeed in the necessary rebirth, the breaking free, the proud arising of the new naked soul from the morass with the declaration – 'here I am'.

You are sincere, but it is not enough. More important is it to find one's own truth.

And with all your sincerity you lie when you describe your heredity and then say – 'result' – I am this, that and the other. It is the devil's own subtle lie which is so easily imposed upon us to excuse ourselves to ourselves. You must be able by the force of your own individual *emotion* (not by your thinking) to repudiate your parentage, your country, all that has gone before, in the rising of that self which Christ so well understood when he told people to forsake all while at the same time 'all these things would be added unto them'.

To intellectualise is the temptation and the disaster. You stay dallying with ideas and not once does the clear urgency and emotion break through.

Have to go now. Shall write another time. All news then.

Love from *Cathie*.

TO F. MARIAN MCNEILL   *30th April 1928*

Dearest Flos

Just got home today – and after a day of it feel *dead* tired. I'm delighted to hear you are coming up. It will make a break for you. This apart from our looking forward to seeing you. And I do hope we shall have a chance of a talk. I'm afraid till we have had a talk we shall only plunge deeper in by putting things in writing. To take a single instance I can see we have a different notion of what I mean by 'intellectualising'. The *essentially* intellectual being does not 'intellectualise', as it is natural and therefore right for him (if he exists!) to deal with life through the intellect. But for a woman or any being whose nature it is to live through the emotions, clarity of mind can only be got by taking the natural order. And I do think many of us thinking and educated women of this age – go against our natures by striving to *force* ourselves to deal first through the intellect, living too much with ideas and not sufficiently trusting ourselves to the truths that would come to us through the deeper sensual and emotional channels. So we get confused, uncreative, and 'pathological'. This is not very well put. I wonder if it conveys anything to you. You see I feel that all those remarks about 'primitive types' and so on are a kind of jargon, and an adding of confusion to the issue.

To *think* for me is entirely different from to 'intellectualise'. One can and should *think* with all one's being – *thought* to be real must be linked up with the stream of the blood. The intellectualising business uses *other people's* experience and borrowed stuff and is a sort of cutting off and cowardice. But perhaps you will feel this is twisting words . . .

                                        Love from *Cathie*.

TO F. MARIAN MCNEILL   *8th May 1928*

Dearest Flos
Let us conspire together to be truly courageous. In spite of all my talk, my troubles and temptations are much the same as yours. From today I am going to put up a better fight. I'm going to sit down to Burns before I give my little strength to journalism or even household duties or any other distractions. This is *very* difficult for me both practically and by habit and temperament. More than you

think. But I'm going to try and to go on trying even after repeated failures.

Try you each day *before* doing any work for your employer, to spend anyhow one hour in writing. Don't attempt to tackle your novel just now. Write down your observations and feelings – principally your observations – of each day. Note significant incidents and scraps of dialogue. Begin a character sketch of Miss——, of the tired housekeeper, of her two old parents. Add to them as new material occurs in the course of each day. *Watch* them like a lynx. Note down your own clear reactions of contempt, pity, amusement, disgust. Try to describe boredom by noting incidents and sayings. Avoid abstract emotion in your notes as far as possible. Do not once look back into your own life unless for an apposite incident. Write a description of Sunday dinner and the visitors. Describe your day, Miss——'s day, the housekeeper's day. Don't bother about style, but be as exact as you can and select the significant things. Don't invent at all.

Even if stories or a book do not eventually come out of this (and I believe they will) I'm certain the exercise will be good for you, interesting, clarifying. Forget all about your novel for the present. This will help you in it later if it is to be at all. You *can write* as you show in your letters. Don't waste your substance just now in long letters to friends. Get a big MS. book or whatever suits you in that way. Probably you will soon find yourself wanting to write in it a bit at night as well. But you must give the best morning hour to it.

My love to you, *Cathie*.

P.S. Also make careful exact nature notes, garden notes, etc. – the look of things as they strike you. Do not force anything or *try* to write about them. But look carefully and listen and *wait* till something really strikes you through your eyes or emotions (not through something you have read). Describe the rooms, the house, the food . . . *C.*

[Outside the envelope]
Keep as well a little diary just as a record of the day's work
and to record faithfulness or failure. One must fail fairly
often and not care *too* much. *C.*

TO F. MARIAN MCNEILL   *15th May 1928*

Dearest Flos
. . . Thanks very much for sending off the notice. We look
forward to seeing it. There have been one or two quite useful
ones about last Sunday's performance[1] which everyone
seemed to think went better than the first. By the way, it
was I, not Don, who advised the fingers to nose attitude.
And it was not intended as a particular attitude towards
specific things – God forbid! but as a *general* attitude when
up against people and life in general.

How are you getting on? I have really been working very
steadily every day and neglecting all else and though dog
tired at night have the satisfaction that it is the right kind of
tiredness. And I'm giving up my sleep in the day time and
not being overcome with sleep. I'm convinced that a good
deal of my horrid exhaustion is due to my not working at
the real right thing. So it is – severe illness apart – with
most of us, I do believe.

Don is going on with the play and has begun to rewrite
it. Thorndike seriously wants it. So we must just go in for
the gamble. Besides Don is keen now, and full of ideas.
No more now.

Much love from *Cathie.*

TO F. MARIAN MCNEILL   *16th June 1928*

My dear Florence
The flowers came yesterday – all right except the yellow
broom which does not seem to like travelling – the

1. Of her husband's play, *Count Albany*.

love-in-a-mist, beautifully fresh. The box more or less
'kaput', but I have posted it back today enclosed in a
sound one to make up for the box before.

The play goes on – is pretty nearly done and so far
Thorndike says he likes it very much. Don has been
sending scenes on to T. as he writes them. The other
night J——[1] came in – 'well disguised in liquor'. He
told us Don's play had put him on to reading up Prince
Charlie who had always been his great hero, he had had
a pile of books sent him from the Advocates library in
Edinburgh, etc., and had been forced to the conclusion
that Charlie was a 'twister' and N.B.G.! Not only this, but
practically everybody connected with him (of any repute)
in Scotland, were twisters too! At the same time J. holds
that the romantic business ought to be and must be upheld
at all costs!

  Burns goes on, though not at all fast. I'm horribly tired
these days. We have both been pretty hard and steadily at
work, but earning practically nothing, which is a worry.
And Doran refuses to advance anything on the Scott book
– rather a blow . . .

Much love and thanks, Cathie.

TO F. MARIAN MCNEILL   *3rd April 1929*

My dear Florence
I know . . . I had always wanted to write and answer your
letter, but . . . well you know how if there is nothing urgent
to say and one is tired and working, letters get shoved on
one side!

About half the Burns book (nearly 50,000) is written and
Gollancz has read it and thinks he will certainly want to

---

1. James Fairley, a Scots senior journalist on the
Beaverbrook press.

make an offer when he sees the rest. Bell is keen too and my agent Pinker is going to try some others with this first half. If only the rest were written! But for weeks I have done practically nothing at it and now John is at home on holiday and it is all I can do to get through my various jobs. The trouble is I am tired – feeling my eyes too and having headaches fairly often, and I have been fearfully depressed of late about the book and most other things. But I *will* get on with it and finish it somehow or other. I had to spend weeks revising and re-typing that first half to make it presentable for sending round. Anyhow I have found out why the existing lives of B. are – to my mind – so unsatisfactory, and incidentally why I should be surprised if anybody else is trying to do him just now – it is a damned difficult life to write, even adequately. I shall be awfully interested if anybody else does do it. An essay – yes; a long, formless collection of facts – yes again. But to build up the life fully and in true proportions – well I'm not sure that it can be done, still less sure if I can do it. An attempt shall be made. That's all I can say. – Don sends much love.

So do I, *Cathie*.

TO F. MARIAN MCNEILL　　　　　　　　*19th July 1929*

Dearest Florence

. . . I'm in the train coming back from staying two nights with Phyllis Clay down in Surrey. It was lovely, peaceful, orderly, and I was taken over a house and garden that caused one or two pangs of jealousy – but no, I don't specially want all that and I could not have stayed long without breaking out in some way. Phyllis is so sweet and an old friend, but oh they are rather among the people who think we should be more decent if we had our navels sewn up in infancy and so obliterated.

I'm having a dose of the country as we are going, all three, to the inn at Kingshill for this coming week-end – John's half-term holiday. Work goes on hopefully, even excitingly but still lots to do. Since writing to you I truly believe I have straightened out, without taking any liberties, the story of Burns over his crucial period (covering the Jean business, Highland Mary, the publication of the poems, etc.) *for the first time*. This simply because not one other biographer has taken the trouble to grapple afresh with the existing evidence. They have one and all followed Lockhart and L. has been in certain vital questions mistaken. He has, for instance, given an admittedly supposititious date to an undated letter upon which much turns and *I'm sure* after long, long pondering and re-examinations that he has dated it wrongly and so has gone astray. The interesting things are – 1. That the whole story now becomes simple, free from 'mysteries' and altogether credible and moving – where before all was question and confusion, and 2. that with all the attention Scotsmen have paid to Burns, not one has taken this amount of trouble to ponder over the evidence. I don't say my book is well written and I know it is full of faults, but if ever I get it done I shall have contributed an honourable and honest piece of research to my country, and *how furious* they will be to have R.B. brought out of the mist they have loved to keep about him! Well, well.

Scott – *Gott sei lob und dank* – is finished! But perhaps I have already told you this. I've only finished typing it though. Now there are the short essays – Hogg, Lockhart, etc., to be done. Can they be finished in time for Autumn publication is the question . . . If only we were a bit quicker!

Just getting into Charing X. so adieu. Life thrills me just now but things are no easier. Why is this?

Love from us both, *Cathie*.

TO F. MARIAN MCNEILL   *13th September 1929*

Thank you so much for the poems which I've read, enjoyed and instantly forgotten. She seems to me to have technique, sensitiveness, but no special impulse. There is not one *fused* poem in that book. Of course she may have done others that were. But after reading say Charlotte Mew's poems or Edna Millay's – what a difference! All the same thanks and I shall carefully return the book. I've been very seedy – like a lot of other people here – up to now, but better now. The other 2 very well. No rent from the studio and now we hear it has been burgled! By God's grace I had pawned the few bits of silver we had and left the clock at Fanny's flat, so they took mainly our non-paying tenant's things and some plated spoons of ours. All the same it is a nasty feeling. I've been very depressed here in spite of the loveliness and the superb weather. Work goes terribly slowly.

Love from *Catherine*.

TO F. MARIAN MCNEILL   *16th October 1929*

Dearest Florence

. . . Yesterday we spent several hours of the afternoon talking to your friend Mrs. Wells from Oxford on 'Le Mouvement Écossais'. What an attractive little thing she is. However once more I am going to deny myself the luxury of a long letter, and go to bed. I've done five hours good at Burns today and a good whack of journalism and was feeling well satisfied and determined to go to bed when – at 10.30, in comes J., dead drunk! Now he is by the fire talking rot and before there is any rest for us he must be humoured, given tea and conveyed on his way home. It is damned things like this that always scupper me when I feel I'm getting under way steadily. Last night a similar demand, though of a different sort; and the night before, Don's parents. Even with refusing invitations it seems almost impossible.

Never mind, I go every morning to a lovely secret room where I have the right to be sole undisturbed occupant all the hours of daylight. It is in Keats Grove, with no telephone and with a French window opening on to a quiet old autumn garden. It is so wonderful *knowing* that one can't be called upon. Long may it last . . .

Love from *Catherine*.

TO F. MARIAN MCNEILL   *27th October 1929*

My dear Florence

The postman brought your honey safe. He was in fact covered with it and smelt 'Of Scotia and of Aberdeen' –

in spite of which there was any amount of it left for us and we are eating it with the greatest enjoyment. It really does taste and smell of heather. Thank you *very* much.

I think there's no use in worrying over publishers and their shortcomings. One just has to do what one can calmly to keep them to it and *go on with producing*. Not to waste any real energy on them (or anyone else's wrong doings) is one of the most important things in life. I have learned this – among many other things – from D. H. Lawrence, whose treatment has been of the worst description. *Not to lose one bit of wool* for them, to get on with one's work. It is the only wisdom and it pays in the end . . .

Love from us, Yours ever, Catherine.

TO F. MARIAN MCNEILL   *4th December 1929*

Dear Florence
. . . Still mostly work and worry here – fortunately the two are separate, the work being mostly great joy; but it is always haunted by the question – can I get it done in time and can we live till we are done? These two days I've been down with a sick headache which has gravely cut into my hours. I've had the satisfaction today of typing the last pages of Don's *Lockhart*. Now there's only Joanna Baillie and he vows she is to be short. I've been having a glorious time with Burns and Clarinda – such fun! But there has been knot after knot to untie all along my way and I *would not* go on till I had done my best with each. Otherwise a new *Life* has no value.

As usual heaps to say, but time and strength fail. I could not resist going to two parties last week and enjoyed both tremendously, but I'm paying now . . .

Love from us, Cathie.

TO F. MARIAN MCNEILL   *30th March 1930*

Dearest Florence
. . . One relief – and disappointment – but more relief. The Burns is not to come out till September. As things are, even

if I killed myself it could not come out till June, which is a bad time for this kind of long book . . .

No more now. Easter plans still undecided. Much depends on if we can shunt John for a fortnight – Love and thanks. Be still my soul! – *Catherine*.

My dear Cousin M—— after my broadcast on B's birthday wrote to the B.B.C. saying 'have we not had enough about this *dissolute* creature'? She consulted her sister as to the advisability of adding, 'have we not had enough of those Carswells?' But prudence forbade. Scotland, my dear, my native land!

TO F. MARIAN MCNEILL   *[? May 1930]*

I've been very depressed. No money, heaps of difficulties. Don's book hung up through no fault of his, my Burns going to take me all my time to get in by the middle of June. I've been *crazy* with exhaustion some days. Somewhat cheered this morning by hearing from Prof. de Lancey Ferguson in America, who has read the ¾ of the MS. that's there, that he thinks 'it gives a juster view of Burns' character and temperament than that has been written yet'. But perhaps he is just being kind. He has been awfully decent going through the MS. for mistakes and I'm glad he finds so few. I don't think he really approves of my *method*. However—.

We have been seeing Aldous Huxley. There has been a painful-comic *geschichte* over the literary executorship of D. H. Lawrence. Great snakes – what a business of intrigues and recriminations! Huxley is decent I think. Murry is *not*, but thinks he is . . .

I am compelled to break off here

My love, dear Florence, *Cath*.

TO F. MARIAN MCNEILL   *13th June 1930*

Dearest Florence
I long to write to you and keep thinking a lot about you, but it will have to be next week before I can write a real letter.

Working 6 to 7 hours a day at the last chapters of my MS. partly dictating to a typist. Hope to get the end off by Tuesday if I keep at it. Proofs already coming in and I hear they have had really good enquiries from the Scotch trade.

Constant headache and a bad cold and frightful exhaustion.

I do hope you have got away and that you are feeling and sleeping better. I have been sleepless also – damnable! Try to *die down* – die to emotion and reasoning and all. Just be a winter plant and have faith and wait.

Love from Catherine.

TO F. MARIAN MCNEILL   *16th July 1930*

Dearest Florence
Every single flower is blooming in exquisite freshness now in the studio – the roses in particular as if they had just been picked. I know a thing or two also about how to deal with travelled flowers (*hot* water for the newly cut stems I use anyhow for the roses) but I expect your way is as good. Anyhow they could not be lovelier or sweeter or more glowing. *Thanks.*

I've just written my preface – which you will notice is intended to meet my native critics on the threshold and give pause! Please return with the proofs as this is my American MS. and I have not kept another copy.

As dedication I want if possible to have:

> Without D. H. Lawrence, my friend, and Donald Carswell, my husband, this book could not have been. I therefore inscribe it to them both.

What do you think?

Have not yet got hold of that last batch of letters and am afraid to stir from the house lest I'm rung up about them.

I've dated the preface *for fun* from Paris on the date of

the fall of the Bastille. I happened to write it on that date and I shall soon be in France anyhow!

Love from *Catherine*.

TO F. MARIAN MCNEILL   *17th September 1930*

So glad to hear, though I *wish* things were better. I'll write within the next few days. Are you at Dunoon? Send me your address when you move. I've asked Chatto to send you some prospecti. Thanks very much. What think you of the *Record*?[1] All hashed about, of course, but it comes through wonderfully well and I'm so glad of the chance to get at the common reader for whom the book is fundamentally intended. The highbrows can fall into line later if they like. If not *je m'en fiche*! It is hard getting started again on meals and things. All news presently.

Love, *Catherine*.

TO F. MARIAN MCNEILL   *2nd November 1930*

Dearest Flos

. . . The reviewers here continue to be patronising on the whole when not actually hostile. But a good one by Richard Aldington in today's *Referee* and long good*ish* ones in *Spectator* and *New Statesman*. Horrid and silly ones in *John o' London's* and *Everyman*. Pretty good one in *Weekend Review*. None nearly so enthusiastic as the ones I get from readers – Prof. Nichol Smith, Prof. Ferguson, etc.

What news of your novel now? I've been reading a marvellous first novel – *Look Homeward Angel* by Thomas Wolfe (North Carolina but Scoto-Irish extraction with a dash of German somewhere, barely 30, stands 6 ft. 5 and

---

1. *The Life of Robert Burns* had been appearing in parts in
the *Daily Record*, and had roused bitter opposition from
certain leaders of the Burns Federation.

magnificent – at the same time *very* lovable). He is our newest friend and we are very happy together. We had a good evening here the other night – but one pays later for talking till 3 a.m. He then went home *to work*! Oh youth! To think he might easily be my son! I wish he were.

Have just seen today's *Express* that my Lord Castlerosse finds my Burns very dull, and 'dragging like an ill-made skirt'.

By the way I am making up to date 2 Burns orations in Scotland in January – the second being at the Paisley Art Club on January 27th. I look forward to this though Lord knows if I can do the thing acceptably. Anyway it's a slap in the eye for the B.F.'s.

The other day by a happy chance I was able to read the last (as yet unobtainable in England) Lawrence book – *The Escaped Cock* – theme the coming out of the tomb and going to Egypt of a Jesus who had not really died on the Cross. Originally it was called 'The Man Who Died'. I believe it to be the loveliest and most original story of our generation. Its sheer fragrance and freshness made me hold my breath. Oh why is Lawrence dead! Yet I don't believe that any but a dying man could have written it . . .

Much love to you, *Catherine*.

TO HILDA BONAVIA *5th December 1930*

My dear Hilda
. . . I wish Christmas was over! It seems to be coming on this year like a sort of steam-roller! Did I tell you that Lytton Strachey was praising up my Burns at some highbrow party at Lady Ottoline Morrell's? Still it does not seem to be rushing by any manner of means . . . I don't think, with this visit to Scotland in January, I shall be able to start the novel till Spring. How lovely it would be to roll up in a ball and hibernate till then – so economical too! But no such luck for poor humans . . .

Love from *Catherine*.

TO F. MARIAN MCNEILL   *24th December 1930*

Dearest Flos

Christmas this year has got me fairly beat! Things are *too* difficult. John is in bed with a cold and not eating (he did not properly throw off the last cold and the fogs have done him in). I have had a sort of flu myself and feel no use. Don's father is 'dying' each day and bullying Don by the hour together, etc. etc.

I don't like Christmas! Some kind unknown[1] has sent us a hamper from Fortnum and Masons full of goodies, however, which at least will look cheerful.

    Thanks for the charming little feather which I shall stick in my hat to buck me up . . . *Catherine.*

Ivy Litvinoff missed her train on Monday night and slept on our sofa, getting away last night. This put the final touch of demoralisation to my Xmas preparations!

TO F. MARIAN MCNEILL   *19th February 1931*

Dearest Flos

. . . You will have had my letter crossing yours. Perhaps by now you have heard from Blake or G.M.T.[2] But don't count on anything there. Look forward, forward only to new things. The novel *really* belongs to your past. It is the awful money business, I know. *Tomorrow* I hope to post you the Ovarine tablets, and you should try taking a teasp. of Kruschen each morning half an hour before breakfast in hot water, whole tumblerful. You must sternly *ask* to be paid for those overdue articles. Meanwhile quite soon I may be able to send you along something just to be going on with.

I'm *really pleased* with the opening of my novel and the way the theme develops in my mind. I only wish I could

1. John Buchan.
2. George Malcolm Thomson.

do nothing else for the next 6 months. But the great thing is I'm in good spirits and my headaches nothing to bother about.

Tonight I hear from the *Adelphi* that they are delighted with my suggestion of supplementing Murry's Reminiscences of Lawrence with *my* reminiscences over the same period. It would begin in the June number and run to 12,000 words. Might get about £50 for that, besides attention. There will be a note by me in the March *Adelphi* replying to an attack on my Burns in the February issue by somebody signing G. Brown. It was in a covering letter to this note – dashed off 2 nights ago – that I made the Lawrence suggestion. It gives me a chance if only I can use it. But the difficulties are many and peculiar. Pray for me.

I've sent two poems in the Vernacular (did I tell you?) to Whyte for the *Modern Scot*, but I daresay he won't take them. I've got stories and articles *seething* in my head. All I need is to be financed for a year or so. Don is working hard and I'm *sure* his de Quincey will be good. For one thing he finds de Q. an entirely sympathetic character, so it will be a change. There is too such a good *group* to deal with. It is always the present that is so difficult. But we shall win through if we keep our hearts up. I *know* my novel is a corker if I can keep going and get it done as I see it. It is *really fresh* and the theme makes a vehicle for things I'm longing to say. This, nowadays, is almost the only kind of novel that interests me.

I saw the *New York Times* review – a page with a picture (spurious) of Burns. I'm told it should be very useful.

Bath – bed. After all a long letter! Goodnight, Flos, and get some of them to pay up.

We still hope to come North at Easter. Mrs. Maxtone Graham wrote to say she might call on us in London before then. I've heard from Rafferty (nice boy that and a talent), McVie, Muir, etc. etc. Yesterday a *lovely* letter from a very old apparently bed-ridden man in Kilmarnock who says he couldn't finish his breakfast he was so moved by the end of my Burns.

I had a long letter in the *Irvine Herald*. And the *Glasgow*

Herald did my eight guinea article *at once*. Not sent the money yet though!

More again. *Must* go now. Had a dissipated day.

Love from *Cath*.

TO F. MARIAN MCNEILL   *23rd March 1931*

Dearest Flos

. . . I feel limp, aching, and a bit despairing after two more teeth out and the prospect of two more to come out next week. I don't so much mind the extractions themselves (gas gives me lovely dreams and great exhilaration afterwards for an hour or two!) though I hate losing my faithful old teeth; but unfortunately I'm one of those who ache severely for several days afterwards, and last time I got one of my old sick headaches again (after thinking I was done with them) of the very worst type. I tried to go out in the afternoon, after lying down for 6 hours or so, to fulfil an engagement and was fearfully sick in the bus – this is the last humiliation – but I did it so discreetly that nobody noticed!

We have been seeing far too many people of late really and keeping absurd hours. It has been amusing but bad for work. Nothing goes on. It is depressing and absurd.

We are lunching with Whyte tomorrow and he supped here the other night with Prentice (partner in Chatto's) which went off very well. I expect to see Rafferty this week. Did I tell you of our waif? The American boy who wrote from Germany on having read my Burns to say it had kept him from going off his head? He turned up with a little suitcase, no hat, a short sailor's coat, upstanding curly hair and about three shillings in the world! Oh wise and valiant youth! He slept on our sofa for the ten days, met through us Gordon Craig, Nigel Playfair, David Garnett, etc., and instead of having to tramp to Southampton for his boat as he had intended, went by train, with a whole £1 sent for him by my friend Binnie in Glasgow – it arrived just in time. The boy was charming – name John Parke. Wants to write, of course, and we may hear of him later. We miss him, but were relieved that he caught his boat!

Whyte is putting my two little Scots poems in his next number. Don't know how they will look, I'm sure. But I guess all the pundits will jump on my brand of synthetic Scots and say it isn't anything. What does it matter!

Yes, it is beastly never being able to get new clothes one chooses oneself and how tiresome all the shifts of poverty to oneself, and alas to others. The clown Grock was wise, but what is one to do when one simply cannot hide it? I was talking a good deal to Whyte about you and he obviously likes and admires you and really had no idea of how bad things are with you. He said, 'she always looks so well dressed and so dignified' – so you can put that feather in your hat, Flos! I know he will do anything for you should the chance come along, and has even got schemes in which you will be implicated. We must all hang on a bit longer. I get encouraging news from U.S.A. and more good reviews (no publishers' statements for a while yet) and I have a ticket and a half for the Irish Sweep, which is being run on my birthday. We may turn up trumps yet!

Must get lunch now, make the beds, etc., then I do believe I shall lie down and snooze!

Our love to you, and hoping to see you soon, *Cath*.

TO F. MARIAN MCNEILL   *17th August 1931*

Dearest Flos
We have definitely given up the studio and are now trying to get rid of the very nice flat near Chalk Farm for which we rather hastily entered into a 5 years lease because after long uncertainty I managed to get the Keats Grove cottage, where you slept those nights! We go in there on September 29 and hope by letting off some of the rooms to live there almost rent free. It wants a good deal done but the landlord is putting in a bath and we are putting in electric light. It should be very peaceful and pleasant and is conveniently opposite the Keats House which is now a public library and reading-room. As we were in very low waters I sold

(unwillingly) my Lawrence letters. Got £230 for them and
paid only £10 commission to—— who did the deal for
me. We have paid over £100 off in debt and now will get
a holiday and a fresh start. I know Lawrence would have
said 'sell them'. But I had hoped to leave them to John.
The man who has them will probably get £800 for them
later on. Naturally I have kept copies of them all.

I think I told you that the Burns had really marvellous
reviews in U.S.A. My publisher sent a whole big batch
– all good and long and not one person shocked! But
the sales are not marvellous. Only about 1500 there. Still
selling, however, so I might later get something, accounts
not due till later.

Suddenly (I got breakfast for the family soon after 7 this
morning) I feel overwhelmed with sleep! . . .

My love and blessings, *Catherine*.

TO F. MARIAN MCNEILL   *5th October 1931*

Dearest Flos
. . . I'd like to give you all our news but it would take
many papers and I've had to give up writing letters as
far as possible (eyes) and every bit of the day is spent
strenuously at above address where we are struggling with
dilapidations, etc., and trying to prepare things for our
entry. Had meant to move the furniture in tomorrow but
impossible, so have postponed the actual removal to next
Monday, lots to put straight before then, meanwhile we are
camping at Ivy's two rooms (she at Tangier) and I go to 17
Keats Grove at night to sleep on a camp bed in an attic as
our pet lodger doesn't like being alone in the house.

Otherwise nothing special. I finished my Lawrence reminiscences for the *Adelphi* when on holiday and hope they'll
start in November. Aldous Huxley is coming to lunch (will
have to take him to Hampstead pub) on Wed. to talk about
Murry, Lawrence, etc. Had also an article called 'D. H.

Lawrence, England and Russia' in a magazine called *The Island* (not paid!). That's all at present except flitting. This is fun but v. distracting.

So much I'd like to say but must go to bed

Our love to you, *Cath.*

TO HILDA BONAVIA *15th July 1932*

Dear Hilda

In the *sturm und drang* I went and forgot all about that solid silver épergne I meant to send along in a pantechnicon for your occasion. But I'm afraid there's nothing for it but to keep looking out at the Caledonian Market for a gold one for later on. Anyhow – and in case I don't find this – may fortune smile on you all. Fortune is positively grinning at us – showing every one of her long yellow fangs in fact. Chatto has . . . withdrawn the book[1] . . . and is issuing a public apology. (I was just re-reading their enthusiastic letter of acceptance a few minutes ago, and noticed with amusement that it was dated April 1st!) For the moment I am chiefly concerned not to have my name implicated in the apology – which I gather is to be drawn up by Murry, and though I've asked to see it, I have not been allowed to so far. I'm taking what steps I can beforehand to counter any steps to implicate me.

The next thing is to see how the American publisher takes it. He may back out too. Again, he may not. We can only lay all the facts before him and wait. Pinker seems disposed to side with us, but one never can tell how things will go. It's always something to have said my say to nearly 2000 readers, and later on I daresay something else may come of it. Letters continue to come in, some of them offering financial help towards a fight with Murry. But I hope it won't come to this.

I've just written a long article (on a Scottish subject) for *The Cornhill* and sent it off on the chance there. Also I've

1. *The Savage Pilgrimage*, her narrative of D. H. Lawrence. [J.C.]

been asked to review the Lawrence letters at length in the autumn for *The Nineteenth Century*. The great thing is to get on with one's work.

While I was wildly typing by the window last night in stepped – through the window – Robert Lynd and Victor Gollancz. Don had collected them in a local pub and shepherded them through the garden. We had an amusing conversation. G. had been visiting the L.'s and the two had gone out for a drink. As we were going to bed after 1 a.m. a bird flew in at the window. I failed to assist its exit as it fluttered under the bed. So it roosted there quietly all night and flew out early in the morning. I feel it will bring us luck somehow . . .

Love from *Catherine*.

TO F. MARIAN MCNEILL　　　　　　　*16th July 1932*

Storms here as usual! Chatto's . . . has withdrawn the book from publication. So that's that. They are about to issue a public apology! My chief immediate concern is to make sure that *I* am not implicated in this, as I was never further from apologising in my life. We must wait and see what the American publishers will do. If they run away it is a grave loss to me. If they stand firm they might eventually risk taking over the English rights as well. The book, of course, reverts to me though I don't yet know how Chatto will act over the remaining copies. They may destroy the lot. The edition, 3000, would have been sold out by now as orders were pouring in when the book was first held up by Douglas Goldring! As it is, I suppose some 1600 are sold, which covers Chatto but brings me in nothing above the miserable £75 (less 10%) I had on account. And we were counting on some money. Never mind, I don't care. I feel very *cheerfully* angry. *Lovely review in the Saturday Rev.*

Love from *Cath*.

TO F. MARIAN MCNEILL   *22nd August 1933*

My dearest Flos

No, I'm not for Scotland after all this go. They wouldn't or couldn't send me my fare and I have not got the money, so it has had to be washed out. They did not, in fact, even offer me hospitality, but – lacking any statement to the contrary – I had taken it for granted that, with an audience of 'from 5000 to 6000' and all the rest of it, they would see me in fares. I was giving them my time (terribly precious at present) and strength and 25 minutes' speech, which (for me) meant considerable preparation, etc., etc. And I was willing to go without a holiday to do it. But when I say that *I have not got the money for my fare even by coach*, I'm speaking the plain truth. If they don't believe it I can't help it. Well, that's that. Sorry I shall not be seeing you. But there is a lot to do here, and one way and another I suppose I should have been sacrificing £20 to £25 by my trip to Scotland, even with my fares paid *and* hospitality. Those folk simply do not realise what it is to have to earn one's bread by one's pen. And they can't be made to realise it. So best to 'whistle o'er the lave o't'.

So much waits to be done today that I dare not break off longer for letter writing.

Ever with love, *Cathie*.

TO HILDA BONAVIA   *8th February 1934*

Dearest Hilda

It was rather a scant leave-taking on Sunday but I hope you knew how much I enjoyed being away at the cottage and with you. I only wish I'd been a less tiresome and garrulous visitor. Anyway I *did* enjoy it and was ever so much the better of the peace and country and your company. Ever since getting home I've been hard at it – (a) making up for my time away and (b) trying to cope with an unwonted lot of 'orders'. Besides tackling the Markets book and the new Anthology, which have both to be done in a hurry, I now shall have a column of novel reviews to do every week for a Scottish weekly (25/- for 4 novels or so), the M.G. to keep up, the Homes and Gardens monthly column (which is troublesome), a 'fornightly' 5000 article to be done soon, etc. So you see I have to get down to it and stay there.

This letter was interrupted by a telephone call to ask if I'd go to Berlin for a few days to hold the hand of poor old Madame Dimitroff[1] as part of a relay that is doing this! Don't know yet if I can or will undertake it. I *may* also later escort a group or troop of Lunn's tourists to Oberammergau! It certainly doesn't look as if I was going to get much time for my friends or myself or meditation.

Keep well, dear Hilda, and get rid of that rheumatism once and for all.

Ever with love, *Cathie*.

TO HILDA BONAVIA   *4th April 1934*

Dearest Hilda

I hope the cottage has chased the neuralgia and any other aches and pains away. It would be nicer if the weather would turn kinder and warm our bones and nerves a bit. I'm finding things hard and heavy myself and am disgusted with the smallness of what I can get through in the day without beginning to turn slightly crazy. Women may have been meant to weep. I'm sure they weren't meant to work – in any concentrated brainy way.

I had planned a peaceful busy Easter with John away, but Grieve, a Scottish poet (good poet and remarkable man . . .) came to stay '3 or 4 days' and still with us at the end of a fortnight. His hours and meals are peculiar and

1. The Reichstag fire trial was then in progress and the main defendant was a Communist leader Dimitroff, whose aged mother is here referred to. He was acquitted and it is generally thought the guilty parties were the Nazi leaders, Goering especially. [J.C.]

he has taken up a good deal of time and energy, especially as Mrs. Howard had to have her Easter off, but fortunately I like him and he doesn't get on my nerves as even nice visitors are too apt to do. We had some good talks too. Now I'm endeavouring to get some spring cleaning. There are men in the kitchen and the sweep comes tomorrow for the front room. There seems a lot of cleaning and clearing to do.

The Markets book is held up till another slightly different one comes out. Then it rests with me whether mine goes on or not. I *may* just try to use up the best stuff as articles. Meanwhile the Anthology, reviewing and M.G. fills the day to overflowing and there's a possibility of regular weekly articles for the *New Clarion*. That house in France was a washout – as I feared it would be.

Don has started writing a play. I'm half pleased about this and half in despair – such a gamble! John seems to be enjoying his tour in Scotland.

Much love from Catherine.

TO HILDA BONAVIA   *5th August 1934*

Yes, Wivenhoe is a great success from our point of view. It is rather a place to be when on holiday than a holiday place and that suits us. The sitting-room is grand for writing or doing things in with its huge solid table and the two lovely bow windows, one looking down and the other across the river, so that the tall brown sails of the barges go stalking across the panes. I find the skies very beautiful, the water a constant joy and there's a certain fascination about the mud except when one is actually in it as we have been once or twice. I have done no work as yet (unless you count proof correcting, a little sewing and making up some arrears in letter-writing) and I feel a lot better. But I think this would be a good place to combine real steady work with a little relaxation out of doors and I prophesy that we shall come again. Thank you *very* much. We have had no rain to speak of, though a bit too much wind at times for restfulness or lazing out of doors. They say it's one of the driest spots in England!

And we have bought a second-hand sailing canoe! She has a main-sail and jib, centre-board, half decked, holds 4 but is perfect for 2 and comfortable enough for 3. She was dirt cheap for £4 so we plunged and today John and I went alone together in her for the first time (we are novices) getting up a fair speed now and then (she can rip along) and now and then getting stuck in the mud on the lee shore. Once or twice my heart was in my mouth and we made some shocking blunders. Don isn't a sailor either but he knows a fair amount in theory. The former owner is an old salt at Rowhedge who has sailed in every part of the globe, and was on the *Britannia* with King Edward, God Bless Him, and now sells fish on a hand-cart round and has a shop for wireless accessories. He took us on the trial trip and then we all drank each other's and *The Swan's* health . . .

I must run out, see Don and John set sail and bid them God speed –

Love to you, *Catherine*.

TO HILDA BONAVIA   *21th August 1934*

Dearest Hilda
. . . We are without troubles here so far and are placidly enjoying wind and sun and forest. The hut is just like the home of the Three Bears in the fairy tale except that instead of 3 beds it has one single and one double one which, when you come to think of it, would be eminently suitable for a truly domestic Mr. and Mrs. Bear with but a single encumbrance. Besides the beds there are 2 tables – 1 double, 1 single – 2 chairs ditto, 1 shelf, 3 pegs for clothes, one mirror hung too high to see yourself in, 1 *cabinet de toilette* curtained off, 2 windows, thatched roof, stone floor, outlook over farm yard and across charming hill meadows leading to the forest. Farm 100 yds. or so to the left, where we have meals and use of sitting-room. The Moodys have had awful troubles in their time and lost their only boy aged twelve some years ago in a bicycle accident. Also a baby girl. But they have one daughter married to a

charming youth who works on the farm (60 acres) and they are obviously happy in each other, both talkative, sensitive, careless and with quick wit. We laugh a lot with them. When Mr. M. was called up for medical examination in the War, Mrs. M. trailed up to London to say goodbye to him. He came out and found her waiting for him and in tears. 'Why are you crying?' he asked. 'I suppose I'm crying for joy that you're going away,' she replied. However, he didn't go as the doctors diagnosed tuberculosis. 'And then,' she said, 'I cried a lot more because he wasn't fit to go away.' He was sent to a specialist who gave him a little tube 'with a silver top' into which he was to spit and then post it to have the sputum examined. But though he had been spitting for months and lately had been spitting blood, the tube made him so nervous that he became unable to spit at all and has never spit since. They keep the tube as a souvenir or a mascot. This place has healed his chest and he's had no trouble since. He wasn't in the house one day all last winter and he never stops working except to make some mild but pointed joke.

Off now to the post and to meet Maggie for our evening apéritif at the 'Trusty Servante', Minstead's one pub. I hope you'll come here some day with me. There's a caravan as well with *good* beds and – as you know – the Forest is unendingly beautiful. We sleep with the door wide open and the hens cluck thoughtfully round, and this morning I was wakened by a young cock who came and crowed 4 times. My conscience was greatly relieved when he did not stop with the 3rd crow.

My love to you, *Catherine*.

TO F. MARIAN MCNEILL   *1st February 1936*

Dearest Flos

. . . It's good that you have company as well as country air at Carlops, Flos, and that you have a certain amount of regular work to keep going with. I've had a sort of flu and feel awfully down (sleeping badly and headaches) and our house is extra full with the men on the 1st floor who take a

good deal of attention and a friend who came for 3 days'
rest and has now been here for 3 weeks at least and shows no
signs of moving. One way and another, I've been in despair
about arrears of work, but today, praise God, we have got
the whole MS. of the *Weekend* off, and now will have only
the proofs which will be a nasty job when they come. I
fear the compilation is a bit unequal, but the publishers
express entire satisfaction with the 'Games' and the 'Meat
and Drink' sections, which were 2 under my wing. I think
you'll be amused when you see what I've made of the 'Meat
and Drink'. We have an amusing picture for it too.

Sorry about your Burns not being taken. But I seriously
advise you to drop mentioning me. Why be martyred? My
book has had plenty of recognition anyhow. I'm going to
do a longish essay on R.B. I think I told you for a book
of essays (from Anne to Victoria) sponsored by Bonamy
Dobrée. But it still has to be written.

We are going to have a look at the cottage today and stay
the night. On Monday I'm going – as an experiment – to a
friend in St. John's Wood who will shut me in a room and
let me do as I please – for a week. I want to pull myself
together and get going again on Boccaccio. I daresay it
won't be a success but one must try different ways.

Maxim Litvinoff came along to see us here straight from
¾ of an hour's talk with the King in Buckingham Palace.
It was interesting.[1]

The sun is shining today and the birds singing.

Love to you, Flos, from Cathie.

TO F. MARIAN MCNEILL   *7th January 1937*

Dearest Flos
Glad you liked Tam in that dress. I've *seen* Ian Macnab at
the Samson Press shows, but if I met him it was some years
ago and only just to shake hands. I seem to remember a
young man with a beard.

---

1. Edward VIII. [J.C.]

Dear Flos, when will you realise that conditions are not what matters most when there's work to be done? There are better and worse conditions, of course. But most books have been written in any old conditions and in the rare cases of 'perfect' conditions few good books have been produced. If the work goes on honestly, it *makes* conditions for itself which are, at least, tolerable. That's about all that can be said. But the 2 necessities are impulse and endless grit. I don't mean that it is ever easy. I only mean that one's pathetic belief that it would be easy if conditions were different, is not borne out by experience. Writing is a very tough job – quite frighteningly so. There may be a few happy exceptions to this, but not many. However, it's not for me to advise.

A good New Year and love from *Cathie*.

No news of the play at all. If we can collect the fare, Don hopes to go to Scotland before very long. I want to go to New York in May !!

TO JOHN CARSWELL   *[1942 ?]*

. . . I did a stupid thing, forgetting that the Saturday coach passed earlier, so it whirled past the cottage before I cd. stop it. As I believed J. expected me & had planned to go, I set out on foot with a rucksac at a few minutes after 5 p.m. to try to make the 15 odd miles before dark. There were practically no wheels on the road (I didn't try cycling as I had neither lamp nor pump and my tyres were flat & there wd be the job of getting it back perhaps by coach). It was a grey cloudy, but not unpleasant nor cold evening. I went via Steeple Bumpstead – the longer way as it turned out – which I hadn't seen before and thought attractive. At one point I got a lift of a mile or so in a car, then a mile in a governess cart with a small pony & a family going home. Then, just as I had begun marking haystacks, where I could sleep through the dark hours if need be, a car came along with its lights on, and tho filled with sailors and their girls, they took me on the last 3 miles or so to Stoke, so that I reached the cottage by about 7.30 and found that I was not expected! However here I am . . .

All my love, *Cath.*

TO JOHN CARSWELL[1]   *1st March 1942*

Darling Johnnie

Here I am then! I couldn't keep my promise of writing to you again before saying goodbye to Black House. It was a grim move in bitter weather and under every sort of difficulty, including my first heavy cold of this winter, which I have not yet shaken off! I was up till 2 a.m. 3 nights running and even so, didn't get done half what I had planned, and had to bring far more stuff than I wanted (6 rooms into 2 – no joke!) as it was so hard disposing of things there and Jim kept loading on every bit of old iron he could find. Jim was magnificent and most devoted, not to say full of protestations of impassioned love. The move was achieved by a deaf publican with a moustache from Cornishall End, & a young singing labourer from Tinkers Green – his refrain was

There's a land of Begin-Again!

which you may have heard over the radio. Everything was tied onto a farm cart and I followed in Mr. Potts's car with Jim and the radio, etc. I arrived to find the 2 rooms so full I could hardly get in, much less move when in, and all the things were in the wrong places. Our 1000 books covered the interstices. It was pretty awful. However I think it's going to do me alright and I'm hoping to be a help to the wretched looking anti-aircraft lot in dismal huts down the road. I gather that there are 2 professors among them (probably maths!) but these are on leave and I've only met the Bombardier and some underlings – all keen to borrow books and make use of oddments.

1. All the letters following except the last few were written while I was serving overseas. [J.C]

Our outside text here (like a Wayside Pulpit) is

The Lord is Good
He is a Refuge in Time of Trouble and He
Knoweth those
    who trust in Him.

I hope He knows me . . .
No more now. I must get some food.

All my love, *Cath.*

TO JOHN CARSWELL   *21st November [1942 ?]*

Darling Johnnie
. . . Can you beat this true narrative about the P.B.'s
(Plymouth Brethren) here? My shed from Black House,
where I keep, among other things, Ivy's bicycle, was not
well put together by Mr. O. when moved, & the rain was
pouring through the roof to the ruination of everything
inside. I ought to say that in the recklessness of moving &
the desire to start on friendly terms I had promised to leave
the shed (now worth over £20) to them when I left . . .

Well, I asked Mr. O. politely if he wd house my cycle
with his and Mrs. O.'s in their cycle shed till I could repair
the roof as the weather was so wet. He replied, 'We have
no room in our sheds except for our own things.' I said –
still quite good-naturedly, 'You know, Mr. O., most people
renting my end of the cottage & paying the rent I pay, wd
expect a share of the sheds & the garden, as well as having
the room you use as a store in my half.'

Mr. O. You told us you didn't want the garden. You
        made your bargain. If you are not satisfied you
        have your remedy.
    I. I'm not complaining of my bargain. I'm pointing
        out that I pay a very good rent for what I have,
        & I must say it surprises me that when I make
        a small neighbourly request you always make
        difficulties and are unfriendly. I've lived many
        years in the country & have never come across
        this till now.

Mr. O. We gave you a bit of the garden, and (he
looked accusingly at me) *what did you do?*

I. What did I do? I can't think.

Mr. O. You sowed some flower seeds in a border
belonging to Mrs. O.

I. Oh, dear!

Mr. O. And you took part of a head of our kale.
(They have rows and rows of greens & I have
no place for them, & one day when making
broth I had taken about 3 small leaves of
curly kale (which wd grow again) uprooting
no plants.)

I. How glad I shd be, Mr. O., if I had as much kale
as you have & if you had none, that you should
have some of mine.

Mr. O. I'm a busy farm labourer & I can't stand
talking here.

I. You know, Mr. O., when I came here & saw the
big text outside & knew that you preached on
Sundays, I thought I was coming to live near
Christians.

Mr. O. The Bible says, 'Be not slothful in business'. Giving things is one thing, business is
another.

I. I was brought up to think that religion, if it was
real, came into everything.

Well aren't they extraordinary people? I don't believe they
even know how mean and queer they are . . .

All my love, *Cath.*

TO F. MARIAN MCNEILL   *30th December 1942*

Dearest Flos

The oatcakes have arrived. What a joy! They are now
unobtainable here. Thank you *very* much. I've had so
many lovely presents this Christmas and I feel a bit sad
that I haven't been able to give. It is one of the greatest
drawbacks of being hard up – as you know! I'm sticking

like grim death to the 8 or 9 pounds I earned at the P.O. as I have full uses for it. But I've been tempted to blow it on presents!

Now you must not get the idea that I'm neglected by my family and friends. With the family it is, if anything, the other way. I've had lots of suggestions from them and from others of free living room, etc. But – you'll sympathise with this too – I know by experience that such arrangements always involve complications, responsibilities, etc. And *unless one can't manage* any other way, I greatly prefer to be on my own. If I can't have the companion I want, I'd sooner put up with the disadvantages of living alone. So far I've managed fairly well and everybody is good to me. I've grown quite fond of my funny cellars and there is always the 2 rooms in the country when I feel the need to get out. At the P.O. – an amusing and interesting experience if somewhat strenuous – I found many women whose circumstances made my own to be envied! On Xmas afternoon I slept so long that I couldn't join the family at Hampstead, but I made up for this on Boxing night, and now I'm almost quite rested and enjoyed the show of French pictures today at the National Gallery and Epstein's flower paintings at the Leicester Gallery. His rhododendrons, tulips and dahlias are rather wonderful, but he can't paint a rose, nor a wild flower!

By the way (not that I want to argue the point) I believe I have quite a lot of common sense in the practical ways. I'm not a bad *contriver*, and Camden Town is not a bad place in which to contrive, especially if one is as careless of appearances as I am – and as one can be in London. I mean, for example, I don't mind going with a sack when there is a bit of road up and collecting the bits of tarry old wood-blocks for my fire, I quite enjoy such things! By contrast I sometimes sup in Park Lane or at the Café Royal, which is about equally entertaining. I manage to keep well so far. I don't think I'd like to teach English to Poles – unless I knew Polish! Really I ought, I know, to be writing. The truth is that I'm getting lazy about that! But I hope to start again in the New Year. I've got lots of notes and notions. Thanks for your suggestion re the Scots Magazine.

I'm at this moment eating one of your oatcakes with real butter sent me for Xmas from America. Both are delicious . . .

Ever with Love, Cathie.

TO JOHN CARSWELL   *7th January 1943*

. . . To sharpen one's tools one must waste the superfluous metal. There's no concentration without waste by way of discarding. That's where poetry scores over prose. I've often thought as you do of the Blake poem you quote (same of some of his others). But the answer to the question why it isn't trite lies in 2 things. The subtlety of the repetitions (subtle and daring) and the surprise and originality (and profundity) of the line.

It is right it should be so

which reveals the intense thought Blake had given to the subject. This followed by the last 2 lines with their key words 'rightly' and 'safely'. The triumph is, of course, that he keeps to the simplest, most ordinary words throughout, while conveying a complex train of thought with tremendous decision. This gift of his makes him great. Without the 4 last lines the poem *would* be trite, nearly platitudinous. But the repeated line gives magic – a cry of wonder and questioning. And the 3 last lines give the answer to the universal question.

All my love, Cath.

TO JOHN CARSWELL   *12th January 1943*

Darling John
Before I forget about it I must tell you about my P.O. experience. Usually the early morning walk had to be done by torch, but the last 3 mornings were bright moonlight and you can't think how beautiful those sordid back-terraces of Camden Tn looked – like Italian palaces with the black bulk of Carreras looming up like a Roman palace. Carreras had

a whole pigeon-hole in the sorting to itself! The P.O. was like a dirty out-of-date factory with perhaps 1000 workers men and women, & five flights of iron staircases (no lift except for sacks). Conversation never ceased & there were some rum characters. One handsome, serene woman had brought 14 live children into the world (she ran to twins and triplets), had 11 miscarriages, twice married – having each time to support husbands – yet had enough energy left to go to the country every Sunday 'with a lover'. Up Camden Town! There was only one woman who wore the old school hatband. Her remarks were an eye-opener. She genuinely believed that the 'working classes' had 'different blood from ours, rougher' and that this caused the fugg in the canteen. What ho, democracy! She was 'making do' in a 4½ guinea flat in Hampstead and kept saying she was with us 'purely out of paytriotic motives'. But when we handed round the hat for the Guardsmen who helped us, she stuck to her pay. The work was dirty and hard on the hands and the memory but I enjoyed it – rather like a parlour game done to the clock. I earned more than anybody else. For one thing I was the oldest so didn't pay insurance! Our highclass friend thought Hitler 'more to be pitied than blamed'. Maybe so, as Bysshe says.

Love always, *Cath.*

TO JOHN CARSWELL   *26th March 1943*

. . . What you said in a recent letter about the *disgustful* horrors so prevalent in modern fiction, set me thinking, tho' not for the 1st time, on the topic, and it has struck me as interesting that the ancients, and indeed writers up till fairly late were free from *disgusts*. Physical accidents and physical processes, when writers thought of them, were thought of as either funny or to be accepted philosophically. It wd be profitable to track down the resentment and self torture we find in Swift as a kind of madness. I think it has some vital connexion with the self torture you speak of in the moderns like Huxley, who invent cruel and physically disgusting scenes as if to rub our noses in them. Dostoievsky has a streak in him. There is no trace of disgust in Montaigne, nor in Pepys. Yet they lived in physically gross ages full of cruelties. Were they merely callous or is there in so called intellectual progress and culture a fierce resentment against our inability to alter the cruder fundamental 'facts of life'? Funny that rose-tiled lavatories should perhaps actually give rise to excremental horrors unfelt by users of earth closets.

Cath.

TO JOHN CARSWELL   *6th May 1943*

. . . But one reads what attracts one at the time, I know. Yes, Keats is a richer, greater, more perfect poet than Shelley, yet there are things in Shelley which mean more to me than almost anything in Keats. I think when one is older Keats often seems over-luscious. Shelley at his best is made of air – pure and piercing. Also, with all his comic doings, I find him intensely lovable in life. Keats of course, too, but differently. There is a fiery innocence about Shelley and an abandon that is eternally winning. Then lines like 'Rarely, rarely comest thou / Spirit of Delight' so often occur to me and those lines about the moon – 'On whose last steps I climb' . . .

All my love, *Cath.*

TO JOHN CARSWELL   *23rd May 1943*

. . . Yes, *Servitudes et Petitesses* isn't bad. Neither is *Turpitudes et Longueurs*. But one can always think of clever titles, especially before a book exists for one. I seem to get less and less able to concentrate on writing. However there should be an article by me in this week's *New Statesman*. It is not specially well done. I'm wondering whether I shd risk sending you the book itself by Somerville.[1] Anyhow before leaving Crowborough I'm

---

1. *The Autobiography of a Working Man*, by Alexander Somerville. I later edited an edition. [J.C]

sending you a proof copy of Harold Nicolson's new book about his gt. gt. grandfather, an odd Irish character (of Scotch blood) who met Robespierre in Paris in odd circumstances. The book will interest you if only for its historical sidelights on France, America and Ireland. He's a skilful writer, too, is H.N. in this sort. But the book which has struck me more than any other one this long time is *None But the Lonely Heart* by Richard Llewellyn, author of *How Green is my Valley*. But the enthusiasts for the 1st popular and in some ways sentimental work will get a shock when this 2nd effort appears. R.L. is in the army and must have begun this book before the war and finished it while serving. It has no war interest whatsoever. Is a terrifying but moving study of low London life, recalling Joyce, but entirely original, at least so I find. The novel is not yet out nor reviewed. What colour is your kitten? Are there Singhalese varieties? I hope it doesn't get stung . . .

All love from *Cath*.

TO F. MARIAN MCNEILL   *3rd June 1943*

Dearest Flos

. . . I worry about you and the censorship[1] (I know *I* couldn't stand it long). I should have thought there was any amount of domestic work in Edinb, as there is in London. What about mending? I do it professionally and *could* get enough to keep myself if I made a push. Household linen is all in rags and clothes need repair. The way is to *go out* and to charge by the hour (not less than 2/- an hour). I'm sure a cleverly worded card could be put up in clubs, ministries, etc. People in jobs simply have not time to mend. Of course it is hard on the eyes, or so I find. What about making rag dolls? I'm doing one now. Finnicky job though.

I'm *dressed* and up for the first time today after more than 3 weeks in bed. Extraordinary how weak one feels, isn't it? But I'm going on well, feeling a little less weak

1. In which she was then working.

every day. I did have one really bad week with head pains. Also we had raid alerts most nights. Sometimes 3 a night for 3 consecutive nights. The weather was exquisite till June came in when it turned wild and wet. Most days my bed was close to the big open window and it was almost like being on a summer cruise. I had lots to read and enough visitors and I sewed for the nurses, who were awfully good to me.

My special one – an old dragon – had been in Salonika in the last War. She told me that she often dreamt about the Royal Family and always felt quite at home with them. When the radio played the National Anthem she told me she always stood up 'even if I'm alone in my digs', and she thought perhaps this accounted for her feeling so at home with the R.F. in her dreams!

Try to find some better way of getting a living, Flos. Polishing floors is all right if adequately paid.

Much love from *Cathie*.

I don't quite see how Chris can claim Nicholas Moore as a Scots poet.

I'm given a clean bill of health. *C.*

TO JOHN CARSWELL   *11th July 1943*

My darling John
Your letter of March 21st has just reached me at Warwick. First I'll more or less try to answer it. About Donne, probably such books are useless or worse for you at the moment. Best put them aside. Books and subjects have their seasons, even their moments for each individual. I've come to think that if any given book at any given time proves to be either unentertaining, unpleasurable, uninstructive (in a clear and definite way) or unstimulating – in a word, not an *experience* but a depressing puzzle or bewilderment – the best thing is to let it wait for a more propitious moment or for ever. Of course a lot of one's omnivorous reading

especially when one is young, must be wasteful, must lead along false scents. From this one gains at least some self-knowledge. But I think it is needful to prescribe and recognise limitations as the best way of enlarging one's Kingdom. As to the modern philosophies, one of the most remarkable things about them is the rapidity with which they go out of date and are succeeded by equally evanescent theories. Their study is a special branch and useful only to a special type of mind. One discovers only by degrees what one's own type is and what is most nourishing. Time and energy are precious. Why not take up some specialised line of historical reading and turn your mind to its problems and details? I can send you the books – at least some of them. For instance what about that complex history of the Fronde, etc. in France with its contemporary English history? Have you read Cardinal de Retz's memoirs? Then one gets to Mme. de Sévigné's estimate of him in her letters, etc. In this way one has the muscular discipline of gradually mastering a period and has something solid to show for it. Of course the subject I've mentioned at random is a mere suggestion, partly because it includes reading in French and English. Any other wd do. I've found my *Encyclopaedia Britannica* a great defence against a too great turning inward of thought when this turns to confusion, depression, vague longings and dissatisfaction. About Wordsworth – that quotation about the 2 voices which Don so appreciated is from J. K. Stephen, the brilliant Cambridge parodist.[1] You must get his works. I don't agree with you that the Lucy Gray poems are bad. One at least is a great achievement – the one that ends 'if Lucy should be dead'. And the kitten poem is at least interesting as an illustration of what Wordsworth was aiming at – extreme simplicity and common speech as a break away from the prevalent poetic deadness with its 'feathered songsters', etc. One has to take the whole of a man's work and divine the underlying tensions, not merely pick out the most successful and memorable passages. I'm

1. Two voices are there, one is of the deep,
The other of an old, half-witted sheep,
And, Wordsworth! both are thine.

now reading T. S. Eliot's extremely good book of criticism on the Elizabethan dramatists, including one of the best (coolest) essays on Shakespeare and one on Hamlet that I've yet come across. I'll get a copy for you if I can. It is worth having . . .

It is all terrible but it seems clear that the needful big effort towards an end has at last begun in the open. One can have a rational hope that the Germans (and even the Japs) now fairly riddled, will collapse with a suddenness which will be astonishing when it comes. It is allowable, indeed good that we shd try to dwell less upon that moment of Ending, than on how ready we can make ourselves for the going on afterwards. Thus we have to lead a double existence – waiting for outward events and preparing our individual selves for what must follow. The End of the War must be our new beginning, not an excuse for having wasted what chances we have had. Preaching again!

All my love, *Cath.*

TO JOHN CARSWELL *21st August 1943*

. . . I've just read for the first time most interesting short essays by Rabelais on 'The State of France' and 'The State of Germany' found amongst our books here most appropriately. This morning I tried the experiment of getting on to my bed & writing there for 1½ hours or so. Much less tired after it. Position makes a difference! One gets cramped sitting. Here's an entry in my stray reflections. 'The mediæval child was given no prospects of happiness on earth. Hence, while comforted by hopes in the hereafter he enjoyed each earthly delight as an unexpected accident. The modern child was denied heavenly in favour of earthly bliss. Which was more creative of individual despair?' . . . Here's another. 'Life, still more "talk", consists mainly of futilities. If life is not to be mainly an affliction one must ignore the faculty for ignoring, transmuting or enjoying futilities.' You'll observe that I have no news!

All my love, *Cath.*

TO JOHN CARSWELL   *14th September 1943*

Darling Johnnie

. . . My trying state of over-excitement, tho' a little better, still goes on. But I had a good sleep last night and it's a lovely day and I'm having lunch with Ianthe. Before turning in last night I went for that walk you like round by the terraces in the Park. There was a full moon & almost all the houses are deserted, some with the great pillars shattered or standing up without their pediments or whatever the tops are called. It was extraordinarily beautiful. Will that old dignified London life ever exist again? I'm glad to have known it & to have known London before the era of motor cars when the horses clopped along the wooden setts & the air smelt of horses & the hansom bells jingled, & the 'swells' loitered along in top hats. You missed all that . . .

All love, *Cath*.

TO JOHN CARSWELL   *24th September 1943*

. . . My 2nd hand clothes friend Mrs W. tells me that—— was quite disappointed at his wife's cremation not to see the actual consuming of the coffin which, under the latest arrangements, disappears from view in a sort of service hatch, so that there's only a puff of black smoke to be seen from outside emerging from the top of a factory chimney. He complained that when his mother was cremated he saw 'lovely purple and green flames' and he had looked forward to seeing perhaps different colours this time. He regarded the new method as a fraud on the consumer! It seems that Lady A. against his wish insisted on being present. Otherwise there was only himself and Miss P., his secretary. Mrs. W. was asked but did not go . . .

All my love and more to follow, *Cath*.

TO JOHN CARSWELL   *2nd October 1943*

. . . Today I got a nicely printed and bound Vol of Montesquieu – *Grandeurs des Romains* with a lot of his letters at the end for 3d. It has an inscription in the

fly-leaf dated Sept 20th '73 from a 'Lieutenant au 101e'
– 'à mon bon camarade Eldridge'. You shall have it. It's
good reading. Yes I think a classical education is a huge
benefit. I also think that maturity in thought and style
does involve a *sort of forsaking* all one's education which
then becomes most useful. Aren't you a bit sweeping about
Dartington Hall? I've just been hearing of a boy from there
who swept all before him with a double first at Cambridge
(true Economics was his main subject) and then proceeded
to a most adventurous life, physically and mentally. One
must learn, I think, the difficult art of *saying* something
true and striking while not being sweeping. Sweepingness
is a temptation to me too, but it always fails of its effect,
in writing at any rate. In conversation it can be amusing,
because a certain tone of voice can show one is consciously
exaggerating. This can be done in writing too, but it needs
great care to be effective and not merely annoying. On the
other hand one must avoid over-qualification. Half the art
of writing lies here . . .

TO JOHN CARSWELL   *12th November* 1943

Darling John
. . . So the days have run past and at bed-time I've been tired
out. On re-reading your last 4 communications I don't find
much that needs rejoinder. I still maintain that Gibbon had
in him nothing of the poet, tho' I fully agree about his rising
'to the grandeur of the idea he'd imposed on himself' & the
rest. But surely this can be the merit of a great prose writer.
I feel that there's a distinction between the grandest prose
and the lightest of poetry. It isn't a question of grandeur,
nor even of beauty or imagination. It's hard to define, but
one can, I think, feel it. 'Poetic' writers of prose are usually
not in the front rank, even though first rate prose work as
a whole, may (like a cathedral) inspire some of the same
poetic emotions in the reader . . .

All the more annoying as I had just got down to writing,
and had made a fair start with a funny sort of autobiography.
Never mind, I'll pull through somehow & there's always

Tinkers Green to fly to for quiet and order. In the autobiography I'm trying to do the reverse of what most reminiscent writers have done – *i.e.* to keep my eye, not on the past but on the present (& future even) using reminiscence to illustrate what I now am, think & see, instead of the other way about. Does the idea interest you? . . .

keep your heart up, *Cath.*

TO JOHN CARSWELL   *5th January* 1944

Darling John

. . . Yes, your summing up of Murry is good. He has – or had – real gifts as a critic (none as a *maker*) but they have largely been spoiled by that egoistic sloppiness & self-pity & self-importance, which even affects his phrasing, I find, especially on re-reading, because at a first reading his sympathetic manner (he has real sympathy up to a point, especially with men no longer alive) one is apt to be carried away. He is emphatically not a writer who improves with re-reading. The slime seems to rise and become more evident. Of course if he had no talent he would not be worth attacking, as he would have had no following. I understand that he is a good and persuasive lecturer . . .

My love, *Cath.*

TO F. MARIAN MCNEILL   *11th January 1944*

Dearest Flos

. . . I'm writing this from the Tweedsmuirs where I came down yesterday for a week's work.[1] I, too, feel much at home in this easy and friendly household. All the same I know that by the end of 7 days I shall return rejoicing to my harsh, but entertaining existence in Camden Town.

Thank you so much, Flos, for sending me the copy of Duncan's book, which I've brought with me here to read with all attention and enjoyment. I'll tell you when this

1. C.C. had been asked by John Buchan's widow to help in editing his voluminous papers.

is accomplished. Don't think of sending another copy as I can share this with John.

Yes, I have met and corresponded with young William MacLennan and I was very sorry it happened to be impossible for me to go to his wife's concert in London the other day. Her portrait (on the programme he sent me) makes her attractive. He is certainly doing excellent work and I'm glad he is to do Duncan's new book soon. I haven't yet read Chris's[1] autobiography but I've had various accounts and I thought Janet Adam Smith's *Spectator* review rather masterly both in what it said and didn't say. The critic for whom I have the greatest respect (he did not review the book in print) found it boring in its incessant and irrelevant self-praise, as distinct from the sort of egotism which is interesting. All the same I hope to read it for myself one of these days. Certainly some of the best autobiographies in the world are egotistic – as also some of the worst. As with so much else there's an egotism which entertains and an egotism which bores. I confess I've often found Chris's egotism of the second sort – consisting as it frequently does of a series of quotations from anybody's praise of his work! Such a method adds little to one's insight of the subject. I'm sure, however, that there is much else in Chris's book besides this.

I'm reading Arnold Bennett's *Journals* with great pleasure and interest. What a worker, and what zest of observation! But they make one long to re-visit France. Much of them was written in Paris in the first decade of the century. Probably you've read them.

Dear Flos, keep well and hang on to that post and have a good New Year.

Ever with love, *Cathie*.

TO JOHN CARSWELL   *5th May 1944*

My darling John

. . . Yes, Landru had *style* to the last & his remark is worth recording . . . One might make an amusing article on

1. – *I.e.* Christopher Grieve ('Hugh McDiarmid').

allegedly historic last words, mostly of a pious nature, but I think that often they were either decidedly penultimate, or invented by survivors to the credit of the deceased. It is at all events, a mode of aphorism which has gone out of fashion. I always thought that condemned criminals and politicals must have got some solace out of being allowed to speechify. But of this they seem to have been deprived except in France. There was something to be said for the old public executions from the point of view of the chief actor though they were bad for the onlookers. If I had to swing, I shd like to speechify as well! Could anything afflict the imagination more than the privacy and quiet of our present hangings of murderers?

I've been reading in Coleridge's letters and note-books – wonderfully good reading. But I'm struck by his occasional Pecksniffian style of prose, passages of which could be beautifully transferred to Pickwick. I suppose Dickens killed that style for good and all – in some ways a pity! . . .

My dearest love, Cath.

TO JOHN CARSWELL   *7th July 1944*

My darling John

. . . One thing strikes me more and more in all modern arguments. The new combination of material progress, psychology and the Child of Nature doctrine, simply omits or forgets the traditional Christian (or indeed Pagan) virtues of patience, tolerance, cheerfulness, fortitude, etc. The word *ought* is constantly employed against others, rarely bestowed on one's own conduct. An immense amount of energy and friction is employed in the futile demonstration of the faults, shortcomings and wickedness of everybody except oneself. The result is not productive of happiness or creative power. No doubt the pendulum had to swing thus, and good will result in some ways from its swing. But for personal harmony, achievement, etc. I think we shall have to recover some of that personal responsibility

& faith which relieves one from constant futile carping at the mistakes and misdeeds of others. I rather think that the true interpretation of the 'resist not evil' counsel is *not* so much the Tolstoyan or conscientious objector one but the 'resist evil with good' – *i.e.* Don't waste too much time and energy denouncing evil, but add with all your might to the balance of active well-doing which must always count while evils blow themselves out. This, of course, does not mean do not fight any evil that comes in one's way. But rather 'fret not because of evil-doers', because mere distress and general indignation weakens one's power of good, dissipates useful energy & gives a false sense of righteous accomplishment. Do you agree? The Greeks were right in finding a 'sin' in *accidia* – which is a fruitless bitterness, if it becomes a permanent attitude of mind . . .

All my dearest love, *Cath.*

TO JOHN CARSWELL   *8th November 1944*

A queer thing this memory. If I'm writing anything and think of a phrase or an idea, I must note it down *at once* or 10 to 1, I lose it, and sometimes it's gone for good and all. Most provoking. The same with single words. But I was always weak there and constantly had to *describe* the word to Don so that he could find it for me. Like knowing a tune yet not being able to hum it when one wants to. All these processes are most mysterious. Some people have marvellous word memories. Others can remember visual things exactly. And so on. Then there's the memory of the old, recalling every detail of an incident, place, or conversation, years ago, but unable to think where one's spectacles have been put. I write this late at night at the cottage where I came 5 days ago, after too long an interval, hoping to get a great many things done. But I've actually done only one – the most pressing, which was a review article for *Tribune* which is about to pull up its socks in this line under Geo. Orwell (once an I.C. Magistrate) who is now Lit ed . . . The subject is Trollope and Geo. Eliot whose *The Warden* and

Silas Marner are appearing as *Penguin* books at 9d each.
I've worked on the damn things day and night here (one
night instead of going to bed I just lay down on the floor
and slept a few hours). Today I sent it off and I'm full
of misgivings lest it will be found unsuitable. I shouldn't
mind if it wasn't for disappointing D. and Orwell . . . The
Buchan essay has to go on now. I suppose it is good for me
to *have* to do such things again (how easily and uncritically
I used to turn them out!). But I find it hellish difficult and
of course my own poor old book is quite held up though
I keep thinking of it and making notes. And I'm sure I'll
go on with it if I live . . .

All my very best love, Cath.

TO F. MARIAN MCNEILL   *10th December 1944*

My dearest Flos
I *wondered* – as I devoured it – what good friend had sent
me the haggis pudding without a word. Thank you very
much. It was delicious and kept me going for at least 2
days. I find eating tiresome these days, though it does help
having my housemate to share the evening meal.

I've been and am busy, one way and another. It is fearfully
hard these days to find time and strength for anything like
regular writing. I think *these* and enormous determination
and encouragement matter more than a room in which to
write. After all, *bed*, with a hot-water bottle and a shawl, is
an excellent place for writing. Mrs. Belloc Lowndes writes
all her books in bed. Arnold Bennett wrote some of his best
books at a bedroom wash-stand. But how to get time and
strength, especially when there's no great encouragement!
That's the real problem. Of course it's wonderful how
one manages when one has to write to order. Good or
bad, one turns it out. This seems logically to mean that
if one were strong enough to order oneself and stick to
it, one could write under almost any circumstances (as
one does, for example, to others' orders amid the noises
and interruptions and discomfort of a newspaper office!)

but of course it doesn't quite work out this way. How one admires Trollope, who, with a long and exacting day's work, never failed to put in his appointed hours of writing – even when travelling in trains which were then uncomfortable *and* cold.

By the way, do you know if the Scottish B.B.C. has had a 'dramatic' broadcast based on Boswell and Johnson in Scotland? I'm re-reading the Boswell account now with enormous pleasure, and it strikes me that it would make, if properly treated, a splendid and most amusing radio programme. If you can find out about this – still better, if you can ascertain whether it would be considered – we could collaborate in it. What a splendid scene we could make of the Highland dancing and the Gaelic talk and gaiety smothering Johnson's wisecracks! Then we could have a fine collection of Scottish clergy, chiefs and gentlemen – always with the inimitable Boswell on hot bricks, or getting intoxicated while showing off his hero. Of course it ought to cover several programmes, but I daresay they wouldn't run to this. Find out if you can.

My desire is to creep through Christmas as quietly and cheaply as I can. Presents from the shops are impossible, and I haven't time to make much. Let's hope things will be more tolerable next Christmas. I can scarcely bear to think of what it must be like in Norway, Holland, Greece, Germany. Oh God!

Ever with love and all very best wishes, dear Flos, *Cathie*.

TO F. MARIAN MCNEILL   *26th December 1945*

Dearest Flos

Just to thank you for your letter and all your news and to say I'm in hospital slowly turning the corner after pneumonia and pleurisy. A weary business – and the cure – M & B – almost worse than the disease to me.

I'm so very glad that you've secured at least that bit of pension . . . No more now

but love and a good New Year, from *Cathie*.

Dearest Flos

Good of you to write. I'm still in Wallingford Hospital where I was brought on Dec. 16th, and I'll be another week here yet. But I'm really much better, tho' absurdly weak and a mere bag of bones on unsteady legs. From what the doctor says, I'll probably keep traces in my lung for the rest of my life. Well, I don't worry unduly over that. The arrangements for my convalescence have fallen through. But I'm sure I shall manage all right. I wish it were not this time of year!

This letter was interrupted by a visitor (I get almost none now the children have had to go back to London and work) and it is now decided – I hope – that . . . I go for a week's convalescence to a couple of cottagers near the family cottage at Ipsden, 4 miles from here where I spent most of the summer. (Our own cottage is too cold.) As I dearly love this particular couple I'm delighted at the prospect and I've turned down the offer of a kind friend to send me to a costly boarding-house in the district. When I get my balance again, I shall stay a week in London, with the children and I mean to be frivolous. Meanwhile they are coming this week-end and will convey me to the cottagers above mentioned.

I must now pull myself out of bed and walk once or twice round the ward to tone up my wasted muscles.

The chapter of my autobiography, which is to appear in *Windmill*, won't be out till the June number. It's all one to me –

Love from *Cathie*.

The author died in the following month.